D1384594

The Center for South and Southeast Asia Studies of the University of California is the unifying organization for faculty members and students interested in South and Southeast Asia studies, bringing together scholars from numerous disciplines. The Center's major aims are the development and support of research and language study. As part of this program the Center sponsors a publication series of books concerned with South and Southeast Asia. Manuscripts are considered from all campuses of the University of California as well as from any other individuals and institutions doing research in these areas.

Kinship and Urbanization

Kinship and Urbanization

WHITE COLLAR MIGRANTS IN NORTH INDIA

Sylvia Vatuk

UNIVERSITY OF CALIFORNIA PRESS
BERKELEY, LOS ANGELES, LONDON

University of California Press
Berkeley and Los Angeles, California
University of California Press, Ltd.
London, England
Copyright © 1972, by
The Regents of the University of California
ISBN: 0–520–02064–2
Library of Congress Catalog Card Number: 75–161993
Printed in the United States of America
Designed by Dave Comstock

To My Parents and to Ma

Contents

Acknowledgments

===

ANY people have aided me, both directly and indirectly, in the completion of this book, and I take this opportunity to express some measure of the gratitude I feel to them. First, I owe a large debt to Cora DuBois, who has given me continuous help and unfailing encouragement since the beginning of my graduate studies at Harvard. The Ph.D. dissertation upon which this book is based benefited immeasurably from her incisive criticism and constructive suggestions. It also received critical readings from Douglas Oliver and John Pelzel, of whose efforts I am most appreciative.

My introduction to the study of India came from Morris E. Opler, without whose encouragement I would probably not have embarked upon graduate study in anthropology. In addition I acknowledge with gratitude all that I have learned about Indian social organization from my former teachers at the School of Oriental and African Studies in London, Christoph von Fürer-Haimendorf and Adrian Mayer. I owe special thanks to Frederick G. Bailey, who has not only been a source of knowledge and inspiration for many years, but is the person most instrumental in seeing that this study be published.

The Department of Anthropology of Harvard University, the Radcliffe College Graduate School, and the Radcliffe Institute have liberally provided financial assistance for my graduate studies, for field expenses, and for the original write-up of my data. In this connection I am particularly indebted to former Dean Wilma Kerby-Miller of the Graduate School and to the late Dean Constance Smith of the Radcliffe Institute. I would also like to thank the American Institute of Indian Studies for their grant of a junior fellowship during 1966–1967, which enabled me to undertake the field study on which this book is based. The Graduate College of the University of Illinois at Chicago Circle generously awarded me a faculty summer fellowship for 1971, enabling me to complete the writing of this book.

The kind people of Ganeshnagar and Kalyānpurī have my heartfelt thanks for allowing me to study their way of life. I hope that in this book I have been able to justify their willing cooperation with my inquiries. I hope that those of them who read this book will recognize their neighborhood, disguised though it is in social science jargon, and that none will find anything at which they might take offense. I cannot mention individually each of those who has in some way contributed to this study, but my brother-in-law, Master Sundarlalji, and his wife and children deserve special mention, for their help with the research and, more importantly, for the warmth of their hospitality and concern to provide a home for us during our stay in Meerut.

For research assistance, I thank Subhashini Khullar and Prem Sharma. I am grateful to my father, Christopher D. Dutra, for help with the drawing of maps and charts. Judy Krysko and Zoe Emas ably coped with the typing of the manuscript, and I am grateful for their always cheerful assistance. I thank David Comstock for preparing the final art work and Max Knight of the University of California Press and Harriet Blodgett for their judicious editing.

More than to all others I am indebted to my husband, Ved Prakash Vatuk, and to our children, Sanjaya, Aruna, Sunita, and Jai Dev, for their moral and practical support during field research and the writing of this book. Their patience, understanding, and willingness to tolerate an often preoccupied wife and mother have made it possible to complete this study. To my husband in addition I owe a great intellectual debt, for it has been largely through discussions with him and in the course of work we have done together that I have gained whatever real understanding of the society of northern India I have.

S. V.

Introduction

A LARGE body of theory and much substantive research on the social consequences of industrial urbanization have provided an impetus for the present study. On the level of general social theory, a number of thinkers have sought a framework for contrasting the social organization of the small face-to-face tribal or peasant community with that of the large, densely populated urban industrial center characteristic of the modern United States and Europe and increasingly prevalent in the rest of the world. Some relevant conceptualizations are Maine's distinction between status-based and contract-based societies, Toennies' contrast between *Gemeinschaft* and *Gesellschaft*, Durkheim's mechanical and organic solidarity, and Weber's traditional-rational dichotomy of social-action patterns. More recently, Redfield's concept of folk-urban continuum has stimulated thinking among anthropologists about the changes which occur when former tribesmen or peasants undergo urbanization.

In Redfield's detailed examination of the folk society as an ideal type, the contrasting urban type was defined only in terms of logical opposites (1947: 294). But Wirth's somewhat earlier classic statement on urbanism as a way of life has provided a framework repeatedly used to view that opposite pole: "the substitution of secondary for primary contacts, the weakening of bonds of kinship, and the declining social significance of the family, the disappearance of the neighborhood, and the undermining of the traditional basis of social solidarity" (1938: 20–21). Much of the recent sociological and anthropological research on urban social organization in both Western and non-Western societies has demonstrated, however, the significance of extra-household kinship ties for members of nuclear family households. Further, it has shown that the social functions of the urban neighborhood have not everywhere fallen into disuse, and that both formal and informal mechanisms commonly exist in city neighborhoods to aid the migrant from the village in his adjustment to the new demands of urban living.

The present study was designed to examine, with respect to the white-collar middle class in a north Indian city, the two key controversial points in Wirth's well-known statement on urban social organization: that which postulates a decline in the importance of kinship ties and in the family as an institution in the urban environment, and that which suggests that the neighborhood where an urbanite lives is of relatively little significance for his social well-being. These two statements suggest many related questions about the changing family and kinship system in urban India, and about associational patterns among residents of Indian cities; I have attempted to use in this study whatever information I have been able to gather that has a bearing on larger questions as well.

The Indian educated middle class is a relatively new phenomenon, at least in its present scale, and its recent rapid growth and key position in a modernizing Indian society have given it central importance for anthropologists and sociologists. But relatively few data exist on kinship and neighborhood organization within this class, inasmuch as most urban anthropological research in India has focused on factory labor and the commercial communities, because of interest in the crucial problems of industrialization and entrepreneurship.[1] In planning this research, therefore, I decided to investigate a population of white-collar urbanites, preferably recent migrants with a rural background. I chose furthermore to study them, as a participant-observer, within the context of their home life in a defined neighborhood within a city, because

[1] Some recent examples are Hazlehurst 1966; Ames 1970; Owens 1970; Gore 1961, 1969; Driver 1963; Singer 1968.

of the conviction that the daily observation of ordinary social inter-action on the neighborhood level would provide valuable insights into the essence of urban Indian life that are unobtainable through questionnaires or formal interview schedules alone. Although I had intended to combine accumulating considerable quantitative data on a complete universe of the selected neighborhood with using more traditional anthropological techniques, I was to find that this approach aroused considerable discomfort and suspicion among many of those being interviewed. In order not to jeopardize the collection of data of a more qualitative kind or to endanger my rapport in the neighborhood, I eventually found it necessary to be satisfied with a minimum of quantitative information. However, that which I did obtain has proved useful in supporting — and sometimes in causing me to question — the evidence gathered through observation and unstructured interviews.

Throughout this study I have compared urban and rural norms and patterns of behavior. My research, however, was limited almost entirely to the urban milieu; I am basing any comparisons with rural society in this region on information from other studies, and on such incidental firsthand data as I was able to gather on brief trips into the surrounding rural areas and in conversation with villagers visiting urban homes or with urbanites recalling their rural experiences. In speaking throughout the book of changing patterns of social organization in the city, I do not mean to suggest a belief that modern Indian society can be characterized by a rural-urban dichotomy. Rural society today is itself undergoing rapid change, and many of the same developments which I have noted for urban kinship organization can also be found in villages of the area. In-deed the source of changing urban patterns must be sought in the initiative of the villager who has physically, if not emotionally, broken away from the familiar village environment to make a new life for himself and his children.

CHAPTER I

The Physical Setting

THE CITY OF MEERUT

MEERUT is an ancient city, in the plains of western Uttar Pradesh in northern India. It lies between the rivers Jumna and Ganges, forty miles northeast of Delhi. Several local traditions claim great antiquity for Meerut, associating its establishment with legendary figures of the great epics, the *Rāmāyana* and the *Mahābhārata*. According to one such tradition, the site was first built upon by Maya, father-in-law of Rāvana. Another legend tells of its establishment by the court architect of Yudhisthira, after whom the city was named Mayarāshtra. More recent and concrete evidence of the site's importance in early historic times is the presence of Buddhist ruins within the city, and an inscription on an Ashokan pillar, now in Delhi, which describes its removal from Meerut by Firoz Shah in A.D. 1206.

The earliest written mention of Meerut appears in Ferishta, who reports the capture of the city in 1017 by Mahmud of Ghazni. A prominent local landmark, the Jama Masjid, dates from this period and is said to have been built by Mahmud's vizir. However, shortly after its capture the city was regained by the local Hindu raja and part of his fortifications, built for the city's defense, survived until recent times.

In 1191 Meerut and its surrounding region again faced attack by Muslim invaders, and the city was conquered by Qutub-ud-din Aibak, first of the so-called Slave Dynasty to rule at nearby Delhi. Meerut remained within the realm of his successors throughout the period of the Delhi sultanate. Though sacked by Timur in 1399, the city was soon rebuilt and incorporated into the succeeding Mughal empire. Meerut and its fort are mentioned in the *Ain-i-Akbari*, and during Akbar's reign a mint for copper coins operated in the city. But in the declining years of the empire, effective control of Meerut and its environs reverted to local chiefs, and in 1788 it was taken by the Marathas. It formed part of a tract ceded to the East India Company by Daulat Rao Sindhia in 1803 (Joshi 1965; Imperial Gazetteer 1908; Nevill 1904; Thornton 1854).

The British set up a military cantonment two miles north of Meerut in 1806. In 1818 Meerut was made the headquarters of a district of the same name, and it continued in this administrative role throughout the colonial period and after Independence. Outside the district, Meerut is probably best known as the place at which the Revolt of 1857 began.

The size of Meerut in the early nineteenth century is not certain, but reports of the period indicate that it was a small and not very prosperous town until the needs of the cantonment began to attract population and to give an impetus to trade, manufacturing, and the provision of services. The extension of paved roads throughout the district, the construction of the Ganges canal in 1855, and the introduction of railway lines between Meerut and Delhi in 1864 and later of lines joining the city to points in Punjab and eastward to Moradabad were important to the city's growth as a commercial and industrial center of the region. In the nineteenth century, trade in Meerut was limited primarily to agricultural products, but hand-loomed cloth, leather, and building materials also passed in significant quantities through the Meerut market. Industry likewise was largely limited to the processing of agricultural goods, but the tanning of hides and manufacturing of shoes and the production of cotton cloth were among the early industries developed in the region and in the city itself.

Waterworks which still provide clean piped water to the city were built at a site nine miles from Meerut in 1896. A powerhouse was built on the same site in the late 1920's, and electricity was brought to Meerut in 1931. Sewage disposal throughout the city is effected by means of open cemented drains, connected to large drainage canals, also open, but an underground system is at present under construction.

Dating from the early period of British rule, missions of various British and American denominations were permitted to set up stations in Meerut and to build churches and schools. Local groups, notably the reformist Ārya Samāj sect, private individuals, and the district government also undertook to establish schools and later several colleges to serve the people of the city and its surrounding districts. Meerut College was the first institution of its kind in the district when it was established in 1892.

The population of Meerut has grown steadily during this century, particularly since 1931. Meerut is now the sixth-largest city of Uttar Pradesh, one of seventeen Class I cities in the province.[1] Its area is 21.58 square miles, of which two-thirds is contained within the cantonment.

TABLE I

POPULATION OF MEERUT (MUNICIPALITY AND CANTONMENT)

Year	Male	Female	Total
1901	65,822	52,717	118,539
1911	66,542	50,089	116,631
1921	71,816	50,793	122,609
1931	80,073	56,636	136,709
1941	98,829	70,461	169,290
1951	133,094	100,089	233,183
1961	157,572	126,425	283,997

Source: Census of India 1961, Vol. XV: Table A-IV

Most of Meerut's population growth in recent decades may be credited to migration rather than natural increase. Approximately 37 percent of the 1961 population of the city was born elsewhere. More than half of these immigrants are from rural areas; the remainder have come from urban homes elsewhere in the coun-

---

[1] A Class I city as defined in the Census of India is one with over 100,000 population.

try.[2] Census figures show that fewer than a third have come from
Meerut District itself but do not distinguish those originating in
neighboring districts from those who have migrated from more
distant districts of Uttar Pradesh (Census of India 1961, Vol. XV:
Table D-V). Most of the migration from "Other Districts" is
probably from the bordering districts of Muzaffarnagar, Bulandshahr, Moradabad, and Bijnor, and the migration from "Other
Provinces" primarily from Punjab, Haryana, and Delhi State. The
establishment of Pakistan and the accompanying mass movements
of Hindus and Sikhs from West Punjab into Uttar Pradesh account for a significant proportion of the migrants. Few residents of
Meerut belong to other linguistic regions of India, with the exception of a small colony of Bengalis in the city. The religion of
almost 69 percent of the city's population is listed as Hindu in the
1961 Census, 26 percent is Muslim, and the remainder Sikh, Jain,
and Christian.

The city of Meerut conforms to the morphological pattern
noted by urban geographers for those Indian cities which "have
been exposed both to indigenous and colonial growth influences,
as well as subsequent growth during the period of national emergence" (Breese 1966: 54). This pattern is characterized by two
fairly distinct areas of settlement, each with a distinct layout and
each with its own historic rationale. On the one hand, there is a
densely populated old city, with narrow mazelike passages flanked
by closely built and inward-turning houses, usually two or three
stories in height. There is little visible open space; however, the
design of the houses provides inner courtyards, shielded from the
view of passers-by but admitting light and air and serving as outdoor work and recreation areas for a building's inhabitants. Land
use in these areas is characteristically mixed commercial and residential. In Meerut, as in many other cities of similar age and development, this old city area was once surrounded by a wall and
moat, the former pierced by nine gates which provided access to
and egress from the city. The gates' names are still used to identify
their immediate neighborhoods. Some are still standing, but the

[2] An "urban" area, as defined in the Census of India, has a population of 5000 or more, at least three-quarters of its population dependent
on non-agricultural means of livelihood, and a population density of 1000
or more per square mile.

wall, which was already in ruins at the time of British takeover, has largely disappeared. The old city is now in the southwestern part of modern Meerut. The indigenous area expanded on all sides, but the major direction of growth was to the north, within the cantonment area, and east, as part of the municipality.

In contrast to this old city area, the cantonment and other British-built parts of the city have wide streets, built on a grid plan. Homes are large and widely spaced, with trees and lawns surrounding them. Residence in much of this area was originally intended for British administrators and military officers, but now the homes are occupied by their Indian counterparts and by well-to-do professionals and businessmen. The contrast between the old city and the areas built under colonial direction may be partly gauged by comparing the population densities of the municipality and the cantonment. These are respectively 26,752 and 5,467 persons per square mile (Census of India 1961, Vol. XV–IIA: Table A-I). In making this comparison, however, it is necessary to consider that much of the cantonment area is reserved for army maneuvers and other military uses, and is therefore largely nonresidential. On the other hand, the municipality includes, in addition to the old city, the low-density Civil Lines (an area built in British times to house civil servants) as well as newer "suburban" residential areas built more or less on a Western pattern.

Like other large towns and cities in Uttar Pradesh, Meerut is functionally diversified. As the largest city in one of the most prosperous agricultural districts in Uttar Pradesh, it has long been a center of wholesale trade in the major agricultural commodities of the region, wheat and raw sugar, as in other foodstuffs, and in locally manufactured goods, notably hand-loomed cloth and leather products. Industry is rapidly increasing in importance in Meerut, and its educational facilities draw thousands of students every year from Meerut District and adjoining districts. But the primary roles of Meerut are administrative center of the district and division and military base for the region (Joshi 1965; Singh, K. N. 1959; Ahmed 1958; Saxena 1968; Singh, M. 1964).

Meerut has been headquarters for Meerut District since the early nineteenth century, and is also the headquarters for the division of the same name, which includes the districts of Meerut, Saharanpur, Dehra Dun, Muzaffarnagar, and Bulandshahr. The commissioner of the division has his office and staff in Meerut, as does the district officer, chief executive of the district. Most departments of the district administration have their main offices in Meerut, and here are found the superintendent of police for the district and the district courts, civil and criminal. Some central government departments have regional offices in Meerut, and the Army Sub-Area Headquarters is also situated here, along with a number of military administrative offices and training facilities for several regiments. As Ahmed has pointed out (1958: 56–57), the centralized administrative structure of Uttar Pradesh has given special importance to the district headquarters at the expense of subdistrict (*tahsīl*) ones, and it is largely due to this concentration of administrative functions that Meerut has gained its present importance.

Figures on occupational categories in the city illustrate the significance of administration for Meerut. The census does not break down employment figures so that one can separate those engaged in government jobs from all others, but the census category of Other Services ("public, administrative, educational and scientific, medical and health, religious, welfare, legal, business, community, recreation, personal and other miscellaneous services") includes these and most other occupations that one would class as "white-collar." In 1961, 41 percent of all workers in Meerut were engaged in Other Services, according to census figures (Census of India 1961, District Census Handbook, Uttar Pradesh 18-III: cxii–cxxv).

According to an estimate made by the Department of Statistics in 1964, 43 percent of all nonmanual employees in Meerut were engaged in central and state government administration, the rest being distributed among manufacturing, trade, and banking; postal, medical, and health services; transport and education (Department of Statistics 1964: Statement 4).

Meerut is not one of the more important industrial centers in India, or even in Uttar Pradesh, but it employs 173 out of every 1,000 males in manufacturing, and the number of employees is increasing. Important in Meerut's industrial growth has been its nearness to Delhi. Conversely, the proximity of Meerut to the new industrial town of Modinagar and to Ghaziabad on the outskirts of Delhi probably is detrimental. Some potential industrial expansion is drawn away toward these other more industrialized sites. Meerut has sugar and flour mills, a large paper mill, a major distillery, and a well-known factory for brass musical instruments. Many small engineering works specialize in making parts for sugar mill machinery. Numerous Punjabi refugees who settled in Meerut in the late forties became manufacturers of sporting goods, assisted by government grants; theirs is now one of the more important of the many so-called cottage industries in Meerut.

As an educational center, Meerut is significant both for the people of Meerut District and for those of bordering districts. In the city are Meerut College and four other colleges (two for women only), all affiliated with Agra University.[3] They attract several thousand students annually. The city also offers men and women a number of intermediate colleges (two years of schooling beyond high school) and many high schools and primary schools. All of these, but particularly the facilities for higher education, draw students from within a radius of fifty miles or more. Opportunities for white-collar employment in government offices or in teaching encourage many students to remain in the city after completing their studies.

GANESHNAGAR AND KALYĀNPURĪ: TWO MEERUT NEIGHBORHOODS

Location and Historical Background

Ganeshnagar and Kalyānpurī[4] are two neighborhoods (*mohallās*) less than a mile inside Meerut city limits, and one-quarter mile outside the nearest old-city gate. These two *mohallās* face each other across a main road which leads out of Meerut city. Forty years ago, the land on which they stand was open country, the fruit orchard of a wealthy landowner who lived in the old city. When the city grew, the Baniā landowner sold his orchard to a well-to-do government official, who divided it into plots for sale. Several imposing homes date from this time, when the land sold for only Rs. 3 per square yard. The openness of the landscape, the

---

[3] Meerut University has since been set up and granted the status of affiliating institution for colleges throughout the district.

[4] The names of the mohallās are fictitious. Except where otherwise specified, the present tense is used throughout to refer to the year 1966–67 when the research was undertaken.

fresh air, and the lack of crowding made the neighborhood attractive. The early homeowners were prosperous government officials (among them a police inspector, a postmaster, an assistant to
the collector), contractors, overseers, lawyers, and absentee rural
landlords, all of high castes: Brahman, Baniā, and Kāyastha. Their
homes were intended as single-family residences, and most of them
remain intact and well preserved. Some homes, however, also built
in the early years of these mohallās, have been divided into several
apartments, and are in a deteriorated condition.

By now most of the land in both mohallās has been built upon;
only a few owners of lots have not yet been able to begin construction. The newer homes are smaller and more compact than
the older ones, and from the beginning most of them have housed
more than one family. Few of those now building in Ganeshnagar
and Kalyānpurī can afford to have homes of their own unless they
plan to rent out several rooms to tenants, at least in the early years
of occupancy. Recently, plots in these mohallās have sold for Rs.
35 per square yard, and construction costs have soared because
building materials are scarce and wages have increased. Those who
choose to build homes in these mohallās are no longer the well-to-
do elite, but rather the struggling middle class, for the present elite
of Meerut prefer to build still further out of the city in more ex-
clusive areas of Western-style detached homes.

The Mohallā Settlement Plan

A mohallā is a bounded and named area of the city. A variable
number of mohallās are included in each ward, or administrative
division of the city. The wards are numbered but have no names,
and their boundaries are arbitrarily drawn for administrative convenience. In response to expanding population the number of wards
has recently been increased to twenty, separating some mohallās
which had formerly been included in the same ward. Although
Ganeshnagar and Kalyānpurī border on each other, they belong
to different wards.

The mohallā, unlike the ward, is a locality to which its residents feel a sense of belonging, and although social activity is not
restricted to within its boundaries, residents share a sense of common identity and pursue common social interests. Women and

children particularly spend the greater part of their time within their own mohallā, in association with its other inhabitants.

The boundaries of the mohallā are not clearly marked in any way, nor are they recognizable to an outsider. However, a local resident is well aware of the boundaries of his own mohallā and, to a lesser extent, also knows those of adjacent mohallās. These

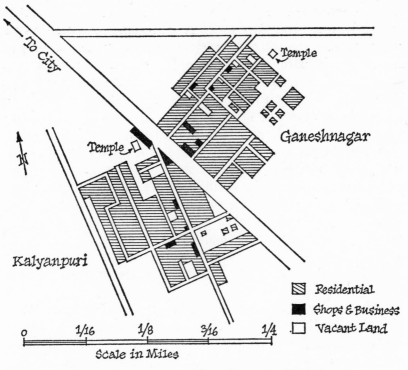

FIGURE 1   Sketch Map of Ganeshnagar and Kalyānpurī

boundaries may be roads or important landmarks such as temples, parks, and markets, but need not be. Ganeshnagar, for example, is bounded on the west by the main road which separates it from Kalyānpurī. The opposite boundary is a subsidiary road leading to an historic temple, a tank, and a cremation site. On the south is a large establishment manufacturing hand-spun and hand-woven textiles, but the remaining boundary is simply a line behind a row of homes, ending beside a gasoline station.

The name of the mohallā provides the address for its residents. Although the mohallā is crosscut by a number of paved streets or alleys (*galī*) on a modified grid plan, these are not named, except informally as "first alley," "second alley," and so on. Houses are numbered for the mohallā as a whole, rather than separately for each alley. Even though Ganeshnagar is cut by three main parallel alleys, partly connected by several cross-alleys, in order to reach some parts of the mohallā from others, one must first go out to one of the main boundary roads. At one corner of Ganeshnagar, where settlement is still incomplete, homes are connected only by unplanned dirt paths through an open field. Kalyānpurī is more self-contained in plan than Ganeshnagar. One main street leads diagonally off the eastern boundary road between the two mohallās to the city fairgrounds. Off this street are a number of slightly narrower alleys, two leading back to the boundary road, the others leading in the opposite direction to cross-cut three long alleys running parallel to Kalyānpurī's main street. All these alleys are dead-ends; there is a single exit to the road on the mohallā's western border. There is considerable vacant land in the southern part of the mohallā, where houseplots have been demarcated with brick walls but have not yet been built upon. There is also a large lot on the main road, owned by a Muslim businessman in the city, which has been occupied by a number of low-caste squatters in mudbrick thatched huts.

The road which divides Ganeshnagar from Kalyānpurī is a wide and heavily traveled artery, always busy with foot and vehicular traffic of every description. Approaching the center of the city, this road is lined on both sides with stalls and workshops. There are two bus stations providing transportation to and from various towns and large villages in the vicinity. On the wide unpaved verges bordering the road, behind the area where buses are lined up, are wheelwright establishments, tea stalls, small flour mills, several barbershops, a pharmacy, and a doctor's one-room office. Vendors of fruit, peanuts, parched grains, and hot fried snacks do a steady business with bus travelers and school children. Several shoemakers daily set up their meager equipment by the roadside and wait for a passer-by with a torn sandal. Often gypsy blacksmiths with their ornamented wooden carts camp for several weeks near the entrance to Kalyānpurī, cooking their meals over campfires on the dusty roadside and earning what they can by repairing and selling iron implements.

Nearer the center of the city, at a crossroads about one-eighth of a mile from the mohallās, the roadside businesses merge, becoming a small marketplace where all but the most sophisticated needs of local residents can be met. Here are vegetable and fruit stands, shops selling grains and spices in retail quantities, stalls for cloth and household utensils, and the workshops of several potters. For major purchases — good quality clothing, jewelry, household furnishings, large supplies of grain, clarified butter, and oil — residents use the specialized markets in the central city. But daily purchases are made here, within easy walking distance, in shops open six days a week. On closing day, a weekly market, which travels throughout the city to a different site each day, is held at another crossroads nearby. Because the specialty of this weekly market is cloth, women often prefer to purchase it here, rather than at the more limited regular shops.

Within the designated mohallās the main alleys are straight and wide enough for two automobiles to pass, not narrow and winding like the alleys in old city mohallās; however, automobiles rarely enter except during fair time, when they pour down the main street of Kalyānpurī each evening. The usual traffic comes on foot or by bicycle and the occasional bicycle riksha. Milkmen often lead small herds of water buffaloes down the street, and donkeys pass by laden with bricks for a nearby construction site; the ironing man and the vegetable vendor pass by slowly with their carts, calling out to advertise their services or wares. The alleys of these mohallās are rarely still or empty of traffic.

Although both mohallās are residential, commerce is not entirely excluded. The only businesses of any scale, however, are a flourishing modern laundry, doing washing and dry cleaning on the premises; a small ink factory, situated in the rear of the owner's home; and a workshop manufacturing stainless steel cutlery. Like the ink factory, the other businesses are owned by mohallā residents.

The numerous small shops in each mohallā, mostly tiny general stores, utilize the front room of a house or a projecting stall; customers stand in the street. Surrounded by his merchandise, the owner barely has room to sit. Goods available in these shops are cigarettes, candies, matches, spices, lentils, tapioca, dried tamarind, thread, needles, buttons, and other items which a housewife might need in an emergency. Each mohallā has a small bread and cookie shop supplied by a baker in Kalyānpurī, who also makes cookies to order for housewives with the ingredients they provide. Moreover a sweetmaker carries on a sporadic trade in Kalyānpurī. Several milkmen set up shop with their buffaloes morning and evening in fixed spots, milking their animals in front of the customer. There are three one-room laundries in Kalyānpurī, run by Muslim Dhobīs. Here ironing is done on demand, while the customer waits, but washing accumulates until the weekly trip to a nearby village pond. The only Muslim household in either mohallā belongs to one of these Dhobīs, who lives in his Kalyānpurī shop with his wife and children. The other Dhobī washermen live nearby, in a predominantly Muslim mohallā, and come to their shops each morning.

Homes and Facilities

Most mohallā homes are constructed of brick, usually faced with a thin layer of cement washed in white or pastel colors, inside and out. Floors are sometimes brick, but more commonly cement or, in newer homes, terrazzo. More elegant older homes may have tile floors with intricate designs. Premolded concrete grilles of varied designs, resembling stonework, are popular as decoration. These are placed just below ceiling level for ventilation or incorporated into rooftop railings. Walls are thick, window openings are protected by iron bars, and wooden shutters over all windows enable the householder to close the entire house securely at night. Glass is not used in windows, nor is wire screening common. The woodwork on exposed beams, window shutters, and doorways in local village homes is distinctive for its elaborate design and fine workmanship, but educated urban residents consider such woodwork rustic and undesirable. They prefer plain paneled doors and shutters, either painted or varnished to a hard gloss.

Here, as in the older parts of the city, most houses abut on the street. The better homes may have a front yard surrounded by a high brick wall and containing trees and ornamental plants, sometimes in pottery containers. Such homes are modeled upon the Western-style ones in the new upper-class districts of the city,

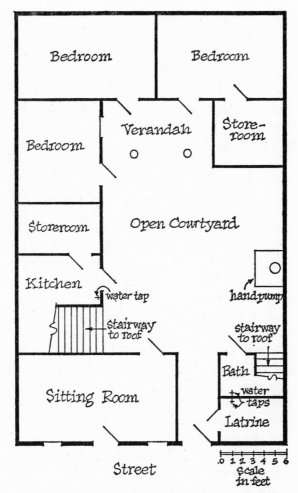

FIGURE 2   Plan of a Mohallā Home (Occupied by Lineal-Extended Household)

except that, like most other homes in these mohallās, they are built around a central courtyard (*āngan* or *cauk*). If the home is large, this courtyard may be completely surrounded by rooms; a passageway (or sometimes two passageways, front and rear) leads to an outside door and permits direct access from courtyard to street. If, as is usual, the house is of two stories, the courtyard is roofed over at second-floor level with a heavy steel grille. This admits light and air and protects the occupants of the first floor from burglars, meanwhile serving as a safety device for the occupants above. In lieu of such a grille, the second-floor may be surrounded by a waist-high railing of brick or grillwork. Because rooms on the second floor are set back one or two yards from the verge, there is space to walk, sit, and work out of doors. Usually a stairway gives access to the roof of the second story, where householders prefer to sleep in the hot summer months. In smaller homes the central courtyard may be replaced by a paved and walled area at the rear of the house. A desired feature of the courtyard, whether central or rear, is offering complete seclusion from the eyes of passers-by. Homes normally cover an entire lot, without provision for side yards or passages between adjoining houses, but the windowless walls of a back court assure some privacy. Complete seclusion for the occupants of a courtyard, whatever its location, is seldom possible because rooftops are used not only as sleeping areas but as work space and for wintertime sunning.

An open roof is important. In fact, each household requires the use of either a courtyard or an open roof in addition to any rooms it may have. Most women's work is done out of doors in all seasons, except during the rains. Clothes are washed daily in the courtyard and hung on ropes or spread on string cots to dry. Grain and spices are spread out in the sun for drying and sorting. Children play for the most part in their own courtyards, and women sit there to knit, mend, embroider, and gossip with friends and neighbors. In hot weather meals may be cooked there, even by housewives who have an indoor kitchen. The many tenants who live in a single room and have no kitchen must cook all their meals in the courtyard or, if they live on the second floor, in the passageway before their room. During the summer heat, those without access to a roof, like ground-floor tenants, must sleep in the courtyard where there is little chance of a cooling breeze. Men in such households often place their cots in front of the house, by the roadside, but women must stay within.

The open spaces of courtyard and roof are also important as sites for most of the social intercourse of mohallā residents. In many buildings these areas are shared by unrelated households, whose members either develop intimacy and close interpersonal ties from this mingling, or else persistently conflict. These are the main informal gathering places for neighborhood women, and the stage for such ceremonies as a household may wish to observe.

Rooms in mohallā houses are small, except in very substantial homes, and usually rectangular. Although most rooms serve for storage and sleeping, if the household occupies more than a single room, one is likely to be set aside as a sitting room (*baiṭhak*), primarily for the men of the household and for male guests. The practice reflects the backgrounds of mohallā residents. In the rural areas from which most of them or their fathers have come, customarily all who can afford it reserve a separate building or a wing of the main house (a *gher* or *baiṭhak*) for men (cf. Hitchcock 1957; Lewis 1965). Such a building, often used also to shelter animals and farm equipment, may or may not be near the regular dwelling. Men and adolescent boys sleep and spend leisure time there, going to the main house only for meals, and, if married, for surreptitious visits to their wives late at night. Such an arrangement is particularly typical of large extended households, where avoidance customs make the presence of older males irksome for the younger married women. Women do not visit the men's house when men are present, but they may enter it in the men's absence to feed animals tethered there or to clean. To continue the custom of the separate men's house in an urban household is of course impractical, but because the custom is associated with social practices (kin avoidances and segregation of the sexes) which are still followed in the city, most households try to reserve a room equivalent in function.

The urban sitting room is typically situated at the front of the house and entered by a door opening into the street or the front yard, an arrangement which enables male visitors to bypass the courtyard where women are occupied with their work. So that household members may also enter the sitting room easily, another door opens from there into the courtyard or, more commonly, into the passageway to it. Unlike other rooms the sitting room does not normally have windows facing the courtyard, a further guarantee of privacy. The typical city house has two entrance doors from the street. Besides the one for the sitting room, there is another for the passageway to the courtyard. If they differ in design, the more elaborate or the larger is the sitting-room door. Unless this door is ajar (which it would be only if the sitting room were occupied), male visitors pause outside the passageway door (normally left wide open unless the residents are absent from the house) and call out so that the sitting room door may be unlatched for them to enter. (Female guests, tradesmen, servants, and the sweeper woman who comes daily to clean the latrine would enter the courtyard directly and likewise call out, but only to announce their presence.) Women enter the sitting room freely in the men's absence and may occasionally entertain female guests or members of their natal family there. Couples in a nuclear household sometimes spend their leisure time in the sitting room. But in many households, especially nuclear ones, the sitting room is treated much like the Victorian parlor and rarely used; its furnishings and bric-a-brac are carefully maintained for impressing visitors.

As such careful use suggests, the sitting room is the most elaborately furnished room in the house. In a prosperous home it contains a metal tubular-frame sofa, with vinyl upholstery, or a highly varnished wooden one, with hand-embroidered cushion covers from the wife's or the daughter-in-law's dowry. Similarly embroidered curtains cover the windows and often too the doors. Two or three chairs — preferably part of a "set" with the sofa — and a low coffee table with a bowl of plastic flowers complete the furniture. On the mantel of the inevitable false fireplace are studio portraits of family members, wedding pictures, and high school and college graduation class photographs, alongside such decorative items as marble models of the Taj Mahal, carved wooden elephants, ivory birds, and plastic wall plaques. Religious posters depicting the major gods and goddesses and illustrated calendars received at weddings or from local businesses often crowd the walls, along with pictures of well-known saints and of political or national leaders. In less well-to-do homes, a large wooden platform of table height (*takhat*), covered with a thin mat and a colorful spread, may replace the sofa. Wicker chairs and stools and perhaps a string cot provide additional seating. If the family has a radio, this too will be placed in the sitting room, as will a table or ceiling fan in hot weather.

Kitchens are small and often windowless, and open off the courtyard like the other rooms. They frequently have built-in shelves along one wall, and sometimes small screened cabinets added for storing perishable foodstuffs. All women cook squatting on the floor in front of the typical U-shaped brick fireplace (*cūlhā*) which burns wood or dung cakes. An alternate stove is a portable, coal-burning *angītī*, made from an iron pail with a grille on top and an opening in the lower side for ventilation. Most housewives have both kinds of stove and use the fireplace only for the morning meal, the angītī in the evening. A modern two-burner plate using bottled gas is now becoming available in Meerut, but during my research none was to be found in the designated mohallās. Many households do have a single-burner kerosene stove, used for preparing tea and snacks without the bother of lighting the cooking fire.

Meals are eaten, either in the courtyard or in one of the inner rooms, as one sits with bare feet and folded legs on a mat or rug spread on the floor, although some people do sit on a string cot or a chair before a small table. It is not obligatory for all members of the family to eat together; when the meal is announced one may declare that he will eat later. Usually the members of a large family eat singly or in groups of two or three, the elder males or perhaps a grandmother being served first. In any case, the housewife, or whoever is cooking the meal, eats when everyone else has finished. In a few households which consider themselves "progressive," a dining table with enough chairs evidences that the family sit together for meals — an unusual practice in Ganeshnagar and Kalyānpurī.

Most houses have an indoor bathroom, although not all households share in its use. The bathroom is similar to a closet with a wooden door, but has a sloping floor and an outlet through which the dirty water passes into the main household drain to flow out the passageway into the open ditch alongside the street. The bathroom may have a faucet, at waist level, but more often water must be brought into the bathroom by the pailful and poured over one's head with a brass pitcher or pot. Ideally, each person takes a daily morning bath, usually a cold one, a practice which is strictly enforced for children in all weather. In the winter, when the night-time temperature may drop to freezing, the water may be heated on the stove for them and for old people. If a household does not have the use of a bathroom, members bathe in the courtyard, perhaps behind a screen of upended string cots, or in an inner room.

Because adults usually bathe partly clothed complete privacy is not necessary, at least for men.

Running water is available in all homes in these neighborhoods; however, the source of water may be shared among several households within a dwelling. Most homes have tap water from the municipal water supply, with two or more faucets for it. One faucet, whose water is used for drinking, cooking, and washing, is normally in the courtyard, near the kitchen. Another is in or near the latrine and reserved for washing oneself after defecation and for cleaning the latrine. Additional faucets may be situated in the bathroom or wherever will be convenient for tenant households. Some homes have a faucet over a porcelain basin, for washing hands and face, but usually there is only the faucet, and water runs directly onto the floor. Because the installation of pipes and taps, like the water itself, is an expense, many householders are satisfied with a hand pump in the courtyard. Others have both pump and faucets, each for a different purpose.

Each house also provides latrine facilities; again several tenant households often must share them. The typical latrine is a small room containing parallel raised steps of cemented brick upon which to squat. Drains leading into the street ditches carry off liquid matter, and a sweeper woman of Bhangī caste removes solid wastes once or twice a day. She also washes down the latrine with fresh water from the latrine tap or, lacking a tap, from a specially reserved pot filled on demand by a member of the household from a metal pail. She may not draw water herself if the building has only one water source. No housewife, even the poorest, ever cleans her own latrine.

Because of local concepts of purity and pollution, and because of the practical problems of odor and flies, the latrine is always placed as far away from the kitchen as possible. It is situated near a door — a rear or side exit, if feasible — so that the sweeper woman need not traverse the courtyard with her open basket of wastes. Since many homes are surrounded on three sides by other buildings, the most common location is directly inside the main entrance, off the passageway to the courtyard. Only an occasional house has a separate latrine, built at the far corner of a rear yard with outside access so that the sweeper woman need not enter the home at all.

Although the section of Kalyānpurī where low-caste squatters live and the newly settled far corner of Ganeshnagar do not have access to electricity, it is available elsewhere in the mohallās. A few of the poorer homeowners have not installed electric wiring because of the expense, but they are exceptional. Principally the electricity provides light, but it also powers the radios found in most homes and the table-model or ceiling fans in common use during summer. A few householders possess electric irons, but these are infrequently used because clothes are normally worn without ironing, and if needed it is done quickly and cheaply by neighborhood washermen. Other electrical appliances are rare.

In retrospect, the living accommodations of the middle-class urban residents of Ganeshnagar and Kalyānpurī are well built and substantial, and most people are supplied with the basic modern amenities, to which they have largely private access. By regional, and certainly by rural, standards, most houses in the two mohallās are comfortable, convenient, and adequately furnished. Crowded conditions do, however, discomfort those who can afford to rent only a single room. Even if perhaps crowding is made more tolerable by the fact that personal privacy is not highly valued here, nevertheless, those with means try to acquire spacious homes without co-resident tenants. Whatever the size of a home, traditional considerations determine its floor plan and the use of its space, but changing cultural values influence the furnishings and household equipment, particularly in the homes of the well-to-do and better-educated residents.

CHAPTER II

The Social Setting: The People of Ganeshnagar and Kalyānpurī

T HE population of Ganeshnagar and Kalyānpurī may be characterized as high-caste, middle-class Hindu. Of local western Uttar Pradesh origin, usually rural, most persons are first- or second-generation Meerut residents. Almost all the men are educated and have white-collar jobs. The population shows somewhat less homogeneity in income levels and life styles. A house-to-house survey of Ganeshnagar provided information on origins and residential history, religion, caste, occupation, economic status, home ownership, and education level for 950 persons in 179 households. No comparable quantitative data are available for Kalyānpurī, but systematic observation indicates that its population is similar to that of Ganeshnagar in all important respects.

ORIGINS AND RESIDENTIAL HISTORIES

Information on place of birth and subsequent residences was obtained from 171 housewives and their husbands (unless the housewife was a widow). Only 20 of these housewives and 30 husbands (not necessarily of the same women) had been born in Meerut, a few in Ganeshnagar itself or in Kalyānpurī and most of the rest in other mohallās in the older part of the city. Some are descendants of generations-old urban families, but most told of the more recent immigration of a father or grandfather from a nearby rural district. The movement of established old-city residents to Ganeshnagar within the past thirty-five years, to build homes in a relatively new mohallā, represents the beginning of a "suburban" migration of the middle and upper classes out of the inner city; in Indian cities the well-to-do have traditionally occupied central locations. Urban geographers have noted such a trend in other Indian cities as well (cf. Mehta 1968).

Most of the remaining housewives and household heads surveyed were born in villages and small towns within a fifty-mile radius of Meerut. They have come from Meerut District itself, or from the adjacent districts of Muzaffarnagar, Bulandshahr, Moradabad, and Bijnor. A few have come from more distant districts within Uttar Pradesh, from nearby rural Delhi State, or from the provinces of Haryana and Bihar. Five households, some related to one another, have migrated from villages in the Himalayan foothill district of Garhval, and one family is from western Punjab, now part of Pakistan.

Some mohallā residents come from urban families in other Uttar Pradesh cities, such as Kanpur, Mathura, Benares, Aligarh, and Agra, and a few are from Delhi. A number have lived in many different cities and towns of North India before coming to Meerut; they were born into civil service families and moved frequently because of the job transfers of fathers or grandfathers. They may continue this pattern of periodic shifts of residence because of their own careers, but in some cases probably will not since they or their fathers or husbands have retired in Meerut or accepted permanent employment.

Even though each residential history is unique, recurrent patterns emerge for the group. The typical middle-aged household head has been born somewhere in rural western Uttar Pradesh. His mother is uneducated and often his father is only minimally educated, if at all. He has come to Meerut during adolescence to attend high school or college and has later found employment in the city. During his school years he may have lived alone or with other students in a rented room, or he may instead have boarded with a family of kin already settled in the city, probably close agnates but perhaps uterine or affinal kin. When the time came for marriage — normally after he had completed his education — his parents arranged a union with a village girl, who remained with them for a number of months or even years after the marriage in their village household. He visited her occasionally until, eventually, "because he needed someone to cook," his parents sent her and any young children to the city. They may also have sent with her a younger son or grandson, in the same process of urbanward migration, to board until he too would be ready to set up an independent home with a wife.

Such a pattern is of course subject to many individual variations. Some Ganeshnagar adults are already second- or third-generation, educated urban residents, and this pattern describes not their lives, but their fathers' or grandfathers'. Conversely, in some families the household head has not yet achieved education and white-collar employment, and did not even come to the city for them, but now has such aspirations for his children.

Because the first homes were built only thirty-five years ago, and the mohallās were developed only gradually (they are still growing and at a fairly steady rate), few adults have spent their entire lives in Ganeshnagar and Kalyānpurī. Most of those who could claim either as a childhood home — the sons and daughters of the earliest settlers — have since moved elsewhere. Only 33 households, out of the 171 for which this information was obtained, have resided in Ganeshnagar for over twenty years. All but 6 of these own the house they occupy. As one would expect, generally homeowners have lived in the mohallā longer than most tenants (see Table II). Their average length of residence is between fifteen

TABLE II

YEARS OF RESIDENCE IN GANESHNAGAR, BY HOUSEHOLD

Years	0–4	5–9	10–14	15–19	20–24	25–29	30–34	35–39	Total
Owners	7	12	21	10	8	8	9	2	77
Tenants	61	15	8	4	3	1	2	0	94
TOTAL									171

and nineteen years, the largest number having lived in Ganeshnagar between ten and fourteen years. Some homeowners built their homes while residing elsewhere (usually while employed in another city) and rented to others until they could retire or wangle a transfer to Meerut. Others lived in rented quarters in Ganeshnagar for years before completing construction of their own homes. Many others, of course, lived elsewhere in Meerut before moving to Ganeshnagar. Thus the above time spans do not reflect the number of years of absence from the place of origin or the number of years spent in Meerut. As Table III indicates, the average Ganeshnagar

TABLE III

YEARS OF RESIDENCE IN MEERUT, BY HOUSEHOLD

Years	0–4	5–9	10–14	15–19	20–24	25–29	30–34	35–39	40+	Total
Owners	4	8	8	4	8	8	8	7	16	71
Tenants	34	23	8	7	6	2	1	2	3	86
TOTAL										157

homeowner for whom this information is available has lived in Meerut for thirty to thirty-four years (these figures include several elderly persons who were born in the city). The median length of residence for these homeowners is twenty-five to twenty-nine years.

The picture is different for those who rent accommodations in Ganeshnagar. Out of 94 tenant households reporting length of residence, only 6 have lived in the mohallā for more than twenty years. The average number of years spent here by tenants is between five and nine, but most have lived in Ganeshnagar fewer than five years. A number of these previously lived elsewhere in Meerut. The average tenant has lived in Meerut for ten to fourteen years, but again the modal length of residence is under five years.

RELIGIOUS AFFILIATION AND CASTE

The mohallās studied are inhabited by Hindus, with the one exception noted earlier of a Muslim Dhobī family, living in its Kalyānpurī shop. Most respondents gave their religion as Sanātan Dharma — indicating adherence to orthodox Hinduism as locally understood. Twenty-two households claimed membership in the

Ārya Samāj, a nineteenth-century Hindu reform sect with considerable following in this region. A few wives declared that they had been brought up in the Ārya Samāj but, being married into an orthodox family, now considered themselves to be Sanātanī. Two sisters took pains in separate interviews to disavow any religious affiliation at all, although brought up as orthodox Hindus.

The religious exclusiveness of these mohallās is not accidental. The Muslim population of Meerut is generally of lower economic status and more sparsely represented than are Hindus in the white-collar middle class. (Several older mohallās, near Ganeshnagar and Kalyānpurī are occupied primarily by lower-class Muslims and accordingly known as Muslim mohallās, although some Hindus also live in them.) But socio-economic class is not the only factor. Upon inquiry, Ganeshnagar residents were almost unanimous in expressing their reluctance to rent to Muslims, ostensibly because Muslims are nonvegetarian. A few stated a personal willingness to have a Muslim tenant, but said they feared the disapproval of others. Of course the question was largely hypothetical because these neighborhoods are clearly recognizable as Hindu and therefore do not normally attract Muslim house hunters. Possibly the fact that these mohallās went through their initial period of growth and social consolidation during the years of Hindu-Muslim conflict has some bearing on the restrictive attitude of older residents toward Muslim newcomers. At least one Muslim family owned a home in Kalyānpurī in the 1940's, but left Meerut for Pakistan. However, very few families even accept Muslims as guests in their homes, and three respondents gave the desire to leave a predominantly Muslim neighborhood in order to live "among our own kind" as their reason for moving to Ganeshnagar from the old city.

Both Ganeshnagar and Kalyānpurī residents are predominantly of two high castes: Ganeshnagar is 40.8 percent Brahman and 35.8 percent Baniā (or Vaishya). With the exception of six households belonging to other North Indian subcastes, all Brahmans are of the Gaur subcaste local to this region. Five of these are of Pahārī origin, migrants from Garhval in the Himalayan foothills. While the subcaste name is identical, the Pahārī Gaurs do not normally intermarry with Gaurs from the plains. These Pahārīs and a single Punjābī Khatrī family in Ganeshnagar (and four Punjābī Khatrī

households in Kalyānpurī) are the only local residents whose
mother tongue is not Hindi (either standard Hindi or a rural
Hindi dialect), but all speak Hindi fluently as a second language.

The Baniā households in Ganeshnagar are largely of the Agravāl subcaste; some are Rājvanshīs. The next most numerous caste
is Kāyastha, with ten households. Seven households have been recorded as Rājpūt, but only four of these are definitely members of
castes generally recognized as entitled to that appellation. For some
time it has been common in this region for certain low and middle
castes to assume the name "Rājpūt" as part of a claim to higher
social status (Srinivas 1967: 94–100; Rowe 1968). Two of the
four households referred to by others as Sunār (goldsmith) gave
their caste as Rājpūt, and the single Chipī respondent did the
same. Because I was aware of all this, I reclassified these three
households. However, in three cases the claim to Rājpūt status
could not be checked and therefore stands.

In Ganeshnagar there is not a single household of a caste
locally regarded as Harijan or Untouchable. In Kalyānpurī a Camār
(leatherworker) family lives in the outer corner of the squatter
settlement, on the main road where it sells wood for fuel. Also
Kalyānpurī contains a hostel for male Harijan college students.
The students from this hostel have little or no contact with mohallā residents, although some local high-caste men who are active
in social reform organizations attend public functions at the hostel
when invited.

TABLE IV

CASTE OF HOUSEHOLDS IN GANESHNAGAR

Caste	Households		
Brahman	73	Nāī	3
Baniā	64	Tyāgī	2
Kāyastha	10	Mālī	2
Rājpūt	7	Chipī	1
Gūjar	5	Jogī	1
Jāt	4	Dhīvar	1
Sunār	4	Luhār	1
		Khatrī	1
		TOTAL	179

OCCUPATION

I have characterized the population of these mohallās as middle class on two bases: the predominance of white-collar occupations, and the average income and income range of household heads willing to divulge them. Little definitive research has been done on urban class structure in India, particularly in discovering qualitative criteria of class stratification (for example, through life styles or self-identification). As Rosen has recently remarked, "Any attempt to define the middle class [for India] can easily become a morass" (1967: 38). Like others including me, he has relied primarily on the two objective factors — occupation and income — in his discussion of the Indian middle class (cf. Bhat 1956: 294; Department of Statistics 1964: 3, 12). Most Ganeshnagar and Kalyānpurī families would fall into Rosen's "lower middle class," inasmuch as household heads are clerks, minor government officials, low-ranking officers in private firms, schoolteachers and other lesser professionals, petty shopkeepers, and small industrialists. As Rosen points out, "Although this lower middle-class group generally has a high rate of literacy and education and an inclination toward white-collar jobs, individual incomes are low" (1967: 39). The ensuing discussion will demonstrate the applicability of his observations to the residents of these Meerut mohallās.

Of the 189 employed or retired males of Ganeshnagar whose occupation (or former occupation) was reported, 163 may be classified as white-collar workers. Some are self-employed (e.g., lawyers, contractors, the factory owner), but most are salaried employees at various levels of city, provincial, or military administration. The telephone exchange, local banks, and private industry employ a few. Although 35 did not specify their places of employment and gave their occupation only as "service," they are also salaried employees, usually office workers of some kind. Teaching in primary and secondary school, more rarely in college, occupies 22 of this white-collar group. There are a small number of other professionals and semi-professionals, but men in the high-status occupations (doctors, engineers) do not set the tone of these mohallās as they do in other, more prestigious neighborhoods.

Agriculture provides a livelihood for 6 Ganeshnagar men, almost all of them large landowners with fairly modern farms who

TABLE V

OCCUPATIONS OF EMPLOYED AND FORMERLY EMPLOYED (RETIRED) MEN

Occupation	Number		
Clerk	37	Engineer	3
Salaried Employee	35	Lawyer	3
Teacher	22	Dairy Worker	2
Shop Owner	14	Bank Clerk	2
Government Officer	11	Police Inspector	2
Farmer	6	Postmaster	2
Accountant	5	Barber	2
Contractor	5	Moneylender	2
Business Manager	5	Factory Owner	1
Office "peon"	5	Mechanic	1
Salesman	4	Shop Assistant	1
Doctor	4	Auditor	1
Construction Overseer	4	Laundry Owner	1
Household Servant	4	Stationmaster	1
Factory Worker	3	Soldier	1
		TOTAL	189

NOTE: Occupations are recorded as given by respondents; therefore some occupational categories overlap.

prefer to live in the city for the convenience of their womenfolk and the education of their children. Business — small shops and factories, a laundry and a dairy — provides a living for a few other Ganeshnagar residents. At the lower end of the occupational ladder, some make a living by pulling rikshas, doing domestic work, or engaging in other manual labor.

WOMEN'S EMPLOYMENT

Rarely are women gainfully employed in Ganeshnagar and Kalyānpurī, either before or after marriage. This situation is consistent with the pattern of employment in the city as a whole: according to the 1961 census, only 40 out of every 1000 women are employed — mostly in household industry and service occupations — and only 62 women for every 1000 employed men. In the mohallās, of 218 women (age twenty or older), 15 reported employment as teachers. Of these, 4 were unmarried at the time of my research, among them a wealthy widower's daughter who, in her early twenties, decided to become a college teacher and successfully resisted her father's attempts to arrange a marriage for her until just before I left, when she was twenty-eight. (A comparable career woman, a spinster in her late thirties with no intention of marrying, is a high school principal. She is not included in the household sample because she lives alone.) The other unmarried teachers are of high-caste families which are in financial need. Their marriages have been delayed because their families need the financial contributions they are making, and because they have been unable to accumulate the funds required for a wedding.

The 4 teachers who are widows include 2 who have opened small primary schools in their own homes. Another 2 teachers are separated from husbands who do not support them, but 5 women teach in order to supplement their husbands' meager incomes, 2 being young and childless women whose teaching also enables them to utilize their education and occupy their time. Of the 15 teachers, only these 2 and the 4 unmarried women are college educated. The other 9 finished primary school or high school only after their financial problems forced them to consider outside employment. As these figures suggest, in these middle-class mohallās teaching (preferably in an all-girls' school) is the only occupation considered respectable for a woman. Such employment, however, is rarely undertaken, except because of real financial need.

Women whose level of education does not qualify them to teach even in a primary school have few opportunities to supplement a husband's income or to support a household. The part-time domestic employment usually available is of low prestige, poorly paid, exhausting, and unpleasant. Many families do hire women to scour the brass cooking and eating utensils after each meal, to sweep once or twice a day, and to wash floors, but the pay is only from Rs. 6 to Rs. 20 per month, depending on whether the women come to the house once or twice a day, and on whether or not the employer provides meals. Three women, two Nāins and a Brahman widow, do most of this work in Ganeshnagar and Kalyānpurī, going from one house to another from early morning until late at night. No women are employed in Ganeshnagar as full-time servants, although four families do have a male servant living in their household. A few others use the husband's office "peon" for domestic tasks.

Finally, women may earn money by doing piece work for the nearby handloom factory. They may finish woven goods for sale, by fringing and tying the ends of blankets, towels, and saris, either at home or at the factory. Although many women from elsewhere in the city gather daily on the factory verandah, most women in these mohallās prefer the more respectable alternative of bringing the unfinished goods home to complete them in privacy. This work is so poorly regarded that none reported it as a source of income, although a number of women were observed doing the work in their homes or transporting bundles of finished and unfinished goods on their heads.

EDUCATION

The educational level of Ganeshnagar and Kalyānpurī residents of both sexes is high by all-India standards, and even by those of the city itself. This fact reflects more than the availability of schools for mohallā residents. Those who have migrated from rural areas are a selective population in educational aspiration and attainment. Education has been both a motive and a means for their present residence in this neighborhood.

The house-to-house survey sought to ascertain how many years of schooling each household member had attained, or, if unschooled, whether he had become literate. The data have some limitations. First, no standard test was used to judge literacy, only self-estimation, which is often inaccurate. Second, the high value placed on education in this milieu probably made some residents exaggerate the number of years of schooling.

To analyze trends in education among Ganeshnagar residents, the population of each sex has been divided by age and marital status into three cohorts. The first includes all persons, aged forty and over, ever married; the second, all similar persons under forty. The third includes all unmarried persons of sixteen years and over. Under sixteen almost all children of both sexes attend school quite regularly, and their age and grade level correlate closely. Few have completed their education. In the sixteen-and-over group many are continuing their schooling. The group has been included to give some idea of the emphasis on higher education for young people in these mohallās. However, I should point out that the inclusion of this group could result in a biased picture of the extent to which girls are educated. Girls over sixteen, if they have stopped going to school, are likely to be already married, and therefore appear in the "married, under forty" group. Any girl over sixteen who is unmarried is likely to be so because her parents have decided to delay her marriage until her high school or college graduation. However, there are in fact only three young women between the ages of sixteen and twenty in the mohallā who are married, and none under sixteen.

A comparison of the three male cohorts shows an increasing literacy rate, from a high of 93.9 percent among married men over forty to 95.7 percent among those under forty to 100 percent for unmarried men. I have excluded from consideration here four mentally retarded men among the unmarried — none were observed among the married. The average number of years of schooling shows a similar rise from 10.6 among those over forty to 11.7 among those under forty to 12.1 among the unmarried. However, whereas in the over-forty group only 78 percent have completed ten years of schooling or more, in the under-forty group 81 percent, and in the unmarried group 88 percent, have done so. The proportion of college graduates (B.A., B.Sc. or B.Com., — fourteen years) rises from 33 percent in the over-forty group to 42 percent in the under-forty group. Only 36 percent of the unmarried males are college graduates, but of course many are still too young to have achieved a bachelor's degree. Only a small number of unmarried persons, as opposed to almost all the married, have completed their education. The holders of postgraduate degrees (M.A., M.Sc., Ph.D.) show a similar pattern, with 13 percent in the over-forty group and 26 percent in the under-forty group. Five of the fifty-six unmarried men have post-graduate degrees and others are now pursuing postgraduate studies.

The figures on women's educational levels show a more dramatic increase in literacy rates and in number of years of schooling attained than do those for men. Furthermore, they show a narrowing of the gap between the sexes in education. Even for women in the over-forty age group, the literacy rate is high for the region (61.5 percent), although the average number of years of schooling is only 2.8. Ten women, who claim to be literate but have had no formal schooling, I have arbitrarily considered to have had the

TABLE VI

EDUCATION OF MEN IN GANESHNAGAR

Years Completed	0	1	2	3	4	5	6	7	8	9	10	11	12	13	14	15	16+	Total
Married 40+	5	0	3	0	1	0	1	1	6	1	28	0	8	1	16	0	11	82
Married 39—	2	0	2	0	2	2	4	0	3	4	18	1	16	0	14	0	23	89
Unmarried 16+	4	0	0	0	0	1	0	1	1	4	7	4	17	1	15	0	5	60
TOTAL																		231

equivalent of two years of learning. Including them, 40 percent of the women in the over-forty group, and 60 percent of those who are literate, have had only four years of education or fewer. The highest level attained by any woman in this group is ninth grade.

In the under-forty married group 25.4 percent are still illiterate. But the greater number with more than four years of schooling brings the average number of school years completed to 6.4. Of the women in this group, 36 percent have completed tenth grade (high school graduation). The unmarried group, however, is 100 percent literate (again, excluding one mentally retarded girl), and its average number of years of schooling is the same as for unmarried men (12.1). The percentage for unmarried girls who have achieved a B.A. or B.Sc. is slightly, though not significantly, higher than for the corresponding men. Note, however, that only thirty-

TABLE VII

EDUCATION OF WOMEN IN GANESHNAGAR

Years Completed	0	1	2	3	4	5	6	7	8	9	10	11	12	13	14	15	16+	Total
Married 40+	30	0	16	0	15	0	5	6	0	6	0	0	0	0	0	0	0	78
Married 39—	29	0	7	0	13	0	11	0	12	1	15	2	11	2	8	0	3	114
Unmarried 16+	1	0	0	0	0	1	0	1	2	2	6	2	8	1	8	1	6	39
TOTAL																		231

TABLE VIII

MEAN YEARS OF EDUCATION AND LITERACY

Age and Status	Men		Women	
	Years	Percent Literate	Years	Percent Literate
Married 40+	10.6	93.9	2.8	61.5
Married 39−	11.7	97.7	6.4	74.6
Unmarried 16+	12.1	100.0	12.1	100.0

nine women, but sixty men, in the over-sixteen group are un-married.

INCOME AND STANDARD OF LIVING

To discuss income and standard of living in these mohallās accurately is difficult because respondents were so reluctant to disclose their financial standing. Most would neither divulge their incomes nor answer questions about ownership of land, number of tenants, rents paid or received, even possession of certain consumer goods. Women were usually interviewed for the house-to-house survey, and many professed ignorance of their husband's income; others appeared cooperative, but gave obviously false information. Because financial inquiries created unease and suspicion which might jeopardize the rest of the study, I eliminated the more sensitive questions early in my research, although I continued to ask the more willing respondents. Ultimately the income of fifty-one persons (in forty-two households) was reported. However, like comparable data in other studies of Indian urban income, this information is highly unreliable (cf. Department of Statistics 1964: 191).

Forty-nine respondents reported income from salaries. The reported amounts probably represent true salaries, but they do not include income from what is colloquially called ūparī ("above"); that is, money regularly earned by illicit means, mainly bribes (rishvat), in the course of official duties. Occasional respondents were frank about having this extra source of income, although usually unwilling to reveal any amounts. As one cooperative man said, "Well, I'll tell you what my salary is, but not what I get above that." In other cases I was given to understand less explicitly that information was being withheld because of its illegal character, and inquiries were unwelcome. For office workers in certain government departments illicit incomes are sometimes considerable, even double or more the official salary. The importance of such earnings in some households perhaps may be inferred from the information volunteered by a young government clerk, who explained that his official earnings of Rs. 150 per month are supplemented by regular receipts of Rs. 250–300 per month in bribes. His brother, employed in another city and in another government department, earns Rs. 350 plus Rs. 600 "above."

In addition to salaries, ūparī, professional fees, and business earnings, rent is a source of income. Fifty-three households of the seventy-seven which own their homes have tenants. In these mohallās rent in new buildings is between Rs. 20 and Rs. 50 per room per month, although rent control regulations on older buildings mean that some long-term residents are paying less. Rarely would landlords disclose their rental income, but sometimes a tenant would reveal what his rent was. However, it is common for landlords to lessen their taxes by agreeing with tenants on an "official," recorded rent considerably lower than the actual rent, a practice which complicates interpretation of my data.

Only one householder who depends on agricultural earnings reported his income. His household is part of a large, rural-based joint family with extensive landholdings, whose combined yearly income was reported as Rs. 60,000. Many other mohallā residents, apart from those whose occupation is agriculture, have some agricultural income in cash or produce from privately or jointly owned rural property, but such income was never reported.

In forty households reported income is from salaries, for nine, the salaries of two adult male wage earners. The range of pay is between Rs. 80 and Rs. 854 per month, with an average of Rs. 280. Although statistically such figures are meaningless, they demonstrate the wide variation in income in these middle-class mohallās. The *Report on the Middle-Class Family Living Survey* of the Department of Statistics, based on nonmanual employees and excluding the middle-class self-employed (1964: Statement 3), found an average income of Rs. 210 monthly among the Meerut

sample and a range of from under Rs. 75 to 1500 per month, with
the modal income in the Rs. 100–150 range (1964: Statement 1).
From observation I would estimate that a small number of households in these mohallās have a monthly income of between Rs.
1000 and 1500. A few households with two or more earning members may have somewhat more, but they also have a greater-than-
average number of mouths to feed. The average income is probably
between Rs. 200 and 250. An average-sized family with this income
must spend at least three-quarters for food, housing, fuel, and light,
even if living in a single room, as these expenses are stable for the
urban family. The remainder purchases clothing, medicine, education, transportation, gifts and ceremonial needs, or becomes savings. Life styles differ considerably among mohallā residents and
purchasing power creates class divisions within the middle-class
neighborhood itself.

   Because I needed an inoffensive indicator of economic status,
I asked a survey question about possession of certain "luxury"
items, the durable consumer goods commonly owned by well-to-do
mohallā families and signifying economic well-being. Unfortunately
a few respondents discerned my purpose and denied possession of
items they probably owned. Others may have tried to make a favorable impression by claiming articles they did not own. More important, possession or nonpossession of these items is not an entirely reliable indicator of economic status because wealthy persons
sometimes avoid conspicuous consumption, even as poorer folk
may spend beyond their means for the sake of an imposing façade.
Furthermore, many of the goods are the typical content of a
"dowry" (dahej, marriage gifts from the bride's family to the
groom's); thus a family may have received them at the marriage of
the husband or son, instead of having bought them. A middle-aged
couple with a rural background may not have received such goods
for their marriage, but may now be saving to buy them for their
daughter's. An elderly couple may have permitted their married
sons to take such goods when setting up independent, neolocal
households.

   Keeping these qualifications in mind, however, the ownership
survey is informative. I have ordered responses to the list of commonly owned consumer goods by a Guttman scale: the order is bicycle, sewing machine (hand-operated), electric fan (table or ceil-

ing model), radio, electric iron, sofa, steel storage cabinet, automobile (cf. Kay 1964; Green 1954).[1] Other items on the list used for the survey were stainless steel utensils, a china tea set, a cow or buffalo. These responses were not tabulated. Possession of a cow or buffalo presupposes a certain income level, but otherwise does not appear to be closely correlated with variations in economic status. Furthermore, the first two items are deceptive. It is difficult to distinguish categorically between the household which uses two or three stainless steel bowls along with its brass utensils and that which uses steel exclusively; similarly, many families who own several pieces of cheap, cracked crockery report owning a "tea set." Motorcycles and motor-scooters were also on the original list. Because they may substitute for bicycles, those few reported have been included with bicycles.

The possessions of 147 households were reported. Of these households 8 reported owning none of the items listed, while 22 claimed only one (in most cases, a bicycle). These 30 households, together with some which own only two items, are among the economically least privileged in the mohallā, judging by their occupation and income (if known) and the impression they created during interviews by their dress and the condition of their living quarters. Conversely those referred to as "well-to-do" in the succeeding pages are the 36 households which possess all items, or all but one, up to and including a steel cabinet. In this category are most of the original settlers of the mohallā, but also many recent ones.

HOME OWNERSHIP AND LIVING QUARTERS

Another at least fairly reliable indicator of economic standing is home ownership. Approximately 44 percent of Ganeshnagar

[1] This list shows a marked correspondence to that used in a study of social class in Bombay by Straus and Winkelmann (1969); namely radio, electric fan, sewing machine, gas cook stove, kerosene cook stove, steel cupboard, stainless steel utensils, cot, water boiler, electric cooker, telephone, washing machine, air conditioner, refrigerator, motor cycle or scooter, bicycle, motor car. In addition, these researchers investigated the presence in the house of a water tap, bathroom, latrine and electric lights, all of which I have considered elsewhere. Some of the possessions listed by Straus and Winkelmann were not found in any home in Ganeshnagar (e.g. refrigerator, gas stove).

TABLE IX

OWNERSHIP OF CONSUMER GOODS

Household	Scale Type	None	Bicycle	Sewing Machine	Electric Fan	Radio	Electric Iron	Sofa Set	Steel Cabinet	Automobile
1	8		X	X	X	X	X	X	X	X
2			X	X	X	X	X	X	X	X
3			X	X	X	X	X	X	X	X
4			X	X	X	X	X	O	X	X
5			X	X	X	X	X	O	X	X
6	7		X	X	X	X	X	X	X	
7			X	X	X	X	X	X	X	
8			X	X	X	X	X	X	X	
9			X	X	X	X	X	X	X	
10			X	X	X	X	X	X	X	
11			X	X	X	X	X	X	X	
12			X	X	X	X	X	X	X	
13			X	X	X	X	X	X	X	
14			X	X	X	X	X	O	X	
15			X	X	X	X	X	O	X	
16			X	X	X	X	X	O	X	
17			X	X	X	X	O	X	X	
18			X	X	X	X	O	X	X	
19			X	X	X	X	O	X	X	
20			X	X	X	X	O	X	X	
21			O	X	X	X	X	O	X	
22	6		X	X	X	X	X	X		
23			X	X	X	X	X	X		
24			X	X	X	X	X	X		
25			X	X	X	X	X	X		
26			X	X	X	X	X	X		
27			X	X	X	X	X	X		
28			X	X	X	X	X	X		
29			X	X	X	X	X	X		
30			X	X	X	X	X	X		
31			X	X	X	X	X	X		
32			X	X	X	X	X	X		
33			X	X	X	X	X	X		
34			X	X	X	X	X	X		
35			X	X	X	X	X	X		

TABLE IX (*Continued*)

OWNERSHIP OF CONSUMER GOODS

Household	Scale Type	None	Bicycle	Sewing Machine	Electric Fan	Radio	Electric Iron	Sofa Set	Steel Cabinet	Automobile
36			X	X	X	X	X	X		
37			X	X	X	X	O	X		
38			X	X	X	X	O	X		
39			X	X	X	X	O	X		
40			X	X	X	X	O	X		
41			X	X	X	X	O	X		
42			X	X	X	X	O	X		
43			X	X	X	O	X	X		
44			X	O	X	X	X	X		
45			X	X	O	O	X	X		X
46			X	O	X	X	O	X		
47			X	X	O	X	O	X		
48			O	X	X	X	O	X		
49			O	O	X	X	X	X		
50	5		X	X	X	X	X			
51			X	X	X	X	X			
52			X	X	X	X	X			
53			X	X	X	X	X			
54			X	X	X	X	X			
55			X	X	X	X	X			
56			X	X	X	X	X			
57			X	X	X	X	X			
58			X	X	X	X	X			
59			X	X	X	O	X			
60			X	X	X	O	X			
61			X	X	X	O	X			
62			X	X	X	O	X			
63			X	X	X	O	X			
64			X	O	X	O	X			
65			X	X	O	X	X			
66	4		X	X	X	X				X
67			X	X	X	X			X	X
68			X	X	X	X				
69			X	X	X	X				
70			X	X	X	X				

TABLE IX (*Continued*)

OWNERSHIP OF CONSUMER GOODS

Household	Scale Type	None	Bicycle	Sewing Machine	Electric Fan	Radio	Electric Iron	Sofa Set	Steel Cabinet	Automobile
71			x	x	x	x				
72			x	x	x	x				
73			x	x	x	x				
74			x	x	x	x				
75			x	x	x	x				
76			x	o	x	x				
77			x	o	x	x				
78			o	x	x	x				
79			x	x	o	x				
80			x	x	o	x				
81			x	x	o	x				
82			o	x	o	x				
83			o	o	x	x				
84			o	o	x	x				
85	3		x	x	x			x		
86			x	x	x					
87			x	x	x					
88			x	x	x					
89			x	x	x					
90			x	x	x					
91			x	x	x					
92			x	x	x					
93			x	x	x					
94			x	x	x					
95			x	o	x			x		
96			x	o	x					
97			x	o	x					
98			x	o	x					
99			x	o	x					
100			o	x	x					
101			o	x	x					
102	2		x	x				x		
103			x	x				x		
104			x	x					x	
105			x	x						

TABLE IX (*Continued*)

OWNERSHIP OF CONSUMER GOODS

Household	Scale Type	None	Bicycle	Sewing Machine	Electric Fan	Radio	Electric Iron	Sofa Set	Steel Cabinet	Automobile
106			X	X						
107			X	X						
108			X	X						
109			X	X						
110			X	X						
111			X	X						
112			X	X						
113			X	X						
114			X	X						
115		O		X				X		
116		O		X						
117		O		X						
118		O		X						
119		O		X						
120		O		X						
121		O		X						
122	1		X				X	X		
123			X							
124			X							
125			X							
126			X							
127			X							
128			X							
129			X							
130			X							
131			X							
132			X							
133			X							
134			X							
135			X							
136			X							
137			X							
138	O					X		X		
139					X					
140		X								

TABLE IX (*Continued*)

OWNERSHIP OF CONSUMER GOODS

Household	Scale Type	None	Bicycle	Sewing Machine	Electric Fan	Radio	Electric Iron	Sofa Set	Steel Cabinet	Automobile
141		x								
142		x								
143		x								
144		x								
145		x								
146		x								
147		x								

Rep. = .94

householders own the dwelling they occupy. The remainder are tenants, usually of rooms or apartments in owner-occupied dwellings. Of 171 households for which this information is reported, 100 share some facility with one or more other households; most commonly the courtyard, water tap or hand pump, and latrine. Kitchens are rarely shared between unrelated households, and the 29 households which have no kitchen must cook outdoors. The rented quarters of 50 households are entirely self-contained, although in a dwelling shared with others.

Usually those households which share a dwelling are unrelated by kinship, but at least 16 households live with kin, in entirely separate quarters or sharing some facilities. Two sets of these related households are tenants, but the others own their respective houses in common. In one case a house is occupied by a brother and sister and their spouses; in all other cases the related household heads are brothers or father and son. Some were originally single household units that have since divided, more or less amiably. Cooking hearths are separate but some income may still be pooled and warm interpersonal relationships persist; at the other extreme, social intercourse has ceased and strict boundaries are kept within the jointly owned residence.

Unrelated households which share a dwelling are likely to be of different castes, although an occasional landlord rents only to fellow caste members. Such a policy is exceptional, however; only a Baniā widow with a large house explicitly stated that she would rent solely to people of her own caste. For most landlords, caste differences appear to be unimportant, but the prospective tenant must be a Hindu (not an Untouchable) who will maintain a vegetarian kitchen.

Three examples will demonstrate rental practices and arrangements. First, a small, newly constructed house in the unpaved section of Ganeshnagar is owned by a young Brahman couple. The owners and their children occupy three small rooms and a kitchen, each opening off the main courtyard. They recently rented a fourth room off this courtyard to a young, childless Chipī couple; the husband comes from the landlady's village and is thus her fictive "brother." This couple shares use of the courtyard, handpump, and latrine with the landlord's family. On the side of the courtyard opposite their room, a door leads to two more small rooms, beyond which is a second, smaller courtyard. Each of these rooms is occupied by a young Baniā couple, a brother and sister and their respective spouses, with children. The two couples are long-time residents of the mohallā, whose parents and younger siblings live in a rented apartment in another alley. The two share the small courtyard for cooking and other chores, drawing water from a pump outside the house, and use a second, separate outside latrine. They use the landlord's roomier courtyard to dry clothes and sort grain and to rest in their leisure time.

For a second example, a large two-story house, one of the first built in Ganeshnagar, is owned by an elderly Kāyastha couple. Their sons are all married and living neolocally but with them lives a granddaughter who attends college in Meerut. They have a roomy apartment on the second floor and share the wide roof area (serving them as a courtyard), the hand pump, and the latrine with a younger Kāyastha family, which rents a single room and a kitchen on the same floor. The two families are unrelated, but the younger man is a college friend of one of the landlord's sons. On the first floor, at the rear of the house, is a roomy, self-contained apartment with its own private courtyard which is occupied by an elderly Baniā widow and her twenty-year-old unmarried daughter, who teaches in a nearby primary school. The front rooms of the lower floor are tenanted by a Pāllivāl Brahman woman and twelve children, her own and those of her husband's elder brother. Part of a rural-based family which provides support and occasionally visits them, they live in Meerut for the sake of the children's education. This tenant's husband had himself been a tenant here when he was a high school student. Another room is rented by a young Kāyastha couple with one small child. The husband, a clerk in a government office, located the room through the brother of his wife's mother, born in the home village of the landlord's son-in-law. The remaining ground-floor room is occupied by two unmarried Brahman brothers, also government clerks. They have come from a town in the eastern part of Meerut District, but their mother was reared in Kalyānpurī, where their maternal grandmother and two uncles still live, and their mother's sister also has a home in Ganeshnagar. The three above households share a paved front and side yard, a hand pump, a latrine, and a partially enclosed outdoor bathroom.

A smaller old house owned by an elderly Baniā, a retired college teacher, is occupied by two families. With the landlord live his son — owner of a shop in the city — his son's wife and young children, a widowed daughter who teaches in a girls' elementary school, and a second son, twenty years old and mentally retarded. The second floor, with two small rooms and a kitchen, its own water tap and latrine, is rented to a Gūjar family: a young government clerk, his wife, their four school-aged children, and his two brothers and sister. They formerly rented quarters nearby in the house of a Brahman couple.

These examples illustrate not only the close juxtaposition of households of various castes in many mohallā homes, but also the importance of previous relationships between landlord and tenant or tenants themselves. Occasionally a family enters an attractive-looking mohallā and asks about possible rooms for rent, but more usually one inquires and rents through kin, close or distant, through contacts from one's home village or that of one's mother or wife ("village kin"), or through friends or acquaintances in the neighborhood. Many tenants have a history of several different occupancies in the same mohallā or in mohallās adjoining their present one. Tenants dissatisfied with their accommodations seek out a vacancy nearby with local help. The Gūjar family in the third example was disturbed by its former landlord's drinking habits and learned of its present quarters through the workman renovating them. Another family moved on the suggestion of its sweeper, who knew about a forthcoming vacancy in another house which she serviced.

TABLE X

NUMBER OF ROOMS PER HOUSEHOLD

Rooms	1	2	3	4	5	6	7	6	9	10	11	12	13	14	Total
With Kitchen	28	44	29	9	7	4	4	5	6	3	0	1	1	1	142
Without Kitchen	25	4	0	0	0	0	0	0	0	0	0	0	0	0	29
TOTAL															171

These examples also show that most households occupy only a small number of rooms. The modal number of rooms per household is two plus kitchen: twenty-five households have merely one room without a kitchen and twenty-eight have one room plus a kitchen. Fourteen households, however, have between eight and fourteen rooms plus kitchen for their own use. Some are large extended households, but others are elderly couples whose married sons have left home, or young families of means.

CASE HISTORIES

A discussion of the mohallā population in terms of averages, percentages, and general features, gives an exaggerated picture of social homogeneity within Ganeshnagar and Kalyānpurī. In fact, of course, each resident has a unique background which, within the framework of the regularities outlined above, accounts for a degree of cultural heterogeneity immediately apparent even to the outside observer. Mohallā inhabitants themselves are very much aware of this heterogeneity, and it has important consequences for their social interaction, as I shall show later. A few brief case histories[2] may serve to illustrate this point in more detail.

[2] The names of all persons described here are fictitious, and details of the personal histories have been slightly altered to disguise the identity of those described.

Shāntī Svarūp Sharmā, a Brahman aged forty-five, is a lecturer
at Meerut College. He was born in a village in the nearby district
of Moradabad. When he was twelve, he was sent to the town
of Muzaffarnagar for schooling, living alone there in a rented room
until at fourteen he joined his brother and sister-in-law in their
Meerut household. This older brother had finished college and
obtained employment in Meerut. Shāntī Svarūp also continued
his studies and later took a high school teaching job in the city.
When he was twenty-four, his parents arranged his marriage to a
twenty-year-old girl, a student in one of the local intermediate
colleges, who had been brought up in the nearby town of Modinagar but was then living in Meerut, where her father was employed
by the provincial government. He brought his new wife to live
in his elder brother's household, and the two couples and their
children lived jointly for six years, until Shāntī Svarūp was transferred to a school in a village of Bulandshahr District and moved
there with his wife and child. Seven years ago he acquired his
present position and moved back to Meerut, but rather than re-
joining his elder brother, set up an independent household in
rented rooms in Ganeshnagar. After some time he was able to buy
a house plot in the mohallā and began construction of a small
house. As soon as one room was ready, the family moved in, and
during the next two years continued to expand and improve their
home. Their four children are in school, their eldest son at the
academically selective government high school, and they have high
educational aspirations for them. The younger sister of Shāntī
Svarūp's wife also lives with them; she is twenty-one and is studying privately for her M.A. in English. Because her father is now
deceased, Shāntī Svarūp is currently helping her brother to find
her a suitable husband.

Sushīlā Devī Guptā, a Baniā woman, was born about forty
years ago in a village in Meerut District. She was married at seventeen and in the early years of her marriage lived in the household
of her husband's parents, who owned a small village shop. Her
husband had been educated up to the eighth grade in the village
school and was considered very intelligent; she was not educated as
a child, she still cannot read. One of her cousins, her paternal
uncle's son, had moved to Meerut some years before and invested in
a bus and a license for one of the rural routes. After he offered

Sushīlā Devī's husband a partnership in this business, she and her husband moved to Meerut with their three children. Because the business prospered, soon they were able to build their own large house, close to the cousin's in Kalyānpurī. The partnership has since broken up, but her husband now has his own successful bus line. Their first daughter is married to a contractor and lives with her young children in a city some 200 miles away. Their eldest son, recently graduated from engineering school, is being sought as a bridegroom by a number of wealthy, cultured families. The remaining five children are still in school. An older daughter, next to be married, is doing well in school and would like to attend college, but her parents are not encouraging her. She is learning classical singing and is already an excellent seamstress, and Sushīlā Devī hopes that with the large dowry they can provide in addition, they will be able to find her a young man comparable in education and earning capacity to her sister's husband and her brother.

Rām Lāl Agravāl, a retired contractor of Baniā caste, sixty-seven years old, was born in a village in Meerut District. He was married at fourteen, and when he was sixteen his wife came to live with him in his parents' home, where also lived his married brother, his sister-in-law, and his elderly paternal grandmother. Soon after, Rām Lāl was sent to college in Meerut, but his wife stayed behind. After he had received his engineering degree, he took a job in Agra and lived alone there, until after two years his wife was sent to join him. During his career he had so often been transferred that when, after ten years, he was sent back to Meerut District, he decided to establish a permanent home in the city. His wife and children could enjoy a more settled life and benefit from good educational facilities. He built one of the first very large homes in Ganeshnagar. Here his wife and children remained while he worked in various cities until his retirement several years ago. His younger son, employed as an engineer; the son's wife, a girl from an old Meerut family; and their two adolescent sons share the Ganeshnagar house. Rām Lāl's elder son, also an engineer, married a girl from Bihar and now lives in Aligarh with his wife. Rām Lāl's only daughter, holder of a B.A., is married to a doctor who works for an international agency and therefore lives abroad.

Jai Singh Sainī is a Mālī from a village in Meerut District, who, with his wife, grows vegetables for sale on land she owns near

Ganeshnagar. Because his wife spent most of her childhood here, helping her parents cultivate this same land, she considers Ganeshnagar her natal home. Married when she was fourteen and he was seventeen, they lived for many years with his parents in his village, where their four children were born. Several years ago her father died, leaving his house in Ganeshnagar and considerable garden land to be divided between her and two half-brothers. After the property settlement had allotted her the Ganeshnagar house and part of the land, she and Jai Singh moved to Meerut, leaving his share of the village land to be cultivated by his brothers. They rent out most of the old house to seven families, each living in a single room, and keep only two rooms for themselves. Jai Singh's entire household works in the fields. The Sainīs say that they want their children to become educated, because they are both illiterate themselves. Their girls attend school irregularly in practice, but their eldest son has completed seventh grade and they hope to see him graduate from high school.

Gautam Dev Ponwār, a central government employee, is a forty-year-old Sunār from a village in Meerut District, thirty miles from the city. This village was his mother's natal home; his maternal grandfather, who had no sons to help manage his extensive land holdings, had brought his son-in-law to live in the household. Gautam Dev earned a B.A. in Agra, where he lived in a college hostel. At twenty-five he was married to a girl of nineteen, a high-school graduate from a small town in Meerut district, and a year later she came to live with him in the large joint household that included his maternal grandmother, his parents, his two married brothers, and their wives and children.

When the family's land was largely expropriated, under the Uttar Pradesh Zamindari Abolition and Land Reform Act of 1951, Gautam Dev and his brothers sought white-collar employment. (His father and mother remained in the village home.) He settled his wife and children in Meerut. His government career has meant several transfers and living for long periods away from them; he returns only on weekends and holidays from his present post, in a small town fifty miles from the city. Gautam Dev's family has occupied three different Ganeshnagar apartments in the last ten years. Although the Ponwārs own a small unfinished house in the mohallā, which they rent to a Nāī family, they prefer to occupy rented quarters because their house has not yet been wired for electricity. Gautam Dev's five children attend school regularly, he and his wife keeping careful check on their progress because they plan to send both the boys and the girls to college. To supplement his income, Gautam Dev has recently set up a small engineering workshop with the help of a government small-industries loan. He employs six workers, some part-time, and is struggling to market his product profitably while continuing to work full-time at his government job.

Chandra Prakāsh Gaur, a thirty-year-old Brahman schoolteacher, was born in a village in Bulandshahr District. He was sent to Meerut at twelve to attend high school, arrangements having been made for him to board with the widow of the brother of his father's elder brother's wife, who lived at that time with her children in a mohallā near Ganeshnagar. He stayed in her home for five years, then at seventeen moved to the home of his mother's sister, newly married to a lawyer in Ganeshnagar. After his aunt had borne two children, he moved out to live by himself in a rented room in the same mohallā. His parents soon arranged his marriage to an educated girl, daughter of a district magistrate, from a small town near Delhi, and three months after the wedding his wife joined him in his rented room, where they still live with their three young children. Chandra Prakāsh teaches in the city of Modinagar, twenty miles from Meerut on the road to Delhi, but because his eldest son, who suffers from a chronic ailment, is being treated by a Meerut doctor, he prefers to keep his family in Meerut and commute by bus to his job. Although Chandra Prakāsh's mother stays in the home village, living on the family's agricultural holdings with his younger brother, his father lives more or less regularly with Chandra Prakāsh in Meerut because he is no longer able to farm.

Urmilā Devī Atrey is a Brahman woman in her late twenties. Married at fifteen, she left her home village in Meerut District at seventeen to join her husband and his well-to-do family in another village, twenty miles away. Her widowed father-in-law and the three elder half-brothers of her husband with their wives and children shared a common household and a joint income from the family-owned cloth business. After her father-in-law died some years later, her husband, the only son of his mother, quarreled about the inheritance with his half-brothers. Despite a settlement, her husband decided to move his own household to Meerut, where he had several relatives, in order to go into business for himself. The Atreys lived in rented rooms in Ganeshnagar at first, but have since built their own house, several rooms of which they rent out. Two of their three children, preschool boys, live with them. The oldest, a girl, has been informally adopted by the husband's childless elder sister and her husband and lives with them in another Uttar Pradesh city.

Mīnā Devī Garg is a Baniā woman in her fifties, widowed five years ago. She was born in a village in Muzaffarnagar District, but spent her childhood in a number of large north Indian cities, including Bombay, Calcutta, and Lahore, because of transfers for her father, a bank treasurer. Married at seventeen to a widower with two children, an accountant in a government office, she came to live with him in a mohallā in Meerut's old city area. By now Mīnā Devī has lived in Ganeshnagar for over twenty years, renting accommodations in various homes. Although her husband bought land for a home in the mohallā many years ago, he could never accumulate enough money to begin construction. Three years ago her elder stepson sold one lot and bought a house plot for himself and his wife in a more elite residential area of Meerut; the other lot in Ganeshnagar remains vacant, overgrown with weeds. Mīnā Devī's eldest son and his wife share the one-room rented house with her, her unmarried son, and her three daughters. Her sons have both completed college and are employed as clerks in a government office, although she has only a primary-school education. She is making plans to arrange the marriage of her eldest daughter within the next two years, but anticipates difficulty finding a suitable husband because her own resources are meager, and the remaining agnates of her deceased husband are distant kin who cannot be expected to help with the expenses.

CHAPTER III

The Household

IN Ganeshnagar and Kalyānpurī, most households contain a
small number of close relatives: parents and children and
sometimes a widowed grandparent or an unmarried uncle or
aunt. Large households containing several generations of agnatic
kind are unusual, and few have more than one married couple. People who share living quarters and eat food cooked at a common
hearth or stove usually refer to the living group of which they are
part as their "house" (*ghar*), rather than by any term which has a
specifically kinship connotation. But this term does not clearly distinguish the household from other, larger groupings of kin who do
not live and eat together. For *ghar* is commonly used also in a
broader sense to denote the three-generation agnatic extended family (even if its members are residentially dispersed), or even to sig-
nify the larger agnatic lineage of several generations' depth, together
with inmarried wives, which is otherwise called *kumbā* or *khāndān*.
There is no specific colloquial term for the group commonly referred to in sociological and anthropological writing on India as the
"joint family" — an agnatic extended family of three or more generations' depth which shares a common household and forms a

single productive and consumption unit (cf. Mandelbaum, 1949; Kapadia 1966; Kolenda 1968a; Desai 1964; Gore 1969).[1]

Yet the concept of such a large, co-residential kin group, "joint" rather than separated into its constituent nuclear family units, exists nevertheless, and is important in the normative aspect of family organization. Residents of these mohallās speak nostalgically of such traditionally ideal households as characteristic of "the old days," when people in an extended family cooperated with one another and were willing to sacrifice their personal desires in order for the entire group to live together in harmony. Reference to the "jointness" of the extended family is usually made by employing the adjectives *sānjhā* ("joint" or "shared") or *ikatthā* ("together") in statements such as "We are together" or "We are joint," rather than by having them modify any noun meaning "family" or "house." The respect in which the designated group is "joint" or "together" is not always specified, however. Depending upon context, being "joint" may mean maintaining a common household with joint income and common budget, or retaining joint ownership of landed property while living apart, or merely recognizing mutual obligations within the agnatic extended family long after residence and property have been divided.

There are corresponding terms to refer to the segmentation of the extended family or to the division of the coparcenary: the jointly held estate of land, business, or movable property. Thus one hears the expression "We are separate [*alag, nyāre*]" in reference to an extended family divided as to meals, residence, or property. Usually the segmentation of an extended family occurs gradually rather than abruptly. Segmentation by stages is particularly typical of rural areas, where an agricultural estate provides a livelihood for all members of an extended family even after the nuclear units have set up separate cooking hearths and dwellings. When residents of a common dwelling, who own property jointly, decide to have more than one cooking hearth, they say, "Our hearths

---

[1] There is a standard Hindi term for this group of kin when its members conform to the coparcenary norms: namely *sanyukt parivār*, a literal rendering of the English term "joint family." As Gore has pointed out, "it is doubtful whether this term is of Indian origin" (1965: 211), and in these neighborhoods I have rarely heard it used. Occasionally it is used by educated persons explaining the ideal Indian family system to the outsider, or describing their own family structure in terms of the ideal model.

[cūlhe] are separate." When segments of an extended family move into separate houses or partition the family residence but continue to cooperate economically, they speak of their "living apart." And when the ultimate stage of division has been reached, and the jointly owned property is divided, they say, "We have been divided [bate hue]." This last phrase indicates the formal, legal division of the family estate, and the distribution to each of the former coparceners of his appropriate share.

HOUSEHOLD TYPES

For collecting and later analysing data on the kinship composition of households, I have taken that group of persons who regularly eat from a common hearth as the basic unit, utilizing the local term and corresponding concept of the "cooking hearth" (cūlhā). This familiar usage does not involve ambiguity for informants. Moreover, my definition of a household resolves the problem of classifying cases in which close agnates — father and son or two brothers with wives and children — live in the same house (which they usually own jointly) but cook separately and have separate incomes and budgets. For this study each constituent commensal unit would be considered a separate household, regardless of the agnatic kinship tie between the men and the common roof.

As already indicated, those who live in a common household in these neighborhoods are almost without exception close kin. Relatives beyond the nuclear family rarely include anyone more distant than grandparents, grandchildren, uncles, aunts, nephews, or nieces. First cousins rarely live in the same household, even as young children; more distant kin may occasionally be accommodated as visitors or temporary residents, but they do not normally remain on a permanent basis. Usually relatives living with a married couple are kinsmen of the husband rather than of the wife, in accordance with the patrilateral emphasis of the kinship system (cf. Vatuk 1971).

Almost unknown here is the practice of keeping unrelated boarders — common in some newly urbanizing societies where migration to cities is predominantly male. Some men in these neighborhoods have left their entire families behind in their home villages, but such men ordinarily live alone, with close kin, or with one or two other men, rather than boarding with an unrelated family. Most are students or young office workers who rent a room in the neighborhood, but take their meals in a restaurant or tea-shop, prepare simple fare at home, or eat with close kin living nearby in return for a weekly or monthly payment. Generally such men, who have little place in the social interaction of the neighborhood families, spend their leisure time either together or with relatives living in Meerut.

Women in this social stratum rarely live alone. Parents are careful to make arrangements for their daughters to board with a related family or to live in the school's hostel before they agree to send them away to high school or college. Few young women are employed before marriage, and those who are customarily live at home or with close kin. The Ganeshnagar census found only one spinster living on her own, the previously mentioned principal of a girls' school. The census, however, did not cover single-person households or households of two unrelated men exhaustively; therefore such population has been excluded from the tables which follow and from the quantitative analyses.

Just as many married men live and work in the city while their wives, children, and aging parents remain in the village, so other married men have established their wives and children in Meerut while they themselves remain in the village or work in another city or town. I noticed eight such cases during the household census of Ganeshnagar, and I am aware of others in Kalyānpurī. The agriculturalists who make such arrangements are well-to-do. They send their wives and children to the city because of its schools and remain in the village to supervise their estates. These men, who provide the funds to support the urban household, typically make frequent visits to Meerut, bringing money and supplies of home-grown produce. Sometimes an urban arrangement is made by an extended family as a whole: one of the wives of a set of brothers runs a "branch" household in Meerut to which are sent all the school-age children of the family. Finally, because many men in these neighborhoods are government employees subject to periodic transfers, there are also a number of families whose head lives away because he has been transferred elsewhere. A man will be reluctant to uproot his wife and children every time his job requires him to move, particularly if the transfer has been made to an isolated outpost or a rural location where schooling is unavailable or presumably inferior. Households in which the head is normally absent for occupational reasons have been tabulated as if he were present, since the men involved provide the household's financial support, make its primary decisions, and visit frequently.

To allow comparison of my material with the data in the only extensive survey of writings on Indian household composition, I use with only minor modification the typology developed by Kolenda (1967, 1968a):[2]

1. *Nuclear:* married couple, with or without unmarried, widowed, separated or divorced offspring.

2. *Sub-Nuclear:* group of kin lacking any married couple.

3. *Supplemented Nuclear:* nuclear household plus one or more additional kinsmen who do not themselves constitute a married couple.

4. *Collateral Extended:* two or more married couples, with or without offspring, between whom there are sibling bonds.

5. *Supplemented Collateral Extended:* collateral extended household plus one or more additional kinsmen who do not themselves constitute a married couple.

6. *Lineal Extended:* two or more married couples, with or without unmarried offspring, between whom there are lineal links.

7. *Supplemented Lineal Extended:* lineal extended household plus one or more additional kinsmen who do not themselves constitute a married couple.

8. *Lineal-Collateral Extended:* three or more couples, with or without offspring, linked both lineally and collaterally.

9. *Supplemented Lineal-Collateral Extended:* lineal-collateral extended household plus one or more additional kinsmen who do not themselves constitute a married couple.

[2] Because I wanted this typology to be more consistent with terminology used in studies of the domestic group outside India, and because proper definition of the term "joint family" has been the subject of much inconclusive debate (cf. Madan 1962a, 1963; Bailey 1960), I have substituted "extended" for Kolenda's "joint" types and "household" for her "family" (see Kolenda 1967: 149–150; 1968a: 346–347). Kolenda's typology makes no specification as to the laterality of the lineal and collateral links in extended households, that is, as to whether links are through men or women. However, in my data they are with only one exception agnatic links between males (father-son or brother-brother) in accord with the patrilineal descent and patrilocal residence characteristic of this region.

DISTRIBUTION OF HOUSEHOLD TYPES IN GANESHNAGAR

Table XI illustrates the point made earlier that most households in these neighborhoods are small and include only close kinsmen. In 58 percent of the 179 households in Ganeshnagar only

TABLE XI

HOUSEHOLD COMPOSITION IN GANESHNAGAR

Household Types	Number of Households	Percent of Households	Number of Persons	Percent of Persons	Persons/ Household
Nuclear*	104	58.1	475	50.0	4.56
Sub-Nuclear	12	6.7	35	3.7	2.91
Supplemented Nuclear*	46	25.7	293	30.8	6.47
Collateral Extended	0	0	0	0	0
Supplemented Collateral Extended	3	1.7	26	2.7	8.67
Lineal Extended	12	6.7	103	10.8	8.58
Supplemented Lineal Extended	1	.6	6	.6	6.00
Lineal-Collateral Extended	1	.6	12	1.3	12.00
TOTAL Extended	17	9.6	147	13.4	8.64
TOTAL	179		950		5.30

* Includes one polygynous household.

members of the nuclear family are present. These households account for half the surveyed population of 950 persons. Most of the remaining households are either remnants of a formerly nuclear household — one of the couple has died or has left — or nuclear families which have one or more close kinsmen living with them, usually parents or siblings of the male household head. We see, then, that 90 percent of all households in this mohallā have only one married couple or no couple, and these households include 85 percent of its population. But otherwise considered, the data summarized in Table XI also show that almost half (46 percent) the people in this mohallā share a household with relatives who are not members of their nuclear family (or their conjugal nuclear family, for married people).

Nuclear Households

Traditional family theory, drawing on the Parsonian model of the "isolated conjugal family" with its peculiar appropriateness for industrial urban society, has been applied to the study of Indian society in recent years in such way as to stimulate controversy over a postulated "breakdown of the joint family" under the combined influences of urbanization, industrialization, and Westernization. Some recent studies simply assume that such a "breakdown" is occurring and that the traditional Indian "joint family" is giving way rapidly to the isolated nuclear family associated with Western urban society. Ross (1961), for example, begins a major work on Indian urban family organization with the statement that her purpose is to analyse "the factors which are tending to break up the large joint family and . . . the main ways in which these changes are affecting family roles" (280).

Even though Ross provides commendable insights into the processes of substructural change within the Indian family system, she makes two assumptions questioned by many other investigators: that the "large joint family" was once in fact typical of Indian rural society, and that the "breakdown" of such units into small, isolated nuclear segments is characteristic of the urban milieu. Studies provoked by such assumptions have emphasized developing quantitative measures of the extent to which the supposed traditional and rural pattern of large extended households (taking the "household" as measurable unit in preference to the vaguer "family") is giving way in the city to small households composed of a single nuclear family. A recognized difficulty in attempts to test this hypothesized decline of the joint family is the absence of an adequate base line from which to measure a change, although Orenstein's study of Indian census data from the late nineteenth century to 1951 is an attempt to provide one. From a comparative examination of figures on household size, mortality rates, and number of married and widowed males per household, he concludes that there has been no clear trend toward small or nuclear residential units during this period, and that "the extended family in India has not been weakened . . . it may possibly have become even stronger in recent times" (1961: 349).

Because of the difficulty of locating appropriate data for the same place at two or more widely separated points in time,[3] most of the relevant studies either compare recent data from different parts of India or compare rural and urban samples from the same region.[4] The most ambitious example of the former approach is Kolenda's examination of data on household composition taken from twenty-six sociological and anthropological studies done in India since 1949 (1968a). In this, and in a later paper based on 1961 census data (1968b), she is able to show significant regional variation in the relative frequencies of extended and nuclear households, and comes to the general conclusion that the nuclear household is in fact the household *type* found with greatest frequency in India, although in most parts of the country most *persons* probably live in households which include other relatives who are not members of their nuclear family. Kolenda's study, however, most of whose data come from villages, does not make specifically rural-urban comparisons, nor does it try to measure how much patterns change in time.

Since the influences presumed to cause the postulated "breakdown" of the traditional family system are concentrated in urban areas, a significant number of studies have investigated specifically urban family life. Others have compared rural and urban or rural, fringe, and urban samples for a single region. Results of these studies vary greatly, even as to the percentages of nuclear or extended households. Mukherjee's investigations in Calcutta and rural West Bengal (1964) show 63 percent nuclear households in the villages and 52 percent nuclear households in the Calcutta sample (if we exclude his single-person or "non-familial" households). Kapadia's studies in Gujarat (1956) likewise show a higher proportion of nuclear households in rural than in town samples. Yet Driver's investigations in Nagpur District (1963) show a

---

[3] The only such study of which I am aware is Kolenda's comparison of figures for household composition in a single village in western India in 1819, 1958 and 1967 (Kolenda 1970).

[4] Gore 1969; Mukherjee 1964; Kapadia 1956; Driver 1963; Kapoor 1965.

slightly larger proportion of nuclear households in the city than in rural areas. For urban areas Desai's extensive study (1964) of the family in a Saurashtra town (a study which does not stress household composition as the key to change in family organization) finds 40 percent nuclear households as against all other types. And Sarma's study of two Calcutta neighborhoods (1964) shows approximately one-third of all households to be nuclear. Despite the varying conclusions of these and similar studies, all report from one-third to one-half nuclear households in their urban samples, figures clearly within the range of variation of rural Indian samples. However we wish to interpret these data, they certainly show no very clear tendency toward increasing "nuclearization" of the household in urban areas, as determined by household composition alone. Some of the data in fact indicate the reverse process for given regions.

None of the studies support the generalization that the nuclear family is rapidly becoming structurally isolated in the urban milieu in India. Nor do my own data, for even if they show a clear predominance of nuclear households, they also show a very large percentage of households in which relatives from outside the core nuclear family are present. Although large households including two or more married couples are indeed few in these urban mohallās, we cannot assume a "decline" in the importance of the "large joint family" as a commensal and co-residential unit because we do not have comparable data from the rural area to buttress such an interpretation of the figures. Data from the residential histories of mohallā residents does suggest that most have at one time lived in an extended household, usually in a village, but retrospective descriptions of household arrangements cannot be relied upon for a quantitative comparison of rural and urban patterns.

A question crucial to the interpretation of figures on household composition is, do the male heads of the nuclear households actually have agnates with whom the traditionally ideal patrilocal extended household could have been formed? Unfortunately my genealogical data on Ganeshnagar household heads is not complete enough to treat this question statistically (cf. Driver 1963; Orenstein 1965; Ames 1970). However, data on the ownership of joint property and the residential histories of these household heads

do show that many have one or more agnatic kinsmen still living
(father, brothers, sons) with whom they could conceivably share
an extended household. Most of these close agnates have been
left behind in the village by the migrant to Meerut; others live
in distant cities, also engaged in urban white-collar jobs. But in
at least twenty-five cases, some close agnates live in Meerut. In
fact, twenty Ganeshnagar household heads have a father, son, or
brother living in the same mohallā, either in a separate house or
under the same roof but with a separate cooking hearth. Varied
reasons are given for what is recognized as a departure from the
ideal in these cases. In some families, conflict between mother-in-
law and daughter-in-law or between sisters-in-law has led to the
breakup of a formerly extended household; in others, dissension
between brothers over the management and disposal of joint property or simply personality clashes between father and son or older
and younger brothers. Some nuclear families have never lived
jointly, even though traditionally their relationship would have
dictated doing so. For example, a middle-aged Brahman couple
has always lived neolocally because the husband already had a job
in Meerut when he married, but his father was in government
service in another city. The younger couple with its two children
lives in a house in Ganeshnagar built about eleven years ago. When
the husband's father retired in 1964, he brought his wife and his
younger, unmarried son to live in the house. It has been enlarged
and partitioned to accommodate them, but the two women cook
separately and each household is independent in income and expenditures. In another Ganeshnagar family, the eldest son of a
prosperous contractor was educated as an engineer and afterwards
found employment in Agra, where his wife joined him after their
marriage. Upon his father's urging, he returned to Meerut to take
over the family business, but rather than return to his childhood
home, where his widowed father and unmarried sister still lived,
he built his own Western-style home in a newer, more prestigious
suburb.

Obviously the proportion of nuclear households in these
Meerut neighborhoods is high partly because of the geographical
mobility of their heads. Many of these men have left village households or city households elsewhere in order to take jobs in Meerut,
and their close agnates, with whom they would have ideally shared

an extended household, have either been left behind or have migrated elsewhere. Thus we might say that some of these people are living in nuclear households out of necessity; practical considerations alone prevent their meeting the ideal of "joint family" living. But what we know of the divisive forces inherent in the structure of the patrilocal extended family and of the fission which commonly occurs also in this region's rural households that are not divided by the necessity of migration, suggests that this explanation would be too simple. Furthermore, there is evidence that the divisive pressures within the extended family intensify in the urban milieu, where members no longer have a strong mutual interest in the management and maintenance of a jointly held estate. If each nuclear unit has its own income from separate sources and success depends upon individual initiative rather than cooperative endeavor, affection and a sense of duty are delegated a heavy burden: ensuring sufficient harmony so that the extended household remains intact.

Supplemented Households

Households that I have called "supplemented" result either from the truncation of a formerly extended household by death or from the incorporation of a widow, widower, or young unmarried kinsman into a formerly nuclear household. In about half such households, the supplementary kinsman is the husband's parent, usually his mother. In the rest, he is a younger brother or sister, a nephew, niece, or grandchild. Households which include a husband's widowed parent are most similar in internal organization and role definitions to the extended form of household, because the locus of authority typically is this surviving representative of the senior generation. (This point will be discussed in more detail below.) Conversely, if the additional person is the husband's or wife's junior kinsman, he is clearly subordinate to the central couple and usually assumes a "child" role in the household. Such households are similar to fully nuclear households in their members' personal interaction.

So too are households in which the wife's mother is present. There are only three in Ganeshnagar, however, because the arrangement is not customary practice. This society deems it most unfortunate for anyone to be forced by circumstance to live with a married daughter. The attitude derives from the asymmetrical relationship maintained between bride-givers and bride-takers and the notion that the former should never take anything of substance from those to whom they have given a daughter. One should avoid a situation in which he must rely for support on a son-in-law. Those women in Ganeshnagar who do live with married daughters are all elderly widows without living sons. They assume a clearly dependent status in the household, deferring to their sons-in-law and generally remaining unobtrusive. They take no overt management role, although their actual influence varies according to their daughters' respective personalities. One of these women spends her entire time in religious worship.

The presence of junior kinsmen in urban nuclear households usually results from the practice of boarding young relatives from villages or small towns so that they can attend school or take a city job. Sometimes an older brother or uncle assumes responsibility for orphaned siblings or nephews and nieces. It is unusual for young people to live with an older sister or a mother's sister or brother, although there are exceptions. Normally a person's "proper" place is with "his own people" (i.e., his agnates or other patrilateral kin), and if agnatic kin are willing to take in one's child, as ideally they should be, then it is improper to send him instead to be fed by matrilateral kin or a sister's husband. Parents who send children to live with the wife's kin, in preference to available agnates, will probably create dissension within the extended family, or more likely their choice itself reflects prior dissension. My conversation with a village family which contemplated sending a son to Meerut for high school is indicative. Both the wife's married sister and the husband's elder brother live in Meerut. The wife said that she preferred to send the boy to live with her sister; there was room for him, and she felt he would be welcomed and carefully looked after. She was reluctant to send him to her husband's elder brother because his wife is bad tempered and incompatible. "But," she said, "if we send him to my sister, my sister-in-law will say that we don't think our own people are capable of taking care of him, they will be hurt and insulted and there will be trouble between us." Ultimately they decided to send the boy to his paternal uncle's home; he later became unhappy there and was sent to school in another town, where he lived in the school hostel.

Individual families vary in how they share the expense of caring for widowed or otherwise dependent kinsmen. A parent will usually be supported by the son with whom he lives, but often the other sons will be expected to assist periodically, either by sending money or by taking turns at lodging the parent. Daughters are not expected to contribute anything toward their parents' support in old age; indeed their help would not even be accepted unless an unusual emergency arose. Rather, an elderly person with few resources usually hoards the small amounts of cash or gifts of clothing he receives in order to make presents to his daughter when she comes to visit. To give presents to daughters throughout one's life is considered a prime obligation. As for junior kinsmen, it is usual for grandparents or an elder brother to assume the expenses of a grandchild's or younger sibling's board and education in the city. But for a brother's child or a relative of the wife, the child's parents will normally be expected to bear part of the cost, at least of such items as school fees, supplies, and clothing. Frequently they will also be expected to pay a regular sum for his meals or to send staple foods from the village to augment his board. If a junior kinsman is employed rather than studying, he will be expected to contribute his share of expenses to the urban household in which he lives, unless the agnatic extended family is a closely cooperating unit with significant joint property. In this case he may send most of his earnings to the head of the family in the village and depend for his needs on the branch of the family with which he lives.

In five households classified as supplemented nuclear, paternal grandparents are sharing their home with one or more grandchildren for whom they take full responsibility of support and education. The parents of all these children are living, and the children have not been formally adopted. Although such arrangements sometimes occur because good educational facilities exist only in the grandparents' locale, the parents of some of these children live in cities where an excellent education could be obtained. In no case does it seem that the grandparents have taken in grandchildren because of the parents' financial need, although the grandparents' ability to lighten the burden for a family with several children to educate may certainly be a partial factor in the arrangement. Primarily the children have been entrusted to their grandparents in order to provide company and some help in the house; the older couple would otherwise be left alone after their sons accepted employment elsewhere. This practice will probably become more common in urban areas when neolocal residence for young couples increases in frequency because of occupational and hence geographical mobility.

Extended Households

The 9.6 percent of Ganeshnagar households with two or more couples — households I have termed "extended" — are in most cases "lineally extended" households. One of these includes two married sons and their parents, and another includes four generations of patrilineal descendants: a very old couple, their son and his wife, their grandson and his wife and children. But the typical extended household in Ganeshnagar (or in Kalyānpurī) consists of only the parental couple, one of their married sons and his wife, and the unmarried children of one or both couples. Ordinarily the junior couple has been married for only a few years. In eight of the extended households, unmarried children of the elder couple still live at home. In six, the younger couple has been married less than two years and is childless. In only one of the lineally extended households does the junior couple have a child who is either married or considered to be of marriageable age. In all the others preadolescent children form the youngest generation.

It is very unusual in these neighborhoods to find married brothers sharing a common hearth, whether or not their father and mother are alive or the brothers live under the same roof. Only four households in the Ganeshnagar data include married collaterals, and one is an unorthodox grouping: a man and wife, the wife's mother's brother's son and his wife, and the wife's father's brother's unmarried son. The tendency is clearly for only a single son, if any, to remain in the parental household after marriage, while any other sons set up independent households, either within the same dwelling or elsewhere. Although several homes in Ganeshnagar contain two or three married brothers and their elderly parents, each filial couple maintains a separate household, and the parents live with one of them.

The data also suggest that lineally extended households typically occur during the early years of sons' marriages rather than later. This might mean that married sons normally break away from the parental home after several years of extended household living, rather than remaining until their own children are ready to marry. However, these data may only reflect the fact that when a man's children are finally ready to marry, probably at least one of his parents has already died. A full explanation would have to rest on more detailed demographic data, particularly regarding the mortality of the older generation, the number and spacing of children, and trends in marital age.[5]

HOUSEHOLD TYPE, CASTE, AND LANDED PROPERTY

Some anthropologists have postulated a positive correlation in India between high caste and extended household residence (e.g., Mandelbaum 1949; Dube 1963). A recent study has failed to support such a correlation for an urban area, however (Desai 1964), and a review of the publications on the rural family in various parts of India gives it only partial support (Kolenda 1968a). The low incidence of extended households in my data and the high proportion of high-caste residents precludes a meaningful test of this hypothesis here. Fifteen of the seventeen extended households found in Ganeshnagar are in fact made up of members of high castes (Brahman, Baniā, and Rājpūt); the other two are respectively Nāī and Sunār. Of course, however, the three former castes together constitute eighty percent of the mohallā population.

A correlation between land ownership and extended households has also been suggested (Dube 1963; Beteille 1964; Desai 1964; Mandelbaum 1949), although again the evidence seems inconclusive, judging by Kolenda's review (1968a). If we consider the ownership of homes in Ganeshnagar, we find that all but three extended-household heads own the dwelling they occupy. Furthermore, all but one of the sets of agnatically related households which share a common residence if not a common table also own their residence jointly. Sarma has noted a similar association of extended households with home ownership in two Calcutta wards (1964). If we compare these data to those on nuclear households, we find that only one-third of the latter are owner-occupants of their home.

[5] For a pioneering attempt to amass such data and relate them to household composition for a single caste in a south Indian village, see Montgomery 1971.

However, most owner-occupants of Ganeshnagar homes live in nuclear or supplemented nuclear households.

Rural landholding provides a different picture. Only four of the seventeen extended-household heads report ownership of rural lands; they also own their homes in Ganeshnagar. Conversely, forty-four of the nuclear household heads (42 percent) report having landed property in their village of origin, and only one-third of these own homes in Ganeshnagar. Doubtless rural land ownership was underreported in my survey, but the figures are suggestive. The extended households in Ganeshnagar are mostly found among families which have severed property rural ties. One reason for this may be that generally these families have also lived away from their original village for many years. When we note that the heads of half the extended households have resided in Ganeshnagar for between fifteen and thirty years, and that five extended-household heads — almost one-third — were born in Meerut, it becomes even more evident that these households are otherwise unrepresentative of the total mohallā population. But if we examine the figures on home ownership, birthplace, and length of residence for the population at large, we also see that most household heads who own their own homes, were born in Meerut, or have lived in Ganeshnagar for fifteen to thirty years do not head extended households.

Once families have settled neolocally in the urban mohallā, have built homes there and given up rural holdings, there are a number of alternatives possible in subsequent generations. The practical advantages of remaining in the urban family home, combined with the cultural ideal of extended household living, will ensure the formation of some examples of the lineally extended household type. In other cases, however, the same conditions may produce a situation in which agnatically related households separate while continuing to live in a jointly owned dwelling. And in still other cases, despite the fact that the family has a home in Ganeshnagar and no strong roots elsewhere, married sons will go off with their wives and children, either to set up housekeeping in another city or to build a home of their own in a more fashionable and "modern" section of Meerut.

The preceding discussion, like much other writing on the subject of change in the Indian urban family, assumes that a comparison of figures on household composition which uses a defined set of household types can inform us about the nature and direction of trends of change. Yet many scholars (e.g., Fortes 1949a, 1949b, 1966; Goodenough 1956) have criticized reliance on typologies in the study of household structure and residence patterns, and several have suggested that an adequate study of change in family structure must first take into account the existence of a normal pattern of rearrangement in domestic organization, a so-called normal domestic cycle of the household (cf. Goody 1966). Inasmuch as a high proportion of nuclear households will occur in any sampling of Indian households, rural or urban, one should not be too quick to assume structural change due to urbanization. Finding a high proportion of nuclear households in a given sample may simply reflect the fact that a high proportion of the population is in the stage of family development at which a nuclear household structure is normal (cf. Gould 1965a, 1965b, 1968; Cohn 1961; Nicholas 1961; Collver 1963; Orenstein and Micklin 1966).

I use a technique developed by Hammel in the study of the family cycle in urban Peru (1961) for my Table XII, which gives figures, by household type, for age and for status within the household of all ever-married women surveyed in Ganeshnagar. Graph I illustrates the same data in another form. I have compressed the household types into four, by combining all extended types into one, and have added the dimension of super- and subordination of the respective women in the household, following Hammel's procedure. This dimension distinguishes the statuses of two or more ever-married women in the same supplemented or extended household. A woman is considered subordinate in status if another woman of senior kinship status (husband's mother, wife of husband's elder brother) lives in her household, or a man of senior kinship status to her husband (husband's father, brother of husband's father, husband's elder brother). She is also considered subordinate if she has no co-resident spouse and lives in the home of her own parents or with a married brother or a married daughter. These assignments of status are made without regard to the actual interpersonal relationships existing in any given household.

An analysis of the figures, based on the 235 women in my data who have ever been married, suggests the following developmental pattern, with each developmental phase reckoned as a decade in the life of the women concerned:

TABLE XII

HOUSEHOLD TYPE AND STATUS OF MARRIED WOMEN BY AGE COHORT

AGE	Nuclear		Sub-Nuclear		Supplem. Nuclear (Sub-ordinate)		Supplem. Nuclear (Super-ordinate)		Extended (Sub-ordinate)		Extended (Super-ordinate)		Total
	Number	Percent	Number	Percent	Number	Percent	Number	Percent	Number	Percent	Number	Percent	Number
15–24	22	52	0	0	6	14	5	11	10	23	0	0	43
25–34	37	53	1	1	12	17	13	19	6	9	1	1	70
35–44	21	40	2	4	10	19	13	24	4	7	3	6	53
45–54	17	49	3	8	2	6	8	23	0	0	5	14	35
55–64	4	23	1	6	3	18	6	35	0	0	3	18	17
65+	0	0	1	6	1	6	10	59	0	0	5	29	17
TOTAL													235

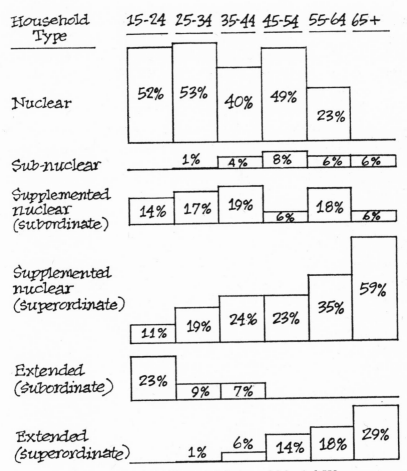

FIGURE 3   Household Type and Status of Married Women

1st decade: Half the married women in the age group 15–24 live in a nuclear household, while only slightly over one-third live as subordinates in the home of a husband's parent or parents. This suggests a significant tendency toward neolocal residence in the early years of marriage for young women of these neighborhoods, a possibility which is supported also by observational data.

2nd decade: The proportion of women in nuclear households is somewhat larger now, though not significantly so. In both decades it is close to the figure for the proportion of people of all ages and both sexes living in nuclear households. However, there is also a substantial increase in the percentage of women who are super-ordinate in households of the supplemented nuclear type. This probably reflects the addition of junior kinsmen to settled urban households prepared to take in rural relatives for studies or a first job. Interestingly the proportion of women with a subordinate status in extended households declines sharply. The decline may reflect the separation of young married men from the parental household after a short period of co-residence or may instead result from the death of one or both parents of the women's husbands. The senior generation's passing would also help account for the increase in nuclear households and in the proportion of women who are subordinate in a supplemented nuclear household.

3rd decade: Here there is indication of a significant decline in the proportion of women who live in nuclear households, accompanied by a rise in the proportion of those who live in either superordinate or subordinate status in supplemented nuclear households. In this age group, some women begin to take on the superordinate position in extended households; it is the beginning of the period in which sons marry and bring their wives into the parental household. But four of the seven women in this age group who live in extended households are still in a subordinate position.

4th decade: In the age group 45–54, the proportion of women living in nuclear households rises again to one-half. This rise probably reflects the death of elderly parents during the preceding period and the departure of young relatives for independent households of their own. The sons of women in this decade are usually married, and some live with both parents in an extended household. But 25 percent of the women in this age group are widows living with married sons.

5th decade: The majority of women in this age group are widows. Widowhood has caused some nuclear households and extended households to change to the supplemented nuclear type with the women of this age group in superordinate position. But some households of this type reflect the practice of elderly couples, whose sons reside neolocally, to take grandchildren into their home. The number of women in this phase is small, however, and percentages have little meaning. An equal number of women are respectively widows living with married daughters and matriarchs in patrilocal extended households, and four women live with their husbands in nuclear households.

6th decade: By this decade, nearly all women are without a spouse. None of those whose spouse is alive live in nuclear households; they have married sons, grandchildren, or other junior kinsmen sharing their household, just as do the widows in this phase of the domestic cycle. Notice finally that although the numbers for all of this developmental analysis have been low, their distribution does suggest a pattern which is supported by other kinds of evidence in my study.

NEOLOCALITY AND THE CARE OF AGED PARENTS

From the perspective of the norms for rural north-Indian residence, the most striking fact about household composition in Ganeshnagar is not the high proportion of nuclear households, but rather the prevalence of neolocal residence in a formally patrilocal society. Neolocal residence in these mohallās is of course directly associated with the occupational mobility that has drawn so many to Meerut from rural and small-town homes. But young couples do not always set up independent households reluctantly, because circumstances leave them no choice. Increasingly young people, particularly women, express a preference for living neolocally, free to run a household as they see fit, without needing to defer to the older generation. Even if urban parents of unmarried sons often speak of the time when their son's bride will join their household, they know that very probably their educated son will leave them either before or soon after his marriage. "The young people nowadays want to be free," the old women lament; "they don't know how to listen to their elders anymore." They mourn the passing of the old-time daughter-in-law, replaced by the educated girl who dares to disagree with her mother-in-law and persuades her husband to separate from the parental household so that she can socialize with neighbors, dress up in the latest styles, and go out to movies instead of staying home to do housework.

But the prevalence of these changing values should not be exaggerated. Young people also realize the advantages of living in an extended household: the security in case of sickness or financial difficulties, the companionship of a closeknit family, the possibility of sharing the housework rather than carrying the entire burden. Young women are still brought up to accept — even if they do not always prefer — the likelihood of their living in a household run by a mother-in-law, and much of their training is explicitly directed toward enabling them to adapt to this eventuality and to recognize its virtues. An important bar to acceptance of neolocal residence for young couples as a new norm is the strong sense of obligation sons feel for aging parents and the disapproval they elicit by leaving parents to live alone, particularly if parents are widowed, ill, or in financial distress. The concept of the life cycle whereby parents care for children who will later return their care is an integral part of socialization. Even very young boys are constantly reminded in varied ways that their parents are relying on them for security in old age. A boy who exposes himself to danger may be chided, "If you are gone, who will care for us later?" or an angry parent may reproach a disobedient or an inconsiderate son by saying, "What is the good of having a child like you, who will leave his parents alone in their old age?" Traditionally all a man's sons would be expected to remain either in the parental household or close by, but because urban conditions often make this arrangement impractical or impossible, in the mohallās at least one son is expected to remain with his parents until their death. If all sons are educated and no work is available near the parents' home, at least one son is expected to take the parents into his own household when they become unable or unwilling to manage for themselves. This pattern is evident in the figures for extended households in Ganeshnagar: only a single household includes parents and more than one married son. This situation suggests the emergence of a stem family pattern in the urban setting; however, this stem family is only structurally, not functionally or developmentally, similar to the classic one of Europe or Japan. Neither primogeniture nor any other regular principle of succession is effective here. (In fact it is probably inappropriate to speak of succession at all, since no office or headship of estate is involved.) Any son may be the one to remain with the parents. Some people claim that usually the youngest son "stays behind." As his elder brothers successively are educated and become employed, they leave home; being last, he must remain. It is also said that "the youngest is always loved more by his mother" and is therefore more willing to be the dutiful son. I did observe some younger sons responding as described, but to assess the regularity of such a pattern I would certainly require additional documentation. I also observed several eldest and middle sons living with elderly parents, either in the village or in Meerut, and helping to educate younger brothers for the white-collar job market. Academic ability and inclinations are certainly important determinants of which son stays at home.

A common solution to the problem of combining occupational mobility with family obligations is to have a widowed parent or both parents distribute time among the sons' households. This arrangement seems to be most common when the parent is a widowed mother; she will make visits of several months' duration to each son's household, often hundreds of miles apart. Aged parents do not always remain together. When both parents are living, and cannot or do not wish to stay alone, frequently they separate, the wife going to live with one son and the husband with another.

The traditional pattern of patrilocal residence and extended households in northern India serves a number of important functions. Primarily, it maintains for as long as possible an undivided, jointly worked and jointly managed estate; its second valuable function is providing ready care for the aged. When sons are employed in salaried occupations or as independent professionals, the primary function of this form of residence loses meaning, but not the secondary one. The need to provide sustenance and the warmth of a home for the elderly remains a problem. Various solutions have been indicated, notably the patrilineal "stem family" and the "touring" widow or widower. Even the practice of sending children to live with paternal grandparents as substitutes for oneself can be seen as an attempt to meet the demands of filial duty acceptably. But such adaptations to a changing situation are not always made: a number of elderly couples live in independent households in Ganeshnagar and Kalyānpurī. A number of widows and widowers with minor children have all their married sons living away, and the parents of a substantial number of young mohallā couples live alone or with younger unmarried children in the village or in another city. Presumably when these elderly people become incapacitated or seriously dissatisfied with their situation, they will be taken into one son's household or asked to share out their remain-

ing years among several sons' households. But such interim arrangements do not completely resolve the conflict in values surrounding the question of post-marital residence for educated and
upwardly mobile young urbanites.

CHAPTER IV

Marriage in the
Urban Context

T
HE broad outlines of family and kinship organization among Hindus in northern India are familiar from village studies and more specialized writings on Indian kinship.[1] Because these are readily available, detailed discussion of rural kinship patterns would be redundant. But I will describe some significant features of these patterns in this and the following chapter because they are the necessary background to a discussion of changing trends in middle-class urban neighborhoods.

I should first stress that, whatever the minor modifications, the urban setting does not cause any major rejection of traditional values and behavior. Adherence to familiar values and traditional roles within the family and extended kinship network is natural for

[1] For general works on the kinship organization of this region, see Karve 1965; Kapadia 1966. Some more specialized regional studies are Hitchcock 1957; Rowe 1960; Gould 1960, 1961, 1965a, 1968; Gore 1961, 1965, 1969; Singh, R. D. 1962; Luschinsky 1962; Dumont 1962, 1966; Vatuk 1969b, 1971. Studies of village life and kinship organization in other, nearby regions of India not only reveal important regional differences, but also provide much descriptive and analytic material useful for understanding family and kinship organization in this part of India. See, for example, Dube 1955; Mayer 1960; Madan 1965; Klass 1966.

a population largely of first- and second-generation migrants with a rural background. However, one can discern incipient trends which suggest the emergence of new patterns of social interaction and changing values and normative expectations, particularly within the household and between affinal relatives. Mohallā residents themselves are fully aware of changing times and new conditions, and their awareness hastens the pace of change.

THE RURAL BACKGROUND

In this region, as in most of India, descent is reckoned patrilineally, and patrilocal residence is the rule. Occasionally a married couple will be invited to live with the wife's parents because she has no brothers to work and inherit the land. But the position of a matrilocally married man is anomalous. Typically the village consists of a core of agnatically related males with their in-married wives, and an in-married husband is necessarily an outsider. Most villages include members of various endogamous castes, who cannot actually be related to one another but who are linked by a fictive genealogy which makes all those born in the village fictive agnates (cf. Freed 1963). The village itself is strictly exogamous; men and women of the same village and generation consider themselves "village brothers and sisters," regardless of caste.

Ideally, close male agnates — fathers, sons, brothers, and sometimes paternal uncles, nephews and cousins — should share an extended household and a jointly owned and managed estate. But provision is made for the partition of such an estate if the coparceners so desire, and typically cousins, and often brothers, divide their joint property after the demise of their parents.

Marriage is arranged for young people by the elders of their family — the initiative in arranging a marriage is formally taken by the father or paternal grandfather of the girl, although indirect inquiries may also be made by a boy's family when they consider him ready for marriage. Nowadays for girls of the higher castes in the rural area marriage typically occurs shortly after puberty; for boys, in late adolescence. Cohabitation, delayed for several months or even years after the wedding, is marked by a distinct ceremony, until which the girl remains at home, her life basically unchanged.

Young people are not consulted in the choice of a mate, nor do they normally see each other before the wedding ceremony. Careful chaperoning of adolescent girls, keeping them close to home after they reach the age of ten, and maintaining the fiction of siblingship among all village youngsters are intended to prevent their developing personal attachments, or engaging in sexual experimentation.

In choosing a mate for their offspring, usually parents do not especially consider personal attributes; they emphasize ancestry and the local reputation and prosperity of his family. Minimizing personal traits is largely unavoidable because marriages are customarily arranged between families which are not closely acquainted and have no opportunity to observe a prospective spouse's everyday behavior. While a girl's father and male agnates ordinarily do meet and talk with the prospective groom, the boy's elders, men or women, usually do not see the bride before the wedding. Nevertheless, there are positive notions of the personal traits desirable in a mate. A good bride is industrious, submissive, respectful, and obedient to her elders. A good husband works hard to support his family, does not waste money on drinking, gambling, or other "bad habits," and treats his wife considerately. However, since one cannot always determine beforehand whether a prospective mate will fulfill these expectations, it is considered best to rely on one's knowledge of his family: a "good" family presumably has been able to bring up children according to its own standards. The girl's family also wants the prospective groom's family to be able to maintain its daughter at least as comfortably as it has done. If possible, it will try to marry her into a family somewhat better off than itself, but most marriages take place between families of roughly equal social and financial status.

Even prior to such considerations are the stipulations that a union should not violate subcaste endogamy, clan (gotra) exogamy, or the bar to marriage between two persons known to be consanguineally related in any way. Furthermore, a marriage should not result in the exchange of women between kin groups — in other words, a girl should not be given in marriage to a family if one of its girls has previously come as a bride to one's own family. Such a marriage would confound the asymmetrical relationship which obtains between bride-givers and bride-takers, the latter being considered superior in status.[2] There is no bar to the marriage of a pair of brothers to a pair of sisters, for no exchange of women would be involved here, but such marriages are not preferred and occur only occasionally.

For a woman, marriage ideally takes place only once. The re-marriage of widows is traditionally proscribed for Hindus and in the higher castes is very rare. A man, however, may marry more than once, either after the death of his wife or in a polygynous union. Polygyny, however, is rare, usually resorted to only if the first wife proves barren or there has been a permanent separation. No formal procedure is used to end a marriage.[3] A man sometimes "leaves" (chor denā) his wife, either by sending her back to her natal home or by neglecting to call for her after she has gone there for a visit. A woman for her part may leave her husband and return to her parents' home if she is very unhappy in her marriage, or she may refuse to return to him after a visit there, thus precipitating a separation. But in order to succeed, she must have the cooperation of her natal kin because there are no practical means by which a single woman can support herself in the village. Children normally remain with their father and his kin in a separation, unless they are very young. Separations are not common in the higher castes because strong values support the sanctity of marriage and severe disapproval meets those who violate it. Married couples are generally exhorted to remain with each other despite any differences. The burden of preserving the marriage, however, is placed more heavily on the wife, who should ideally be able to win over even the most recalcitrant husband by forbearance and selfless devotion. When separation occurs, therefore, the wife's inadequacies are usually blamed for the failure of the marriage, unless there is strong evidence to the contrary. In any case, a separated woman of the higher castes is generally not considered eligible for remarriage. For her the marriage remains in effect, even though she is not

    [2] For a description and analysis of kinship terminology and prescribed kin roles, see Vatuk 1969b.
    [3] Since 1955 Indian law has provided for divorce of Hindu men and women, and rural inhabitants of this region occasionally make use of this law, which is described in more detail below. However, divorce is still strongly disapproved of and rarely obtained in rural areas among the higher castes. See also Luschinsky 1963.

living with her husband and he has taken another wife. Occasionally parents will attempt to find another husband for a daughter "left" very soon after her marriage, but it is always difficult for them to find a family willing to accept her.

MARRIAGE IN GANESHNAGAR AND KALYĀNPURĪ

Choice of Mate

In the urban mohallās, just as in the rural area, the families of the young people arrange the marriage. Traditional criteria remain important, but there is some shift of emphasis in response to changing conditions in the city. For the girl's family it is still important that the prospective groom provide economic security. But in the urban middle class his family need not have landed property, a prosperous business, or even illustrious ancestry. Far more important is that he himself be educated and have a well-paying, prestigious job. A young man who has been educated for a profession or holds a salaried position is in demand, even if his background is mediocre, although of course the well-placed son of a respected, well-to-do family has a greater advantage. Asked what kind of man they would seek for a marriageable daughter, people in these mohallās almost invariably replied "a service-vālā," that is, a salaried, white-collar employee. Some with higher aspirations mentioned an engineer or a doctor. A few Baniā respondents, themselves businessmen, suggested that a boy whose father runs a successful business would be the most desirable groom, but even for them the white-collar employee had considerable appeal.

Just as the wealth of the boy's family may matter less than his own earning potential, so his place of origin — rural or urban — matters less than his future place of residence. An educated boy of a rural family who has a good urban white-collar job would be readily considered for a mohallā girl, but a rural boy who intends to remain in the village and work the family land would rarely be of interest, even if his income were substantial. One difficulty in such a match would be the probable disparity of educational levels; few educated boys remain in the village to farm, and no mohallā family would want to marry their daughter to a boy less educated than she. Furthermore, rural and urban people alike consider city girls too delicate for the rigours and labor of country life. Despite

the preference for urban households, some young city wives ultimately find themselves keeping house in a village, because their
village in-laws have decided that to keep their daughter-in-law while
their son works in the city and makes periodic visits home is most
convenient for them and economical for the whole family. The
possibility of such a domestic arrangement is a consideration which
may play a role in the lengthy family discussions about a possible
match.

A boy's family inspects a girl's looks and skills. Her appearance
is important, particularly to the boy himself. Most desired is the
girl of "fair" complexion, with skin free of blemishes or scars. She
should ideally have smooth hair, thick and long, and a well-formed
body, neither thin nor very fat, and should be at least a few inches
shorter than her prospective husband. The boy's family also wants
her to be domestic: able to cook well and economically, to sew and
embroider, and to keep house efficiently. Especially important is
that she be energetic and willing to work and of a home-loving
temperament; not overly interested in movies, fashionable clothes,
and the like. Normally girls of the middle class, reared in homes
with no servants, begin helping with the housework young, and by
their early teens are quite capable of cooking meals, laundering,
and doing all the other usual household chores. In early adolescence
girls also begin sewing clothes for themselves and others and
spending much of their free time knitting sweaters with intricate
memorized patterns or embroidering bed and table linens and un-
derclothes for their trousseau. Nevertheless, there is a stereotype of
the educated girl as knowing nothing about housework and being
in any case reluctant to dirty her hands with cooking and cleaning
inasmuch as she has been trained for higher things. Because the
stereotype persists and a girl's household abilities are difficult to
ascertain before marriage, parents are on guard for any hint of in-
dolence or ineptitude in a prospective daughter-in-law.

Formal education is considered desirable in a bride, as long
as it has not deflected her from the functions and duties of a
woman. The demand for educated women as brides for white-collar
young men is probably largely responsible for the high level of
education reached by most of the girls in these mohallās, because
few of them are seriously preparing for a career. Parents often say
that educating one's daughter ensures her a "good" match — and

up to a point it does. The danger in education beyond the B.A. is that the range of acceptable men greatly narrows. Because her bridegroom must be equally well educated, parents often refuse to allow their daughter to pursue postgraduate studies.

Another reason why parents find it futile to allow their daughter to prepare seriously for a career is that an educated young wife is rarely expected to work to help with her own new household's expenses or those of her parents-in-law. Although some wives do go out to work, most families would consider it shameful and risky to have their daughter-in-law do so. Even if a young educated wife wishes to work, her husband or her parents-in-law rarely permit her to, because of the reflection on the family's prestige. Nonetheless girls and their families often do point out the value of an education for a woman because someday the death of her husband or a separation may oblige her to earn her own living. Although these calamities in fact befall only few women before their children are grown, recognizing that self-support might become necessary is itself a sign of changing times. Traditionally a woman would be cared for by her parents- or brothers-in-law if her husband should die, and in the unlikely event of a separation, her own parents and brothers would assume responsibility for her. The question of her own efforts would not normally arise. In Ganeshnagar and Kalyānpurī, however, widows do not generally live with affinal kin. Only one, a childless widow in her fifties, lives in the household of her husband's elder brother, in accordance with custom, but this family is unusual in that the widow's elder sister is the wife of her deceased husband's brother. Other widows in these mohallās live either with natal kin or in independent households, if they are not old enough to have married sons to support them. Many do have parents-in-law or brothers-in-law with whom they would traditionally have been entitled and expected to live. Some of these women, like others who are separated from their husbands, have relied on prior education to support themselves, but most became educated only after being left alone.

One reason given for educating a daughter is "so that she will have something to do," both before and after marriage. Studying is the only socially acceptable way that she can occupy her time, aside from needlecraft and housework, while waiting for a match to be arranged. After marriage, if she lives neolocally in a single room in the city, especially before the birth of children, she has comparatively little to do while her husband is at work all day. After preparing and cleaning up after the morning meal, tidying the small quarters, and washing the few clothes, she finds that much of the day stretches ahead. Except for visiting nearby neighbors or relatives, she can go nowhere alone respectably to pass the time. The reality of this life does not fulfill the romantic expectations of young marriage, so that loneliness and boredom are common complaints, particularly for young women brought up in large households. Continuing their studies, usually by working at home toward an examination, is one way in which many young married women cope with the need for an activity and occupation.

College-educated young men often explain their preference for educated wives in terms of social advantages. They speak of the greater sophistication of the educated girl, her awareness of things beyond the home and family, her knowledge of modern fashion and home decoration. More important, they praise her ability to entertain her husband's office colleagues in a refined manner, serving attractively prepared snacks or meals, perhaps even exchanging greetings and limited polite conversation. They admire the educated girl's ability to go out walking with her husband in public or to accompany him to the movies occasionally without feeling unduly embarrassed or shy. A gradual shift in the role of the wife — now seen as a companion in marriage — is clearly associated with the preference for educated brides.

Whatever reasons underlie the preference for educated girls, clearly it is increasingly necessary, even in the lower middle class, for fathers to provide their daughters with at least a high school education, or even more, if they aspire to a son-in-law equal in status to themselves, or of higher status. If they want a man who can provide their daughter with the standard of living to which she is, or would like to become, accustomed, they have to encourage — or allow — her to continue studying, preferably to the B.A. level, before completing marriage arrangements.

The Arrangement of Marriage

When a young man of these mohallās is considered ready for marriage by his parents, usually after he has completed his edu-

cation and found employment, his father makes the boy's eligibility
known to kinsmen, friends, and office colleagues, and is soon con-
tacted by men engaged in the even more urgent task of trying
to marry off a daughter. Proposals of marriage — and the delicate
feelers that precede such proposals — are usually, though not invariably, made to relative strangers: families known through a
friend or relative and perhaps by reputation, but not personally
or at least not intimately. To some extent this situation is a consequence of the need to find someone with a variety of desired
qualifications and the unlikelihood that he will happen to be within
one's close circle of acquaintances. But there are also obstacles to
a union linking families already well acquainted. Close associates
of the same caste are likely to be already related by blood or marriage such that another marriage would not be permissible. If not
related, they will have been assimilated into the sphere of fictive
kinship, as is anyone with whom a lasting relationship is maintained. Bonds of fictive kinship would make the young people of
the two families "brother" and "sister" and each other's parents
"uncles" and "aunts." Although such fictive ties may be, and sometimes are, disregarded to permit a marriage, ordinarily they are
taken seriously enough to make a marriage which would violate
them seem inappropriate, though not incestuous. Furthermore,
friend and in-law are considered to be incompatible roles. The restrained relationship between the respective parents of a man and
wife and its asymmetrical character are not consonant with the
ease and equality maintained between friends or fictive brothers,
and there is a natural fear that a marriage between the children
of friends will threaten their amity.

Because the two parties to a proposed marriage usually do not
know each other well, both must make enquiries through mutual
friends or acquaintances. Although once it was usual to employ
formal go-betweens, a man of Nāī caste and a Brahman, now this
role is informal and taken by anyone who knows both parties and
cares to help. Arrangements are often made without any intermediary. After expressing interest and receiving a favorable response, the girl's family customarily sends the boy's one or more
well touched-up studio portraits of their daughter, attractively
posed. The photograph is discussed by the boy and other members
of the family, along with all the other information they have about

the girl's qualifications. If his family is still interested, it will indicate (by letter, through an intermediary, or directly) that it would like to meet with the girl's family for further discussions. It may also send a photograph of the boy to be examined by the girl and her family.

The initial negotiations usually take place with only the most important male members of the two families present: fathers, paternal grandfathers, perhaps also the fathers' brothers. However, other close male agnates whose opinion is valued may also be included, along with one or two respected non-agnatic kinsmen or intimate friends. If a mutual friend or relative has originally brought the parties together, he may also be invited. The group present during the negotiations is not large, but both parties in turn usually consult a much larger number of their respective kin and close friends before reaching a decision. Women rarely participate in direct discussions with the other family, but they are active behind the scenes and often significantly influence the final choice. Usually after these initial talks the two parties continue discussion in their respective households, evaluating all the pros and cons of the proposed match. Often negotiations have been conducted with several parties and the advantages and disadvantages of each proposed match must be weighed before one of the young men is finally chosen and a formal agreement for the marriage is contracted.

When representatives of the two families talk together, they are not only exploring the qualifications of the young people, each side presenting the assets of its own child. They must also sound each other out on expectations about the scale of the proposed wedding celebration, the number of persons to be brought to the wedding by the boy's family and the duration of their stay, and the amount of cash and goods to be given as "dowry" (*dahej*). Inasmuch as most wedding expenses are borne by the girl's family, and it is usually in the disadvantageous position of trying to find a suitable groom whose family will accept its daughter at a price it can afford, these discussions are particularly delicate for her kinsmen. Some men entertaining a proposal for the hand of their son will state directly what they expect in dowry, but it is generally considered crude to "demand" cash and goods in this way. Many, in fact, say proudly, "In our family we never demand anything — whatever they want to give is fine, but we don't believe in demanding dowry." Discussions between the parties may begin with such protestations, but typically soon progress to what was received when the young man's brother or cousin was married last year or what plans are being made for his younger sister's marriage this summer, or more vaguely, "what is usually given nowadays" in "our circle." In this way the expectations of the boy's family are exposed for consideration. The girl's family responds by giving the impression that it is prepared to be most generous, meanwhile not committing itself too far beyond its resources.

At this time the two families also make detailed inquiries about each other's household and extended kin network. They ask about the marriages and the affinal connections of brothers and sisters, aunts and uncles. If any of their own relatives are illustrious or financially successful or in influential positions they will be certain to mention them. They may even tell of any irregular marriage of a close kinsman or give their version of any other blot on the family's respectability that is more or less public knowledge and could possibly cause difficulties later on.

In addition to the qualifications and appearance of the prospective spouses and the finances and reputation of their families, certain other matters come up in the family conferences that precede a final decision. For example, a boy's family usually considers it disadvantageous for him to marry a girl with no brothers because there will be no one to fulfill the gift-giving role of these kinsmen in later years, and after her parents' death neither will the wife have close natal kinsmen whom she can visit, nor will her husband have male affines to receive him in her natal home. Furthermore, there is the danger that, if his wife has no brothers, he will be drawn too closely into her family circle, to the neglect of his parents. However, to marry the only daughter of a well-to-do man who has no son may be an attractive proposition for a boy without extensive resources of his own. The girl's family in turn scrutinizes the composition of the boy's household, and his plans for future residence. Particularly if the girl is to live in an extended household, it investigates the character and personality of her prospective mother-in-law and sisters-in-law, both the husband's sisters and the wives of his brothers. Because adjustment in the early years of marriage in such a setting depends so much on the relationships among the females, learning something about the prospective groom's mother and the other women of his household is important. If neighbors or mutual acquaintances report them to be harsh or bad-tempered, the girl's close relatives will become apprehensive about the match. Her family also considers the boy's obligations. To marry an only son is deemed advantageous if a substantial estate is involved, but not if he is a white-collar worker with dependent parents: he should have brothers to share the burden. Even more serious is his having several younger sisters whom he may eventually have to marry off at considerable expense.

All members of the immediate families of the boy and girl discuss a proposed marriage among themselves, but the elder males — particularly the father, grandfather, or elder paternal uncle — are likely to have the final say. The young people themselves usually do not take an active part in these discussions, but they do have more choice about their impending marriage than do the typical rural pair. Particularly the educated boys are consulted about the kind of girl they want, asked their opinion of the girls' photos, and kept informed about the progress of negotiations. They are usually allowed to reject a displeasing match, and occasionally prevail upon parents to accept a proposal, otherwise not especially attractive, on the appeal of the girl's picture. The extent to which a young man actually becomes involved in the choice of his future wife depends of course on the forcefulness of his own personality and the relationship he has with his parents, particularly his father. Many young men, because of their upbringing, hesitate to express a dissenting opinion directly, or even indirectly through their mother. Or they are simply willing to defer to their elders' judgment on a matter in which they have had no experience of their own.

A girl's participation in the choice of a husband is usually even slighter. Ordinarily she is well aware of the arrangements that are being made, although her father may not discuss his plans as readily as if it were his son's marriage. Because ideally a girl does not concern herself with this matter, most girls feign complete indifference before outsiders and are embarrassed when the forthcoming marriage is mentioned in their presence. But of course they are deeply concerned about the momentous event. They listen avidly to the description of the boy, to the details of his education, job, and income, and to any other information that can be gleaned; they appraise any photographs that arrive. Although a girl is unlikely to tell her father that she disapproves of a particular young man, she can reveal any objections (or preferences) to her sisters or mother, who will in turn speak for her. Parents usually do consider their daughter's wishes, without regarding them as necessarily paramount, particularly if based on physical appearance or other details which they regard as minor. Most girls are eager to be married and unless the proposed young man has a serious defect are easily persuaded to accept their parents' choice.

In many urban middle-class families it is becoming usual for the boy and girl to see each other and for the women of the respective families to meet before the final decision. This occasion is not described as the young people's "meeting" each other, but rather as her family's "showing" the girl and the boy's "seeing" her. Showing one's daughter is not taken lightly and parents are usually reluctant to allow it unless fairly confident that a decision to marry will be reached. They fear that the boy, or some member of his family, will decide against the girl when they see her in person and reject the proposal. Several rejections of this kind may make it difficult to find any suitable match for her, as word spreads about her past failures. Nonetheless, it may be necessary to take this chance if the boy's family refuses to proceed without seeing her. Parents sometimes affirm that on principle, for the sake of respectability and in conformity with tradition, they do not believe in allowing their daughter to be seen before marriage, but this tactic may only result in terminating negotiations and furthermore arousing suspicions of something seriously wrong with the girl.

A girl may be shown in a public place such as a park or restaurant, but more usually the "seeing" takes place in her home. The boy's household — both men and women — together with any other close relatives they choose to include will be invited for tea or dinner on a prearranged date. The men are entertained in the men's sitting room (the baithak) while the women of the party are visiting with the girl, her mother, and other women of her family in the courtyard. On this occasion even the most vivacious girl is shy and retiring and untalkative, but the visiting women try to draw her out (to see if she has a speech impediment) and make her laugh (in case any teeth are missing) and display her bracelets (to check for skin diseases and missing fingers). They may also request a brief song, an instrumental demonstration, or a dance (which she will repeatedly refuse to perform so as not to be thought bold). She may be asked to display examples of her sewing or embroidery; meanwhile her relatives praise to the visitors her modest, respectful, and hardworking nature; her unusual skill at homecraft; and her excellent school examination results.

The girl is supposed to prepare refreshments by herself on this occasion, so that her cooking ability may be appraised; she also helps to serve the guests. Thus sometime during the visit she can be called into the men's sitting room, perhaps in the guise of bringing another pot of tea. Now, although her head is bent and almost covered by the end of her sari, her husband-to-be has a glimpse which must last him until their wedding day. Very rarely, families in these mohallās also allow a boy and girl to talk to each other. In the company of other members of their families, they may exchange information on courses of study, numbers of brothers and sisters, hobbies and special interests, and anything else that they can think of to say under such awkward circumstances. During their talk, they and the assembled relatives are alert for any additional clues that can be used in making the final, irrevocable decision.

A boy may choose to reject a girl whom he has seen, and his parents normally respect his opinion if he is firm and has a convincing reason. Sometimes other members of his family, particularly his mother or sister, notice some defect that had not been mentioned earlier and raise an objection. More rarely, the girl finds the boy unacceptable, or at least voices some doubts at this stage of the proceedings. But her doubts may not be heeded if her parents showed her only because they were already prepared to assent to the match, if the boy and his family would have her.

The "Love Marriage"

Some writers on the modern Indian family have suggested a contemporary trend away from the arranged marriage as I have described it toward greater participation or even initiative in the choice of a mate by urban young people. Ross, for example, maintains that:

In consideration of the feelings expressed in the interviews it would seem that the change that has so far taken place is that instead of the former practice of parents and relatives making the complete decision or giving their children the opportunity of selecting from a group of picked candidates, now the young people themselves tend to select the person they want to marry, and ask their parents' approval for their choice. (1961: 253)

Such a statement is not at all applicable to the population of this study, and does not, in fact, appear to be well substantiated by Ross's own tabular and interview data, although it is true that marriages arranged as Ross suggests are becoming more common in Westernized upper-class circles. Even in Ganeshnagar and Kalyānpurī, marriages based on personal choice are not entirely unknown. But they are rare — considered deviant and regarded with strong disapproval, both in abstract discussions and for actual cases. Older conventions prevail even though many young people, particularly boys in their late teens and early twenties, profess a desire for more control over the choice of their mate. Despite some romantic fantasies, few young people do not ultimately submit to an arranged marriage without outward rebellion, and many even evidence relief that the responsibility is not on their own shoulders. There are several reasons for this discrepancy between verbal commitment and actual practice. The chance to select one's own mate is part of the "modern," "progressive," and "forward" social ideology associated with the West and encouraged by the fanciful and romantic Indian movies which are an important part of the leisure life of the young educated Indian. It is not surprising that these young people would express such a wish in replying to a sociological survey, talking to a Western anthropologist, or even conversing among themselves, without being in the least prepared to carry it through in practice. Young people of middle-class families are effectively socialized for submission to parental authority and reliance on parental judgment, and even when disagreements with parents are serious and the urge to rebel is compelling, most young people find themselves unable to act in disregard of their parents' wishes on an important matter. Not only fear of their parents' anger or the wish to avoid causing pain is involved here. Strong feelings of emotional and material dependence upon parents produce unwillingness to take the consequences of defying them, if this means losing their support. And often, of course, there is an uncertainty:

perhaps the parents really do know best, perhaps their longer experience has really given them the insight they claim. If so, acceding to their wishes will ultimately prove the wiser course.

For most young people the issue of choosing their own mate never arises. In Ganeshnagar and Kalyānpurī, and in similar middle-class mohallās, the sexes are quite strictly segregated from pre-pubertal years. Coeducational schooling is not offered, except sometimes in the early grades. After the age of eight or nine girls and boys play together only within the family. Adolescent girls are carefully shielded from any contact with unrelated boys, taught to keep away from young men of the neighborhood, not to greet them on the street or engage in any conversation. They may greet friends of their brothers' who come to the house but are not supposed to sit in the room with them to talk. A nice boy is one who passes a girl in the street with averted eyes and makes no attempt to socialize with the sisters of his friends. These norms create uneasiness between unrelated members of the opposite sex, and preclude most young men's even meeting an eligible girl. Some boys compensate by standing in groups outside the girls' colleges, near movie theaters, or on busy streets and making suggestive remarks to girls who pass by. Thus they strengthen both girls' and their parents' conviction that only protection and isolation from young men can preserve virginity.

Nonetheless, romantic attachments do occur. They are called "love affairs," often using the English term, although premarital sex is rarely involved and very commonly no physical contact at all occurs. A love affair may be only a mutual attraction between neighbors or college classmates buttressed by an exchange of romantic letters and a few brief private conversations. Or it may be a deeper, enduring relationship between two young people who have found a way to meet often without arousing their parents' suspicions. But most of the affairs fail to end in marriage; many times the pair never even reach the point at which they dare to broach the subject to their respective families.

Marriages of personal choice are usually called by the English term "love marriage." The same is implied by the Hindi expression "married according to his own wishes" (apnī marzī se shādī kī). Since premarital love is socially disapproved of and must be hidden or denied if discovered — for it is often earnestly sought in private — these terms have derogatory connotation. One does not usually refer to one's own marriage in these terms, even if they are in fact appropriate. Commonly a distinction is made between a "real love marriage," which is akin to an elopement because it occurs without the cooperation or knowledge of the respective families and therefore without the traditional Hindu rites, and a marriage that was initially proposed by the couple themselves but was effected — however grudgingly — by their parents, with the decorum of an arranged union. In the former, the marriage may be solemnized by civil registration or occasionally by an accommodating priest, willing to forego parental consent. Two such unions of which I have knowledge took place in an Ārya Samāj temple. The ceremony may be kept a secret from the respective families for some time, or the young man may simply bring his wife home afterwards, presenting his parents with a *fait accompli*. Because of the disgrace which surrounds this type of union, most marriages of personal choice are performed in the traditional manner, and the "choice" aspect is later minimized as much as possible.

Because there were few instances of love marriage in the mohallās I studied, I can offer only limited generalizations about the circumstances in which marriages of personal choice may occur. Of four such marriages I have personal knowledge; others were described to me by mohallā residents as having occurred within their circle of relatives and friends. All the marriages involved either fellow students in a coeducational college, fellow workers in an office, residents of the same dwelling (children of landlord and tenant or of two tenants), or close affinal kin. Only one or two girls from these mohallās attended the coeducational Meerut College at the time of my research. Parents regard the attendance of girls at this college as too progressive and risky just because they may become involved in a love affair or be taken advantage of by some more sophisticated male classmate. But many boys from these mohallās attend the college and a few have developed romantic attachments there, two of which led to marriage in recent years. Both were intercaste marriages, one between a Brahman boy and a Jāt girl, another between a Brahman boy and a Bāniā. Neither occurred with the cooperation of the parents, although in both cases an uneasy reconciliation took place soon afterwards.

To my knowledge the only marriages which have taken place

between two residents of the same mohallā have been love marriages between occupants of the same or adjacent houses. Sharing
a roof offers one of the few situations in which young people may
mingle with a nonrelative of the opposite sex, although intimacy
must develop surreptitiously. Most such dalliance is blighted by
watchful parents. Those who allow their daughter to become involved with a young man in this way are sharply criticised.

Romance between affinal relatives may develop when lengthy
or frequent visits are made to the home of a kinsman in which an
eligible partner lives. The only close affines eligible for marriage
would be the brothers or cousins of a sister's husband or, for a
man, the sisters or cousins of his brother's wife, but more remote
kinsmen of the same kin categories (jījā/sālī) would also be permissible mates and might have the opportunity to interact informally with each other on such visits. A Brahman girl of Ganeshnagar was married some years before my visit to the younger brother
of her sister's husband. Their neighbor reported to me:

> They got to know one another when he used to come with his older
> brother to fetch home his older brother's wife. Sometimes he
> would stay with the family for a few days, and nobody minded if
> they talked to each other since they were jījā and sālī. But once her
> mother found them alone together, talking privately in the sitting
> room, and the family decided that under the circumstances it
> would be best to arrange for their marriage.

The one marriage of personal choice between office colleagues from
these mohallās is necessarily unusual because so few young women
are employed before marriage and those who are usually work in
girls' schools. The woman in this case was in her late twenties
when she married, well advanced in a career in government service,
and living on her own.

Finally, there are marriages of personal choice which do not
result from any real friendship between the pair, but occur when
a young man comes to know a girl from a distance or from a brief
meeting — a neighbor perhaps, or the sister of an acquaintance —
and without approaching her directly asks his father to look into
the possibility of arranging a marriage. If little or no communication has occurred between the two young people — nothing suggestive of scandal — and both are acceptable otherwise to the re-

spective families, they may agree to the match. Occasionally a girl may similarly suggest the name of a young man when her father is seeking a husband for her. Matches thus instigated by the young people ordinarily do not come to be arranged, or if they do, usually are not called love marriages, even by those who might be aware that the initiative came from the boy or the girl.

Horoscopes and Setting the Wedding Date

The middle-class people of these mohallās do not place very much importance on the matching of horoscopes which is customary in rural marriages. Many disregard this procedure entirely; others may have the horoscopes compared, but in the event of a negative prognostic will ignore the astrologer's advice or consult another expert if the match is otherwise suitable. Alternatively, they may use an unfavorable report as an excuse to break off negotiations when the real reason for refusing the match is financial or otherwise. Traditionally the date and time of the wedding should also be determined astrologically. An auspicious timing of the ceremony is traditionally considered crucial for the success of the marriage. But increasingly, as one woman explained, "they decide what day they want to have the wedding and then tell the priest 'figure it out for the twentieth of June.' " Because of job responsibilities, the timing of school vacations and examinations, and the need to rent accommodations for a large bridegroom's party during the busy marriage season, weddings must be planned to suit the convenience of the families concerned. Should they conflict, practical considerations often outweigh religious ones for the middle-class urbanite.

Caste Endogamy

Two basic traditional requirements in the arrangement of marriages are subcaste endogamy and endogamy of the region or linguistic community. Although regional endogamy occurs as a matter of course in the north Indian rural setting with its "marriage circles" of fairly limited geographical range (see Rowe 1960; Gould 1960, 1961; and Klass 1966), in urban areas which shelter people of varied origin, regional differences become a matter of notice. In these neighborhoods, Punjābīs and Pahārīs are the only "foreign" groups found in any numbers, and each tends still to retain its

endogamous identity even when the same named subcastes occur
in all regions and are accepted as equivalent for most purposes, as
are, for example, the Gaur Brahmans in each of the three regions:
Western Uttar Pradesh, Punjab, and Gahrval.

Marriages which cross the endogamous caste or regional boundaries are almost always marriages of personal choice, according to
my own observation and other's studies; thus in the only extensive
study of intercaste marriage in India, which analyzes a sample of
two hundred such unions, ninety-five percent were "love marriages"
(Kannan 1963: 53–54). During my study, not a single arranged
intercaste marriage was observed or reported in the two mohallās
or among the kin and acquaintances of mohallā residents. In discussing this matter, several men independently admitted their in-
ability to practice the egalitarian ideals they professed by arranging
an intercaste marriage for any of their children, their excuse being
the unwillingness of "society" or of the women of their family to
accept such a union. Others said that while they do consider intercaste marriage socially desirable, they feel that in practice such
unions have little chance of success because of cultural differences
between the partners.

Only one intercaste couple lives in these mohallās. Its marriage
was one of choice, performed without the knowledge of either set
of parents in a local Ārya Samāj temple. Shortly after the ceremony
the husband, an only son, became reconciled with his parents, who
are well-to-do, educated, Brahmans, highly respected in the neighborhood. He and his Jāt wife, a girl of a rural family who studied
with him at Meerut College, moved into the household of his
parents and paternal grandparents and live there still with their
young children. His family has gradually adjusted to the marriage,
despite its original opposition and the disapproval of kin and neighbors which it suffered when the marriage became known. This
process of adjustment has doubtless been made easier because
the family has high economic and social status and other close
relatives have also contracted intercaste or interfaith marriages.
Although this marriage still raises eyebrows when it is discussed —
I was told many versions of the story before ever meeting the
couple — the family has ceased to suffer any social ostracism and
the couple's children do not suffer any obvious disadvantages, although their caste status may cause difficulties when the time for

their marriage approaches. But this couple is upwardly mobile; it considers itself modern and Westernized and sends its children to an English-language convent school in Meerut which caters primarily to the upper and upper-middle classes of the town and to the families of military officers stationed there. This couple may well be in a position in later years to find mates for its children within a more Westernized circle where their mixed ancestry is of minor importance.

Breaches of the endogamous boundary between subcastes are somewhat more common than between different castes and arouse no particular adverse comment in the community as a whole, although many people would be strongly opposed to such a marriage if it took place within their own family or close kin network. I recorded a considerable number of marriages between members of different Baniā subcastes and between Gaur Brahmans and people of other Brahman subcastes, although only a few of these involved mohallā residents. The local Vaishya Association, to which leading Baniās of various subcastes belong, formally approves the breaking down of subcaste barriers among Baniās in this way, and the trend seems to be toward an increasing incidence of intersubcaste marriage, as it becomes increasingly difficult to make suitable matches for educated young people within the subcaste.

Gotra Exogamy

The rule among most of the castes of this area is exogamy of the patrilineal "clan" (*gotra*)[4] with a bar to marriage into the gotra of the mother (referred to as the "clan of the mother's father" or "clan of the mother's brother"). According to the traditional rules of some castes the father's mother's gotra and even the mother's mother's gotra should be avoided as well.[5] But few informants in these mohallās claimed that they actually do consider the mother's gotra nowadays when arranging marriage, and none professed any concern with the gotra of the father's mother. While

---

[4] Some scholars disagree as to whether the gotra may properly be considered a clan, in the usual anthropological sense of the term. However, for the present purpose, and with reference to its function as an ascribed exogamous group, this translation will be used (cf. Madan 1962a).

[5] For an excellent discussion of this so-called "four-gotra rule" and its implications in the kinship system of one caste in this region, see Tiemann 1970.

recognizing the existence of the traditional rule, they explained current laxity among urban educated people like themselves as resulting from a narrowing of the field of choice because of non-traditional considerations such as education, occupation, and income level.

My information on the actual frequency of marriage into the mother's gotra is limited to those instances in which a man and his wife's mother or a woman and her husband's mother were both included in the census, and even among these some women proved unable to name their natal gotra. However, sufficient cases of the marriage of a man or a woman into the gotra of the mother's father are present in this data to lend support to informants' assertions that this rule is no longer rigidly followed in their social stratum and that typically the question of the mother's gotra is not even broached during the premarriage negotiations.

More surprising perhaps is the incidence in these mohallās of breach of gotra exogamy, again apparently in direct response to a shortage of suitable mates. Out of 163 marriages in which the gotra of both spouses is reported, nine are *sagotra* unions, that is, marriages within the gotra. The percentage is not high, but it is indicative of a loosening of the rigid gotra exogamy reported by students of Indian rural social organization (Mayer 1960: 203; Klass 1966: 957–958; Gould 1960: 480–481; Orenstein 1965: 62–63). Explanations for these breaches of exogamic rules were not obtainable in every case, since the persons who had arranged the unconventional unions were generally not available to me. However, discussion with the sagotra couples themselves, with persons still arranging their children's marriages, and with others who had once engaged in negotiations, together with limited observation of actual marriage negotiations, showed a distinct pattern in these breaches of exogamy. Positive rejection of the rule of gotra exogamy is rare. Most of those interviewed on this subject agreed that one should not marry within the gotra "because persons of the same gotra are like brother and sister." People of the same gotra refer to one another as "gotra brother" or "gotra sister" and consider themselves distantly related even if they share no known genealogical links. Two older men, both Ārya Samājīs, dissented from this almost unanimous view, and professed not to believe in gotra exogamy. One of these had himself been married to a woman of his own gotra forty-two years before — the only case in my data of a sagotra union which took place more than ten years ago. The other maintained: "Our whole family is very progressive. We don't believe in caste and gotra and things like that, and I have married my daughter and two of my sisters to men of our own gotra." Whether these marriages were intentionally arranged in this way because of his convictions, or his statements are a justification of his unorthodox actions is not clear.

Most people feel that adherence to gotra exogamy has a legitimate rationale — that sagotra unions are distantly incestuous — but when the rule impedes an otherwise ideal match, a way is sometimes found to circumvent it. Two strategies were reported. The first is known as "marrying from the gotra of the mother's father" (nānā ke gotra se shādī karnā). The two parties (and probably also the officiating priest) agree that when the priest arrives at that point in the wedding ceremony at which he asks for the gotras of the pair, the guardian of the girl will reply, "We are marrying her from her maternal grandfather's gotra, which is ——." I have never personally observed this procedure, but two sagotra couples independently described its use in their own marriages.

I was once present when a family visited the home of a prospective son-in-law, an engineering student and son of a well-to-do Baniā businessman. While the men of both families discussed their terms in the men's sitting room, the girl's mother and paternal aunt were invited into the courtyard with the boy's mother and her brother's wife, who lived nearby. After some exchanges about the talents of their respective offspring, the girl's mother asked for the boy's gotra. On realizing that it was the same as the girl's, her mother shrugged and said: "It doesn't matter. We were thinking, anyway, if the match is good, we will marry her from her maternal grandfather's gotra." Negotiations for this marriage later broke down, but the boy's family did not give coincidence of gotra as the reason; it found that the girl's family could not provide sufficient dowry. Yet gotra problems can impede marriages. A Brahman widow alluded to this procedure of claiming the maternal grandfather's gotra when discussing the negotiations for her daughter's marriage. Her father-in-law had married for the second time after her own marriage and had young children of his own. Although he and his wife also lived in Meerut and he should have undertaken the responsibility for the marriage of his late son's daughter, he had not done so, ostensibly for financial reasons. The widow's father, a retired engineer living nearby, therefore decided to find a husband for the girl. He finally found a suitable young man, but when serious negotiations began the two proved to be of the same gotra. The widow recalled how, "Many people suggested to him, when they heard this, that he should marry the girl from his own gotra. But he refused. He said, "It isn't right. After all, her own people [i.e., her agnatic kin] are still alive." He eventually rejected this match because of the gotra problem and later arranged his granddaughter's marriage to another young man.

Another way to evade the exogamous rule without flouting it is to find some difference in the gotras, even though they are apparently the same. For this, the connivance of the priest is necessary. He typically finds a difference in the pronunciation of the gotra name which enables him to make a judgment that two distinct gotras are involved — not difficult to do in view of local dialectal variations, differences between dialect names and Sanskrit names, and the variant names for some gotras. Most of the sagotra marriages of which I have any background knowledge had been rationalized in this way, with at least some of the people involved fully cognizant that the procedure was an evasion. Assuredly gotra exogamy is not being abandoned; it is still considered important. But evasion of the traditional rule is increasingly practiced by those who pursue other, more worldly considerations. Even in rural areas, when educated offspring are being married, observance of gotra exogamy shows signs of weakening.

Marriage to Consanguineal Kin

Another traditional bar to marriage is known consanguinity. Although the conventionally quoted rule refers only to an impediment to marriage within five degrees on the maternal and seven degrees on the paternal side (these kin being referred to as *sapinda*), the rule is interpreted in practice as barring marriage to anyone known to be a blood relative. It is impossible to assess the precise degree of adherence to this rule, but I have no evidence that it is ever disregarded in the neighborhoods I studied. The feeling of common blood between members of the same gotra is often purely formal whereas the marriage of known consanguineal kin arouses intense abhorrence. Hindus are aware that close kin marriage is practiced and even preferred by Muslims in this region, and some know of the custom among south Indian Hindus, but they say that such marriages are unthinkable for them. Furthermore, because of limited numbers it is easier to avoid consanguines in arranging a marriage than to avoid members of the same gotra, given other considerations and preferences.

The one case of kin marriage that came to my attention occurred in an adjoining mohallā between a man and his patrilateral cross-cousin. It was a marriage of personal choice for the man, who is said to have forced the girl and both sets of parents to agree through threats of violence. The couple have children now and live together in an apparently stable relationship. Public opinion was shocked by the marriage, but generally there is pity for the girl and for both sets of parents, forced by tragic circumstances to agree to a clearly incestuous union.

Local Exogamy

One might expect to find a rule of mohallā exogamy in the city neighborhood to parallel the village exogamy maintained so strictly in the rural areas. However, it does not exist in the neighborhoods I studied, although I have some evidence that it does in the long-settled mohallās in the old city area (and see Lynch 1967: 146–147). Despite the absence of an explicit rule, no marriages, to my knowledge, have ever been arranged within either of the mohallās studied. I have mentioned above some love marriages which did occur. These were criticized because the young people had chosen their own spouses, not because the pair were neighborhood brother and sister.

Marriages between residents of adjoining or nearby mohallās do occur by arrangement, but they are unusual and are not preferred. The distinct attitude disfavoring marriages within the neighborhood is consistent with the general preference, already mentioned, for marrying one's child to the offspring of strangers or slight acquaintances rather than friends, and furthermore for marrying one's child geographically far rather than nearby. It is felt that if a girl's parents live nearby, her ties to her natal home, reinforced by frequent meetings with her parents and siblings, will interfere with her adjustment to her conjugal home and the shift of loyalty from her natal to her conjugal family. She will have frequent opportunity to complain to her parents and brothers about the way she is treated by her husband and in-laws and will encourage her parents to intervene in the affairs of her conjugal household. She will tell her parents secrets of her conjugal household which could lower its prestige if broadcast in the neighborhood. It is also said that the bride who marries near will take things — money, clothes, foodstuffs — from her conjugal home for her natal kin. A boy's parents are particularly cautious about proximity when they are arranging a marriage, but a girl's may prefer a near marriage so that they will be able to see their daughter and grandchildren as often as possible. Obviously as neolocal residence becomes more common, the proximity of the respective parents does not create the same problems as in the rural setting, although it does intensify the conflicting family pressures on a young married woman.

Dowry

In urban India the extent and importance of the dowry (dahej), appear to increase according to the groom's education and white-collar status. This circumstance is largely a response to the diminishing number of eligible mates for girls in this class — particularly the relative scarcity of sufficiently qualified young men of the same caste — and also, as Gould suggests (1963: 436–438), serves as a means of maintaining the social exclusiveness of the aspiring elite. There is evidence that in other parts of India also the dowry is playing an increasingly prominent role in marriage arrangements (Karve 1965; Srinivas 1966; Khare 1970), and even among those few idealistic families which verbally oppose the giving and taking of dowry as a "social evil," the marriage of a daughter requires a large financial outlay.

In rural parts of this region dahej consists primarily of clothing (for the bride, the groom, and members of his family), household goods (cooking and eating utensils of brass, bedding, and table linens), jewelry (of silver and gold, for the bride herself), and other personal items for the bride's own use, such as cosmetics and ribbons. A large trunk for the storage of her possessions in her husband's home is traditionally included as well. Other gifts for the groom are given in addition to his one or more suits of clothes:

a ring, a watch, often a bicycle, and in recent years, a transistor radio. Moreover, the groom and members of his family expect to receive cash gifts at specified stages in the marriage proceedings.

The wedding of a daughter is an expensive undertaking, and saving for their daughters' marriages is a major concern of all parents for years before the actual event. Although cash and goods are accumulated over a long period, money must often be borrowed to cover the expenses, which also include the cost of feasting the wedding guests. The ceremony is always held at the bride's home. The brother of the bride's mother contributes a substantial gift of cash and goods (*bhāt*), and friends, neighbors, and relatives contribute cash at the wedding ceremony called "gift of the virgin" (*kanya dān*), but these contributions return only a small part of the total outlay. The wedding of a son also requires expenditure on gifts of clothing and jewelry for the bride and feasting of friends and relatives of the groom at his own home, but typically the costs incurred by the groom's family amount to considerably less than those of the bride's.

Among the urban middle-class people studied here, the cost of a wedding is greatly inflated over the rural standard, even though incomes are not appreciably higher because of the rapidly increasing cost of living in the city. Inasmuch as the cost of a wedding is directly related to the level of education and potential or actual earning capacity of the groom, one hears semi-humorous references to the "price" of an engineer, a doctor, or a college professor. There is said to be a greater emphasis on the dowry and a tendency to give larger amounts of cash rather than goods among Baniās. However, I do not have quantitative data which would support this generally held belief. Although the most expensive weddings I observed were Baniās', these families were also among the wealthiest in the neighborhood and therefore could be expected to spend large amounts.

To spend two or more times one's annual income on a daughter's marriage is not at all unusual. A wedding locally regarded as "modest" costs a minimum of Rs. 5000, and a Rs. 12,000 wedding is considered adequate, but not extravagant. Most weddings about which I have detailed information are in this range, but many cost far more. At one extreme is a wedding costing Rs. 1000 in which an extremely poor Nāī couple in Kalyānpurī married

both their daughters in a double ceremony to village boys, uneducated and of poor families. The girls were eleven and fourteen,
and their youth (particularly the age of the younger) caused much
shocked comment, although there was sympathetic appreciation
of the fact that the poverty of the family made it impossible to
afford a second wedding at a later date. Besides, the maturation of
the older girl made it risky to wait and still be sure of her virginity.
Girls of wealthier families are protected and chaperoned even into
their twenties, but she would not be. This girl was particularly
vulnerable because she worked as a house servant in a number
of homes to help her parents and was often out alone until late
at night completing her jobs. Some of the cost of the wedding
and many of the goods given in dahej were donated by mohallā
families for whom the Nāin and her daughters did housework and
provided ritual services at weddings and other ceremonies. Some
money was borrowed from a family for whom she had worked for
many years. In comparison, the marriage of a college lecturer to
an army major cost her father Rs. 35,000, including Rs. 11,000 in
cash, a Rs. 3000 motor scooter, a refrigerator, and other goods. At
this wedding a considerable amount was spent on decorations, primarily strings of multicolored lights festooning the front of the
house, and on music, popular records broadcast by loudspeaker to
reach the ears of listeners several blocks away.

A more typical wedding for these neighborhoods is one costing approximately Rs. 12,000: the marriage of a retired teacher's
daughter to an Ayurvedic doctor's son, who is studying in order
eventually to take over his father's practice in a small town in
Meerut District. This wedding had not yet taken place during my
stay, although all the negotiations had been completed and the
initial "reservation" of the boy (roknā) had been made with the
presentation of Rs. 126 (distributed among members of the groom's
family) by the bride's father. The following budget for the forthcoming wedding had been decided upon:

cash (for the groom and his family) Rs.	3201
suit (for the groom)	250
watch (for the groom)	250
bicycle (for the groom)	300
ring (for the groom)	100

jewelry (for the bride)	1000
steel wardrobe cabinet	450
sofa	200
bedstead	100
dressing table	125
clothes (for bride and in-laws)	800
clothes (for in-laws' children)	150
utensils	200
miscellaneous (umbrella, fountain pen, shaving set, tea set, glass pitcher and tumblers, etc.)	125
sweets, fruits, and nuts (for engagement ceremony)	150

Total goods and cash: Rs. 7401

Additionally the family had been saving clothing, bedding, and linens, some of which the bride had embroidered, to be presented with the dowry. It planned to give a sewing machine worth Rs. 250, which had been bought several years ago anticipating this occasion and had been only rarely used. A number of the brass and stainless steel cooking pots, plates, and glasses for presentation were already stored in readiness — many had been received two years earlier when the oldest son was married and had never been used. The family had planned to give a radio and an electric fan as well, because these are standard dowry items, but the groom's father specifically mentioned that his household already owned these things and would not expect their inclusion in the dowry.

The remainder of the budgeted funds were intended for the wedding feast. The parties had agreed that the groom's wedding party would consist of 150 to 200 men, relatives and friends of the groom and of his parents, who would be provided with three meals during their stay. Relatives and friends of the bride's family would come for the ceremony and would also be fed one or more meals. Several hundred rupees would be needed to pay the professional caterers hired to prepare the festive meals, and to purchase wheat, spices, vegetables, clarified butter, sugar, milk, tea, and Coca-Cola, the non-traditional but popular wedding beverage. In addition, miscellaneous amounts of cash would be expended for traditional ritual dues paid to kinsmen of the bride and to kamins or "servants" who have prescribed ritual roles in the wedding proceedings. Colored lights must be rented for decorating the house, and a loudspeaker and popular records obtained.

The groom's family, like the bride's, incurs expenses for a marriage, but, just as in rural areas, their expenses are generally far lower. The groom's parents always provide one or more expensive saris for the bride, as well as gold and silver jewelry, often of considerable value. The jewelry does not become the private property of the bride to dispose of as she wishes; it remains part of the joint property of her in-law's extended family and may be given again to the brides of her husband's younger brothers when they are married at a later date. The groom's family also gives at least one feast, often a catered affair, for their friends, kinsmen, and neighbors at their own home. The procession in which the groom arrives at the bride's home for the wedding ceremony provides an opportunity for conspicuous display. The city groom most often arrives in a hired automobile, followed by his male relatives and friends (some in cars and others on foot) and preceded by a professional brass band playing the latest popular film tunes. The vehicle is often elaborately decorated and members of the party shoot off firecrackers as the group proceeds slowly through the streets. Transvestite dancers are commonly hired to accompany the procession; they flirt with male onlookers and are tipped coins and rupee bills. One procession which I observed had the groom enthroned on a float, a sleigh drawn by four reindeer whose antlers flashed multicolored electric lights. Motive power was provided by an ancient but unobtrusive automobile. The groom's display is rivaled by the colored lights decorating the bride's home and the loudspeaker blaring songs until late into the night.

Conspicuous display for a wedding importantly includes the "showing" of the dahej (in installments, at the time of the engagement and of the wedding itself and at gaunā, the consummation ceremony). The goods are spread out first in the home of the bride, in the courtyard or in a room specially reserved for the purpose; and neighbors, friends, and kinsmen — mainly women and children — come to inspect, admire, and compare the display with the dowry for other marriages they have attended. Later the goods are again displayed and inspected at the groom's home, and judgments are made as to whether the new in-laws have "given well" or not. The harshest criticism of a new bride is that "she has brought nothing at all" — seldom literally true, but a bride whose family has been unable to make an impressive showing may nonetheless suffer for years to come. As display a wedding validates the status of both families for their associates and may affect the success of the marriage itself.

Age at Marriage

The minimum legal age for the marriage of girls is fifteen, and rarely are urban middle-class girls married younger. Of 115 married women under forty, only 11 had been married before fifteen, and of these half waited until fifteen or beyond before gaunā took place. During my research I learned of only one legally underage bride in either mohallā — the Nāī girl mentioned earlier. Adherence to the law is not especially inconvenient because changing conditions have made early marriages undesirable for other reasons. Inasmuch as enforcement of the law is extremely lax, its existence cannot be considered a primary motive for later marriages among the urban middle class.

Mohallā residents say that nowadays young people marry several years later than is usual in the village and later than they used to do in the city. To evaluate the rising age of marriage among mohallā residents accurately is impossible without figures from their places of origin or detailed genealogical data on the age of marriage of their forefathers. But comparing the ages at marriage for residents now over and under 40 years offers some pertinent indications. Despite the common notion that pre-pubertal marriage is characteristic of India as a whole, we find that only 15 percent of women over 40 in Ganeshnagar were married before 15, and of these very few began to cohabit with their husbands until 15. In the under-forty group even fewer women married before 15, all of them among the older women in the group. Yet more than one-third the married women under 40 married at 19 years of age or older, whereas only 7.4 percent of the older women married at such a late age. The average age of marriage for women in the younger age group is 17.4, with gaunā at 18 years; for the older age group it is 15.3, with gaunā at 16.5. For men the difference between the two age groups is less: the younger men married at an average age of 21.8 and had gaunā at 22.4; older men married at an average age of 20.7, with gaunā at 22. These figures show an increase in the average age at marriage for both sexes, an increase in the average age at gaunā, but a decrease in the average length of time elapsing between these two ceremonies.

Significantly a considerable number of unmarried girls in these mohallās are over nineteen years of age. Such a situation is unusual in the village milieu. Most of these young women will probably marry someday, but as I have said, arranging a suitable marriage becomes increasingly difficult as a girl approaches thirty, and is virtually impossible thereafter. Older men who have been married before almost invariably seek a young second wife. Bachelors in their late twenties or thirties exist, but are rare. Most unmarried older girls, as I have commented, are also highly educated and therefore restricted in their choice of spouse. And to be contended with is the feeling that an unmarried girl in her late twenties must have a hidden defect (if not an obvious one) to have been neglected for so long.

In these neighborhoods sixteen is considered the best age for a girl to marry. Although I found the *average* age at marriage to be higher than this for the present generation, sixteen is in fact the *modal* age at marriage for women of all ages, according to the figures from Ganeshnagar. Girls of this age are considered physically most desirable as brides. Furthermore, because they have reached the age when their sexuality is believed to be fully awakened, they "need" a husband. The moodiness, quarrelsomeness, and emotional problems of girls in late adolescence are commonly traced to their sexuality, and marriage is believed to solve them. By sixteen a girl is mature enough to undertake household responsibilities but young enough to be molded to choice by her husband and in-laws. Adaptability is most important in a bride expected to learn and internalize the ways of her conjugal family, and older girls are assumed to have developed opinions and personalities of their own which will hinder their adjusting satisfactorily to a new environment. Neolocal residence makes this last factor less important than it is with patrilocal residence in an extended household, but adjustment to a stranger-husband and his preconceptions about his wife requires considerable malleability of a girl. But despite the fact that people generally say that they prefer to marry their daughters at sixteen, girls in these mohallās, as the cited figures show, are increasingly being allowed to continue their education until seventeen or eighteen, or even later, before they are married.

Boys are expected to marry in their early twenties, after they have completed their education and are able to support a wife or at least make a substantial contribution to the parental household to support her and any children. Because of the emphasis on a completed education, some men in the younger age group either married after twenty-five for the first time, or are over twenty-five and still single.

The Ceremonial Schedule

When girls are married typically between sixteen and eighteen to young men in their early twenties, there is little reason to prolong the various stages in the wedding ceremony. Marriages in the urban middle class usually are arranged only shortly before the parents plan to have the actual ceremony performed. The engagement (sagāī) rarely occurs more than one year before the wedding, and often takes place the previous week, although some time before this, the formal "reservation" of the boy (roknā) has been made and sealed with a cash gift. Between this brief ritual and the engagement the families make their preparations for the engagement and the wedding itself. The period of time elapsing between the wedding and gaunā is also decreasing, as I have shown, and to combine the two ceremonies is becoming common. That is, after the wedding the girl goes to her husband's home for the usual one or two days to be welcomed by her affines. She is then returned to her parents' home, but not for the customary several months or years, only for one or two days. She then returns immediately to her husband's home for gaunā, and may either remain there or, if he is employed elsewhere, accompany him to live near his work. The Western practice of the honeymoon is still not generally accepted in these neighborhoods, although it is becoming fashionable in more Westernized, upper-class circles in Indian cities. Two mohallā couples, both from relatively well-to-do families, took such wedding trips during the year of my research.

Telescoping the various stages in the wedding ceremonies, like shortening each stage itself, is an economizing practice. But it has the disadvantage of causing all the family's expenses to come simultaneously rather than gradually. It also forces upon the young couple a rapid shift to the married state, in place of the lengthy transitional period during which both parties can become accustomed to their new status. The young wife especially may experience a sense of dislocation, because periodic long visits to her natal home are inconvenient if the couple resides neolocally.

In her study on the impact of recent family law on the women of an eastern Uttar Pradesh village (1963), Luschinsky has reported that most women are unaware of the new laws intended for their benefit, disapprove of them when made aware, and disincline to apply their provisions. Although the population studied here is considerably more sophisticated, in general her conclusions apply to it also. Ganeshnagar and Kalyānpurī residents are considerably more aware of the existence and provisions of these laws than the villagers studied by Luschinsky but only slightly more interested in taking advantage of the relevant legislation, which covers divorce, inheritance for women, remarriage of widows, and abolition of polygyny (cf. Derrett 1957, 1963).

Divorce

The Hindu Marriage Act of 1955 applies to all Hindus, Sikhs, and Jains and provides for a formal divorce procedure, to be instigated by either party, after at least three years of marriage. Divorce is granted only on specified grounds: living in adultery, converting to another religion, renouncing the world by entering a religious order, suffering from incurable insanity or leprosy, deserting for seven years, the man's having married again or being guilty of rape, sodomy, or bestiality. Divorce may also be granted to a party whose spouse has not resumed cohabitation for two years after a decree of restitution of conjugal rights, or a decree for judicial separation. The partners are free to remarry if divorce is granted.

The law is very seldom used in this region for relief of an unhappy marital situation, but not only because of its particular grounds. Although mutual incompatibility is unacceptable as a plea, the primary reason for this law's having so little appeal is that the idea of divorce is slow to gain acceptance in a community in which two people ritually united in marriage are indissolubly wed. Formal divorce is known customarily as *talāk*, a word which in origin refers to the Muslim practice of a man's repudiating his wife without her consent. It is thus distinguished from an informal separation of husband and wife, known as "leaving" (*chor denā*). Even though several women in Ganeshnagar and Kalyānpurī have been "left" by their husbands, none to my knowledge have undergone a formal divorce. It is indicative that the number of divorces granted in the Meerut district court under the Hindu Marriage Act between 1956 (when the act took effect) and 1961 is only 62, with no more than 15 divorces granted for the entire district in any one year. Almost three times as many suits were filed as were granted, and about half of these were filed by wives or by their families (Joshi 1965: 81–82).

As these figures evidence, talāk is considered a very serious step. Because of the expense involved, moreover, and the "bad name" usually incurred by divorce proceedings, few people of this class take advantage of the law. Some cases in progress for kin or acquaintances of mohallā residents did come to my attention, but I do not know whether they resulted in divorce decrees. For one, in which suit was filed by the father of the woman involved, the grounds were adultery. Since the husband had persisted in his adulterous relationship over a long period of time and treated his wife badly as well, her parents decided that she would do better to divorce him and have the court decree a monthly alimony for her support. In the other case of which I know, the wife's parents had also instigated the proceedings, this time for failure to resume cohabitation after a decree for restitution of conjugal rights. Shortly after the wedding the husband had rejected the wife his parents selected for him and refused to live with her, so that she remained in her parents' home. Her husband did not contest the suit because he wished to remarry without the risk of being still legally married to his first wife. The husband's reaction demonstrates that the incidence of divorce is directly related to awareness of the provision against polygyny. It could conceivably also be related to changed attitudes toward remarriage for women, since a successful divorce suit in which the husband were shown to be clearly at fault might make it possible for the woman to marry a second time. However, remarriage for a divorced woman is still a very rare occurrence, and I am aware of no such case in these neighborhoods.

Polygyny

The law prescribes monogamy for Hindu men, unless the polygynous union was contracted before the passage of the Hindu Marriage Act, and, as I have shown, it also makes the contracting of a polygynous union by a husband grounds for divorce by his wife. Ganeshnagar and Kalyānpurī residents have little understanding of these provisions of the law, and a common misconception is that polygyny is permitted for all except government employees. To find men who have taken a second wife since the passage of the act is still possible, and their marriages apparently cause little concern among their relatives and associates as illegalities. There are two polygynous households in Ganeshnagar; in both the first wife is barren, the primary traditionally acceptable justification for a polygynous marriage among Hindus. Only one such household was formed before 1955. In most cases of polygynous marriage, the first wife has been "left" and the husband maintains a monogamous household with his second wife. Thus some secondary marriages of which I learned were love marriages, contracted after an arranged marriage had proved unsatisfying for the husband. Such cases are evidently more common in the urban middle class than among people in rural areas, as educated men, married in their youth to uneducated village girls, later seek the companionship of more intellectually compatible women. Normally in such cases the first wife is sent back to her parents' home or is left in the man's village home with his parents and brothers, and the second wife shares his urban residence. In a few cases, such a man maintains two establishments in the city for his respective wives. The husbands of several women in these neighborhoods have remarried and live elsewhere. Most of these deserted women are living with their natal kin, parents or brothers.

Women's Inheritance

Traditional law in this part of India provides that a man's sons shall share in his property equally, his wife having a right to maintenance but no absolute share in the estate. Daughters do not normally inherit, except in the absence of male heirs. The money expended for their marriage and the ritual gifts from parents and brothers for childbirth and the marriages of children are of course taken from the family estate and are considered to constitute the daughters' share of the family property. There is no question of a married daughter's receiving a share of the family land or movable property on her father's death. The Hindu Succession Act of 1956, however, provides that a daughter, a widow, and a mother of a deceased man shall share equally with the sons in his estate. Men and women in these mohallās are aware of the new law, but have little interest in its enforcement, particularly with respect to the rights of daughters. This provision of the act is regarded as threatening to the traditional kinship system, and few women take advantage of it in practice. Women typically sign over their share of the estate to their brothers if asked to. Occasionally a woman will claim her share, however, either on her own initiative or, more commonly, on that of her husband or affines. A woman who does so, is severely criticized by relatives and associates although the law is on her side. Particularly if she is married and has already received a dowry and other traditional ritual gifts, her claim is deemed unfair and she is said to be taking more than her rightful share. For a woman to claim her legal share of her father's inheritance is believed to destroy the warm, supportive relationship traditional between brother and sister. Such a woman can no longer expect to rely upon her brother for periodic gifts of money and clothing, for the traditional ritual prestations, for emergency aid and support, or for refuge in her natal home.

I know of only two cases, involving close kin of Ganeshnagar residents, in which women claimed a share of their father's estate. In one, relatives called in to settle an inheritance dispute between half-brothers suggested that the daughters of one mother might be given shares as well, so that their full brother, a single son, might not have a disproportionately large share compared to the four sons of the other mother. Although the full brother of these women remains on good terms with them, and continues to make the expected ritual gifts, he and his wife are still resentful that they agreed to this settlement. In the other case, a married woman was encouraged against her will by her husband to claim half a thriving business which her father had left for her only brother. Although the court awarded her a share, she later signed it over to her brother without her husband's knowledge. In the talk surrounding this case, everyone felt that the husband was unreasonable and reprehensibly greedy. Even his parents opposed the suit and tried to persuade him to abandon it.

To avoid hard feelings between siblings over inheritance, property may be signed over to a daughter during a man's lifetime, or an agreed amount may be willed to a daughter although the bulk of the estate is willed to the sons. But special provisions for a daughter are usually made only if she has been widowed or divorced, or for some other reason is likely to be dependent upon her brothers after her parents' death. A widow of advanced age living in Ganeshnagar has willed her home (which she owns in her own name) to her daughter, a childless woman left by her husband years ago. This woman's sons have other houses and property in Meerut and are satisfied with an arrangement which partly frees them of the obligation to care for their sister after the mother's death. Another couple plans to make similar arrangements for a badly crippled only daughter. Her parents will leave her their home, rented out to several tenants, and the rest of their property will be divided among their sons. The boys probably can rely on salaries from white-collar jobs, but the girl they fear is unmarriageable. This requires their making special provision for her future security.

Widows' Remarriage

The remarriage of widows has been legally permissible since 1856, although it is contrary to custom in this region, at least among upper and middle castes. Various reform movements, particularly the Ārya Samāj, have encouraged the remarriage of widows in this area, however, and a number of instances may be cited in which young, usually virgin widows have been remarried by their reform-minded parents. However, most widows do not remarry even today, and widows with children almost never do so. People in these neighborhoods realize that widows may legally remarry, but they consider it morally wrong for them to do so. Few widows themselves actively seek remarriage, and some resist it even when their parents are willing to try to find them a second husband. Most people with whom I talked were willing to consider the possibility of trying to remarry a daughter whose husband had died before cohabiting with her — such is the extent of change in attitude —

and in practice they might not even go this far. Significantly, in my Ganeshnagar survey not a single woman reported a second marriage (either after widowhood or divorce). Possibly remarriages were simply not mentioned because of prevailing attitudes; I have no direct evidence on which to judge.

CHAPTER V

Family and Kinship in the Urban Context

THE RURAL BACKGROUND

I N ACCORDANCE with the prevailing system of post-marital residence, children in this part of India typically grow up in the village of their father, among male agnates and their wives. The village of birth is considered "home" for children of both sexes, but when a girl marries it becomes specifically her "natal home" (*pīhar*), which she leaves for her future life in the "conjugal home" (*sasurāl*), the village of her husband. A married woman undergoes a gradual but ideally almost complete incorporation into the extended family of her husband, and her adjustment in marriage is understood as an adjustment not only to her husband as an individual, but to his kin group as a whole. Yet in the early years she spends many months visiting her own kin, alternating with ever-lengthening periods of residence in the conjugal village. Her natal visits gradually become less frequent and shorter, but they should never cease altogether.

There is a marked double standard of behavior for a married woman in her natal home (a "daughter of the village") and a woman in the village of her husband (a "bride of the village"). In the latter a married woman must avoid all family and village males who are senior in age or generation to her husband. This avoidance takes the form of covering her face with the end of her sari or the separate shawl that village women have traditionally worn. Furthermore, the married woman must not speak to or in the hearing of men whom she avoids. Within the extended family this form of avoidance (called *parda* in standard Hindi, *gunghat* in the local dialect) is said to be primarily a way of preventing disrespect by a young wife to male elders — her father-in-law, her husband's elder brothers, and uncles — who may live in the household. Outside the family it protects her modesty and ensures that she will not shame her affines by engaging in idle conversation (or worse) with men of the village. In high-status homes in the village, young married women are kept secluded within the house and its courtyard to minimize the opportunity for contact with unrelated male villagers. As a married woman grows older she continues to observe parda but acquires more freedom to move around in the village, particularly after her mother-in-law is dead. As time goes on she of course has ever fewer men to avoid.

A bride of the village must also defer to all senior women of her husband's family and village as a whole. A new bride must give precedence to all women married to villagers older than her husband and to all adult daughters of his village. There are certain stereotyped gestures of respect with which she expresses deference: the most important is a gesture of greeting and departure in which she bends down to press the lower legs of the older woman with both hands (*ṭāng dabānā*). She must also give certain personal attentions to senior women in the household, rubbing their backs when they bathe and massaging their legs in the evening. Although she may be treated as a guest for a short period immediately after she comes to live with her husband, she is soon expected to begin to relieve the elder women in the household of the most onerous and tiring household tasks and becomes the first to rise and the last to retire at night.

Early in marriage the marital bond is consciously subordinated to the consanguineal one within the extended family. Outward recognition of the relationship between a young man and his wife is avoided. The two are rarely alone except at night, and when others are present she must observe parda before him. For a young man to show interest in or concern for his wife in front of others is considered "shameless," and demonstrations of affection are taboo. If, as is likely, his wife and his mother conflict, a young man is expected as a matter of course to side with his mother, although very frequently his real sympathies are with his wife. As a couple grows older, and particularly when they have their own household (through the death of his parents or fission of the extended household), their relationship becomes publicly less formal and privately more companionable. By this time they are ready to welcome a new "bride" into their home.

The natal home continues for all a woman's life to symbolize warmth, freedom, and comfort. No pardā is practiced in the natal village, and a married woman may move freely there, speaking to all, within the bounds of customary respect for elders and the characteristic segregation of men's and women's spheres of activity. On her visits to the natal home, she is relieved of most household work, and if she has brought her children with her, the responsibility for their care is taken over as much as possible by her mother, unmarried sisters, and brothers' wives. The children learn to associate the mother's natal home with pleasant experiences because they are treated there with special affection and indulgence.

Under normal circumstances, a man seldom visits the natal home of his wife and never stays there for long. When his wife is ready to return after spending a holiday in her natal village, a man comes to call for her and is treated deferentially and hospitably in his in-law's home. But he is not expected to linger more than a day or two. While he remains, and until they leave the boundaries of her village, his wife avoids him strictly. They must not sleep together in her natal home, they should not converse, and she covers her face in front of him. Any overt recognition of the marital bond between the daughter and son-in-law is avoided, even more stringently than when the couple is in the husband's home.

Respect and avoidance characterize the relationship between the two sets of parents of a married couple. The inherent tension in this relationship is handled by diminishing and simultaneously formalizing any opportunities for face-to-face contact between the bride-giving and bride-taking kin group members. The relationship between the two, as I mentioned much earlier, is asymmetrical: bride-takers are superior in status and properly the permanent recipients of gifts and gestures of respect whereas bride-givers are barred from accepting gifts or hospitality from those to whom they have given a daughter. For this reason, the bride's parents never visit the homes of the groom or any of his senior kinsmen. The groom's people may visit the bride's, and will be given a most courteous welcome, but they do not normally do so unless they chance to be in the daughter-in-law's village. A woman must observe pardā before any man to whom she is related through the marriage of a son or daughter — thus the respective mothers-in-law of a married couple strictly avoid each other's husband if they should ever meet.

In these ways the traditional system carefully segregates the contexts in which a woman is daughter and bride, forbidding them to overlap either spatially or socially. Her incorporation into her husband's kin group becomes almost complete in time, but she has always the option of temporarily resuming her status as daughter in her natal home, even after her parents have long since died and she is an old woman. Each role, as a set of expected behavior patterns, is clearly delineated; in many ways the two roles are diametrically opposed, and in the traditional system they cannot be confused.

As urban residence effects changes in the spatial organization of kinship, repercussions on the kinship system and on the playing of kinship roles become unavoidable. Changing patterns of interaction between kin and altered norms for kinship behavior may be observed, both of which can be traced to the combined effects of changing patterns of residence and the impact of education and new social ideologies. They are occurring at each level of the system: within the group of kin who occupy a common household, among the separate households of an agnatic extended family, and between the members of a household and other bilaterally related kin and affines.

KIN WITHIN THE HOUSEHOLD

Just as in the village, relationships between members of a common household in the city vary with differences in individual personality. Beyond this level of variation, general differences in the social organization of the household depend upon its kinship

composition. It is possible to look at household composition from
a slightly different angle than that taken in the earlier discussion,
and to make a broader classification of household types cutting
across the lines of the previous typology and focusing on the place
of the young married couple within the structure. Here the key
variable is the presence or absence of the husband's parent or
parents in the household. In the first type of household, the married
couple shares a household with both parents of the husband (a
lineal extended or lineal-collateral extended household) or with
only one of his widowed or separated parents (a supplemented nuclear household in which the "additional" person is a husband's
parent). In the second type, the married couple either lives alone
with its children (a nuclear household) or shares its household
with a junior kinsman (a supplemented nuclear household in which
the "additional" person is subordinate to the couple). In the first
type one observes a close approximation to the interpersonal behavior generally reported for rural extended households in this
region. As a rule authority remains vested in members of the senior
generation until they are no longer physically or mentally capable
of contributing to the management of the household. Women are
usually able to maintain control until a more advanced age than
men — because their life expectancy is longer, a household is in
any case more likely to have a widowed mother than a widowed
father in residence. And aged women are likely to be able to continue their household tasks, or at least the less strenuous ones,
until long after a man has had to retire from a white-collar job or
leave agricultural labor to his sons. The standards of the older generation in such households usually prevail, particularly in women's
activities, and young couples who want to be "modern" are restricted by the necessity to adhere to the values of the husband's
co-resident parents.

The differing economic base of the urban household, however, commonly influences the pattern of domestic authority. The
younger man in a typical urban household holds a job different
from his father's, if his father is still working, and earns his salary
independently, rather than working cooperatively with his father
for a joint income. In some cases the son hands over all or most
of his salary to his father, who meets household expenses and gives
permission for any personal purchases out of what remains. Such

an arrangement is most common when the father is still active, the son young, and the family lives in the parental home. In other cases, however, the younger man himself handles household expenditures, giving his father an allowance — an arrangement more likely if the father is retired or has little or no cash income (for example, from land being tilled by another son). Many retired government employees have small pensions which they contribute to a son's household expenses, perhaps keeping a small amount for personal spending money. If only the mother remains in the household, an adult son may pay the bills for rent, electricity, and food himself and give her the rest of his salary. He will request spending money for himself and his wife as needed and consult his mother about major purchases.

Family histories reveal how variable practices are. One father in Kalyānpurī earns Rs. 500 (officially) as a government officer, whereas his two sons, one of them recently married, earns Rs. 140 and Rs. 200 respectively. He reports that he meets normal household expenses out of his own salary; his sons give him whatever they have left at the end of the month. "Sometimes they come to me and say they have spent everything, but I don't mind because I know that soon they may be transferred away from Meerut and will have to live on their salaries and that will be very hard for them. So let them enjoy themselves while they are still with us." Another man supports a married son and his wife and his own two unmarried children on Rs. 250 a month. His son earns Rs. 120, which until recently he spent as he wished, occasionally giving money to his mother or siblings when asked. Then the father suggested that his son deposit Rs. 75 each month in a savings account to help defray wedding costs for his younger sister. The son is not dissatisfied with this new arrangement. He recently rejected an offer of a better-paying job in a nearby town, beyond commuting distance, because even with the increase of Rs. 50 monthly he would find it difficult to maintain an independent household on his salary and would have no funds for recreation and small luxuries. In comparison, a contractor who also has substantial agricultural holdings takes the entire pay of his son, earned as a government clerk, and insists that he account for all his pocket expenses. The son has a wife and two children, and is in his thirties, but he has no financial independence at all. In still another Ganeshnagar family, however, the father has no income, having failed in a business venture undertaken late in his life. His younger son, with whom he and his wife live, is a clerk in a government office. On his salary and the rent from two tenants he takes care of all household expenses and gives his father Rs. 200 per month (his clerk's income is usually well supplemented by bribes) for spending money. The father is using most of it to construct an addition to the unfinished house in which they all live. Finally, in a larger extended household which includes two married brothers with their parents, all income is pooled; the father handles all expenditures and meets the individual needs of household members as funds permit. The father, who held a relatively high position in the police department until his retirement, has a government pension, the older son of the household earns a small salary as an office "peon," and the younger son is a doctor. A third son, an engineer living in another city, sends a fixed monthly sum to his father as well, and thanks to him the family has been able to build the house in Ganeshnagar. The doctor's wife explained: "My husband's younger brother earns very little, while the doctor has a good income. It wouldn't be right if we spent our whole income on ourselves while they didn't have enough to eat and to wear. In this house, everything belongs to everyone."

Whatever the financial arrangements within the household — certainly they vary greatly from one urban household to another — the absence of a jointly owned, income-producing estate necessitates adjustments in the traditional relationship between father and son. Urban sons may recognize their filial obligations to remain with and contribute to the extended household, or they may take a widowed parent to live in their own household, but their actions are largely a matter of personal choice. Often a young married man finds it advantageous to live in his father's home, despite having to contribute most of his income to the general pool, because urban incomes are so low and living costs so high that even a childless couple must struggle to manage on its own. Yet living with parents may mean giving up not only money, but independent management of one's household affairs, a sacrifice which some make only grudgingly. For the senior generation, in turn, dependency on an employed son for support means renunciation of some of the authority which the presence of a joint estate confers.

Obvious differences between households which do and do not include a husband's parent occur in women's activities. Almost without exception, married women living with parents-in-law are secluded, just as in high-status rural families and perhaps even more because one need not leave the urban house to perform the natural functions or do chores. These young women remain within the home at all times, except for visiting kinsmen outside the mohallā, making occasional trips to the movies with their husbands or other members of the family, or going on a rare shopping expedition with the mother-in-law or husband in preparation for a wedding or other important event. They are particularly barred from moving about the neighborhood unaccompanied when not headed somewhere outside the mohallā. They do not visit with neighbors, but since women from nearby may freely come to visit them, they can make friends among women of their own age who live neolocally. Women who live with their mother-in-law do not normally attend the neighborhood women's gatherings for marriages and other ceremonial events. All who live nearby are invited, but households are almost always represented by older women. Occasionally, as a special treat a woman will bring her daughter-in-law to attend a celebration at the home of a particularly close friend or send her, the end of her sari pulled well down over her face and breasts, with a younger unmarried girl.

When a woman whose parents-in-law live in the mohallā leaves the house, she must cover her face completely so that it will not be seen by neighborhood men — just as the village wife does outside her home. However, as soon as she leaves the boundaries of the mohallā, she "opens parda," lifting the end of the sari so that it covers only the top of the head in the way almost all married women in these neighborhoods wear it, indoors and out. None of the women who observe parda within the mohallā do so when they go to other parts of Meerut unless there are male family members or friends of their husband or father-in-law present.

Within the home these women usually cover their faces in front of the father-in-law and any other elder male relative who lives in or visits the household. They also observe parda before their husbands in the presence of others. In a number of households, however, parda within the house has been abandoned or was never practiced by the bride, although she observes it outside the house. These are most commonly households in which the mother-in-law is deceased and the father-in-law has encouraged his son's wife to open pardā before him. He has perhaps done so because of his conviction that pardā is an unnecessary and backward custom; it is one of the traditional practices most often attacked by educated men, although heatedly defended by older women. But pardā is also cumbersome and inconvenient for any man, on whom rests the burden of keeping out of the way of women who should avoid him. In the village a man can spend most of his time outdoors and in the men's house, but in a small urban home, a man whose daughter-in-law observes pardā is inconveniently restricted to the men's sitting room or some other secluded part of the house, while she is working in the courtyard and elsewhere. If there has been a love marriage and the daughter-in-law has already spoken to her father-in-law before the marriage, many persons consider it hypocritical for her to avoid him afterwards. The same attitude applies to the atypical arranged marriage between the offspring of family friends; the father-in-law may have been a fond fictive uncle for years. Sometimes educated women simply refuse to observe pardā or their educated husbands refuse to require it of them; occasionally marriage negotiations stipulate nonobservance.

Even when a woman does not avoid her father-in-law or elder brothers-in-law, she does not speak freely to them or engage in casual conversation. With head well covered by the end of her sari and eyes downcast, she discusses with them the practical matters of running a household. She answers questions in a low voice and rarely initiates an exchange. An attitude of respectful deference from the daughter-in-law is considered particularly important if the traditional avoidance customs have been abandoned, because showing respect is the manifest function of pardā observances. As an elderly mother-in-law in an extended household in Kalyānpurī explained to me:

> It is all right for an educated woman to "open" pardā, because she knows enough to behave properly, to be respectful even though she speaks and shows her face. But an uneducated girl, if she doesn't do pardā, the time may come when she doesn't like something her father-in-law says, and words will just come out of her

mouth. For most girls it is easier to keep parda. Then you don't look, you don't speak, and there is no chance of trouble.

This woman, interestingly, had never observed parda before her own father-in-law, although she did before other male kinsmen of her husband and outside the house. Her mother-in-law had died before the woman's marriage to the only son, and her father-in-law, who belonged to the Ārya Samāj sect, wished to put into practice in his own home the teachings of this body concerning parda. However, this woman keeps her own daughter-in-law strictly secluded and has her observe parda in all situations.

Parda is observed in the city in varying degrees by different women. It is not necessary to make a choice between adhering strictly to the rules of parda and ignoring them completely. Most women in these mohallās are selective in their observance of parda, taking into account such matters as the occasion, the place, and the personal preferences of relatives with whom they come into contact. A Baniā widow of Kalyānpurī explained that her brothers' well-educated wives, by their husbands' choice and their own do not observe parda before anyone except their father-in-law, "because he has old-fashioned ideas." Since they do not live in his household, observance is only rarely necessary. The brothers and their wives talk together freely, and the younger sisters-in-law do not cover their faces in front of their elder brothers-in-law. Comparably, another young woman of Kalyānpurī, an uneducated Brahman strictly secluded in her widowed mother-in-law's home, observes parda before her husband's widowed elder brother, who also lives in the household, and covers her face in front of her husband when others are present. But she has ceased to avoid the husband of her husband's elder sister, who often comes to visit the family during business trips. She explained: "He said he wouldn't come here any more if no one would talk to him, if he had to just sit alone in the sitting room and drink his tea. My husband's elder brother's wife is dead [she would not have avoided him, since her husband is older than his wife], and Mother is often out of the house. So I had to begin to show my face and speak to him." Another bride of Ganeshnagar, whose natal home is in Kalyānpurī and who has a B.A. in music, is kept secluded in a household which includes her mother-in-law and several younger unmarried brothers of her husband. Because her husband is the eldest male, she does not observe pardā within the household except when visiting male relatives are present. Her mother-in-law does not insist that she hide her face from her husband in the presence of others. However, on the rare occasions when she leaves the house, usually to visit her parents in Kalyānpurī, she pulls the end of her sari well down over her face and breast until she reaches the mohallā boundaries.

As evident from the observance of pardā, the marital relationship in households which include the husband's parents usually follows the traditional pattern, and authority still belongs to the senior generation. The wife, who spends most of her time with the women and children of the household, is directly responsible in her daily work to her mother-in-law. In some households a domineering daughter-in-law assumes extensive authority in domestic matters: one woman in Ganeshnagar was greatly pitied by neighbors "because her daughter-in-law is so cruel to her." However, the typical relationship is one of the bride's greater or lesser subvervience. In some families this relationship is warm and considerate; in others, fraught with conflict. The husband sharing a household with elders may be emotionally close to his wife, even dominated by her, but he spends little time alone with her, except at night after the others have retired. Usually urban families which can afford it allot couples their own room. This is something rarely provided even in prosperous rural homes, and allows a degree of privacy often unavailable to the young rural couple. But a husband has his own circle of friends and social activities and a job about which his wife knows little, if anything. Only family matters are of mutual interest, and decisions about these are mostly not the couple's to make.

Households which contain only one married couple, sometimes also a young relative of the husband or wife, allow greater leeway in structuring interpersonal relationships. For nuclear households that are also neolocal, residence far away from either set of extended kin has additional important consequences. The neolocally resident man and wife in a nuclear household obviously have more time to spend together than do couples who live with the husband's parents, and they can share decision-making between them because there is no senior authority. In these households couples are more or less free to work out their adjustment to each other, without the problems created by the presence of the husband's parents and elder siblings, though also without the insulation of others to rely upon for emotional support. Because senior agnates of the husband are absent the customary behavior for women living among their conjugal kin need not be followed. In the daily life of these wives, pardā restrictions have little significance and are observed only when receiving male visitors.

Husband and wife share child-rearing responsibilities more in nuclear households than in rural or urban households in which the husband's parents are present. Women of course remain largely responsible for child care and their burden (as in any urban household) is in many ways heavier and longer lasting than it is for village women. Village children spend much time roaming the village with their peer group, but most urban middle-class families keep their children near home when they are not in school, discouraging play in the street or frequent visits to the homes of friends, unless these are close neighbors and the respective parents are well acquainted. Children of both sexes remain with their mothers much of the time that they are not in school. When the father is at home, however, his relationship with his children is often closer than it would be in the rural or even urban extended households. Unconstrained about fondling his child, because his parents are not present, the father in a nuclear household may be seen playing with his young children, carrying them around, or taking them for walks. He may often undertake to entertain them while his wife prepares meals, or he may even share some of his busy wife's minor household tasks, such as peeling vegetables for the evening meal. (Occasionally men also cook for wives who are sick or undergoing their menstrual period because there are no women in the house to do so.)

Although in a nuclear neolocal household husband and wife work out a mutually satisfactory adjustment without direct hindrance or aid from kin, they do act within the framework of a culture which prescribes in some detail the appropriate role behavior for husband and wife. Even in the urban nuclear household, the husband is expected to be the dominant partner, responsible for handling outside affairs and for making major decisions for household members. The wife is ideally submissive. She caters to the needs and whims of her husband and is responsible for the proper care of domestic affairs. Her place is with her children in the home, which she is expected to make a peaceful refuge for her husband at the end of his day's work. The actual extent of a husband's dominance varies from one family to another even in rural India, and many women in fact dominate their husbands in family matters, and sometimes even in outside affairs. But theirs is usually a self-effacing dominance, control attained by managing the husband: being selective in telling him things, approaching him only when he is in a good mood, serving him devotedly before making a "modest request" or a "slight suggestion." Some women use a more direct approach and marital disputes in which the wife dominates occasionally enliven the neighborhood. But both men and women generally disapprove of such methods. Most women prefer to allow their husband to be the publicly acknowledged head of the family, for by seeming to be a good and submissive wife in the traditional sense a woman can achieve social approval from family and neighbors.

Not only do the roles of men and women remain separate in the city, but also their social networks. Men spend their free time with male colleagues, kinsmen and friends. They go to teashops or coffeehouses or restaurants for snacks and meals, and spend as much time and money as they can afford at the movies. Although they may occasionally treat their wives and children to a movie, more often men go with small groups of males. In the evenings men drop in at the homes of kinsmen and friends for conversation, rarely taking their wives along. Likewise they usually go alone to a wedding or other ceremony outside the family circle, perhaps taking a young child along, but rarely a wife. They invite male friends for dinner (or offer dinner to a friend who has come unexpectedly) but rarely include their friends' wives in such invitations. The husband's male callers are invited into the sitting room, where the wife does not join them as a rule; she prepares refreshments to send in with a child. Most women, including those in nuclear neolocal households, observe pardā before the friends and colleagues of their husband, even though they do not do so before neighbors in the mohallā. Therefore, if a husband's friend comes to the house in his absence, he must either be sent away (by a child, if one is present) or left in the sitting room alone to await the husband's arrival. An occasional woman is encouraged by her husband to address male guests, even serve them tea and chat, whether or not he is present. But this practice is considered very forward and is generally disapproved of in these mohallās, so that even if a woman's husband allows her to entertain male guests in his absence, the fear that the neighbors would draw unsavory conclusions prevents most women from doing so.

A woman in turn has her own social activities within the mohallā and her own network of kin and neighbors, although her social life is subject to certain limitations. Women in nuclear households may not be supervised by mothers-in-law, yet the culture prescribes that they stay at home as much as possible; a woman "who never leaves her house" is much praised. Much casual visiting among women within the mohallā nonetheless occurs, particularly in early afternoon after the midday meal has been served and the routine housework completed. Attendance by women at ceremonial observances within the neighborhood is almost obligatory, except for young married women who live with a mother-in-law or elder sister-in-law. Still, a husband may rightfully object to his wife's leaving the house for such a purpose, and his right to deny her permission to go out, like her obligation to obey, is not seriously questioned.

Although recreational activities are largely segregated by sex and the Western pattern of socializing as couples has not especially taken hold, young urban husbands and wives increasingly spend some leisure time together. Men in nuclear households probably spend more evenings at home with their wives than do men living with their parents. Young couples often stroll with children after dinner, and on weekends young families frequently dine with relatives elsewhere in the city or welcome young married relatives to their home for the afternoon. With movies becoming the most popular entertainment for the young (even for the middle-aged, although many still consider films morally unwholesome), increasingly young couples attend movies, either alone or with other young married couples, usually kinsmen. Such outings are still considered slightly deviant in these mohallās, where a young couple's going out together in public, unaccompanied by elders, causes comment. Several women told me that they rarely go out with their husbands for any reason "because the people in this mohallā don't like it" or "because I feel shy going with him in the street." Others, of course, have less concern for the opinions of neighbors, typically the better educated women, who consider themselves more modern and sophisticated than the average mohallā wife.

Symbolic aspects of the husband and wife relationship remain little changed in these neighborhoods. Wives are often heard making the traditional assertion, "My husband is my God," and most of them perform the traditional obeisance of touching the husband's feet upon rising. Wives continue to perform without reciprocation the personal services for the husband expected of them, such as massaging his body with oil, his legs before he goes to sleep or when he is tired, his head if he has a headache.

An important symbol of respect for the status of the husband is that a wife should refrain from eating before her husband has eaten. Men are normally served first at mealtimes, then the children, and the wife (who is of course also the cook in a nuclear household) eats last. Although some young couples eat together, more commonly the wife is busy preparing hot bread while her husband eats. This arrangement permits the husband to eat his fill of whatever has been prepared; the wife afterwards takes whatever is left, often eating from his plate. If a husband has not returned home by mealtime, it is considered most improper for her to eat, although she may feed her children. Ideally she should wait until his arrival, no matter how late, before eating. Yet one of a husband's prerogatives is to leave the house without telling his wife where he is going and when he is coming back. Another prerogative is to remain out after work — although with no telephones, he could scarcely inform his wife of a sudden decision to go out with friends. Often a man will not return until midnight, having dined in a restaurant or at a colleague's and then gone to the movies. Nevertheless, most wives observe the rule strictly and would feel guilty for eating before their husband arrived home. However, they may take their midday meal in his absence if he habitually eats at his office and therefore is not expected home.

Linguistic usages — forms of address and reference between husband and wife — also show little change in the city. Husbands and wives do not use each other's given names when speaking or referring to each other, and a woman will not utter her husband's name even when asked it by an outsider. Only those who have made love marriages may be heard to use the husband's name in reference, or more rarely in address. The usual mode of address and reference is by personal pronoun, the woman using the polite form (*āp*) to address her husband, he using the familiar form (*tum*) for her.[1] A wife typically refers to her husband as "he" (or sometimes even "my he"), with the plural form of the verb to indicate respect, or by teknonymy as "the children's father." A husband refers to his wife as "she," with the singular verb.[2] Although standard Hindi and dialect terms exist for "husband" and "wife," these are used rarely and then only in reference to the spouses of others, never for one's own spouse. However, the educated have an increasing tendency to refer to their own spouse with the English words "wife" or "husband" (with the Hindi possessive pronoun), and these usages are occasionally heard in Ganeshnagar and Kalyānpurī.

Increasingly, as I have shown, young couples in these and similar mohallās begin married life in neolocal residence. Their union, however, falls within the traditional system of arranged marriages, which has always depended upon the selection of a bride who would be adaptable to life in a patrilocal household with her husband's parents and other kin, or at least in close proximity to her affines. The system of patrilocal residence provided for a gradual adjustment of the bride to her affines, and did not require that she and her husband be personally compatible, although of course the development of an affectionate relationship between the two was felt to be desirable as long as it did not threaten the unity of the extended family. Neolocal residence obviously has different requirements, but it is difficult to estimate the precise effect of arranged marriage with neolocal residence on marital adjustment, because I have no comparative data on marital adjustment within traditional patrilocal extended households and because there are so many other variables to be considered. Most information in the writings on rural family life is highly generalized, and little

---

[1] In the local dialect, which many recent migrants to these neighborhoods, particularly the women, use instead of the so-called standard Hindi of the city, the corresponding terms are *tam* ("you," polite) and *tū* ("you," familiar).

[2] There is only one form for the third person singular pronoun. The distinction is made in the verb ending, which marks masculine and feminine gender.

research has been done on the specific question of marital adjustment in either rural or urban India (but see Fonseca 1966; Kapur
1970). My study does not itself deal in detail with marital adjustment, but I can offer some few observations.

Although not all the marriages which I observed in these
mohallās could be regarded as completely successful and satisfying
to both partners, the same is certainly true also for some marriages
in rural India and elsewhere in the world. Partners in most marriages were, as far as I could judge, reasonably content with each
other. The changing needs of middle-class youth in respect to
married life are recognized, and as I have shown earlier, this awareness is reflected in changing criteria and in the increasing participation allowed young people in the choice of a mate. As long as
most young people are convinced of the wisdom of the arranged
marriage, and the young, particularly girls, are trained to expect
adjustment to their mate rather than individual fulfillment and
personal expression in marriage, the new patterns of residence as
such should not cause serious conflicts. The obviously unhappy
marriages which I observed had begun both in patrilocal and neolocal residence. It might be supposed that since neolocal residence
removes one of the most serious sources of marital discord in rural
marriages, the interference of the husband's kin in the relationship
between husband and wife, the marital relationship should improve with neolocal residence. However, neolocal residence places
a heavy emotional burden on partners who in the traditional system
would rely for companionship and solace primarily on other family members of their own sex. Incompatibility, which could be
borne under the traditional system because a young couple had
little time alone together, can cause persistent mental anguish
when they are alone together for much of the time.

THE URBAN HOUSEHOLD AND THE EXTENDED FAMILY

Although the Ganeshnagar and Kalyānpurī household as we
have seen, is most commonly nuclear in composition and rarely
includes more than one married couple, its members usually maintain close ties with other members of a three- or four-generation
agnatic extended family, whether living in the same mohallā, another part of Meerut, the husband's village of origin, or some dis-

tant city. The degree of cooperation, economic and social, with members of the extended family who neither eat nor live with the urban household, varies widely. But usually many mutual obligations among the separate households of the extended family are acknowledged.

In a few rare cases, nuclear households in Ganeshnagar and Kalyānpurī pool their entire urban income with that of other households of the extended family located elsewhere, withdrawing only the minimum required for expenses. Siblings, nephews, and nieces join the urban household from time to time for schooling, medical treatment, or simply a change of scene. The head of the extended family (usually the father or elder brother of the urban household head) remains at the home village, but retains a considerable amount of authority over members of the urban household. Major purchases and decisions about the education, employment, and other important activities of urban household members are made only after consultation with and authorization from him. Women of the urban household are expected to follow behavioral standards laid down by him (or his wife), rather than the perhaps more lenient standards of their educated husband. Most households which have this close relationship to the extended family depend for their main support on the income of a rural estate. The urban household is considered to be a branch of that family sent to the city for the benefit of the family as a whole, rather than a segment of the family which has broken off to take urban employment for its own benefit. Several such "branch" households, established so that children too young to be sent alone to the city might be educated, consist only of a woman and children, the husband and other members of the extended family having remained in the village to cultivate the land which is the sole source of income. For one branch household in Ganeshnagar the extended family is not country-based, but is a Baniā business family centered in a city one hundred miles away. The Ganeshnagar branch is nuclear; the husband's considerable income as a contractor is pooled with his father's and brothers', and all draw from a joint checking account for expenses. They are not limited to a specific monthly allowance, but have mutually agreed to live frugally within the demands of a middle-class style of life and to discuss among themselves any unusual major personal expenses. The harmony (or

apparent harmony) of this arrangement is probably possible because their resources are large; nevertheless, considerable restraint
must underlie it.

It is difficult to draw a sharp line between households like
these, which form essentially a single consumption unit with other
segments of the extended family, and those urban households
which are separate from the rest of the extended family in residence, income, and consumption, but have not yet divided the
common property of the extended family. Such property ordinarily
is agricultural land and may include a house as well. Some extended
families have a jointly owned house, but no land, and a few have
a shop or other business. There is usually also some common
movable property, such as household goods and gold and silver
jewelry which has not been formally distributed among the women.
Households in an extended family like this are part of a legal coparcenary, a "joint family" in the usual sense of the term. In addition to retaining a claim on jointly owned property, members of
such households also feel obligated to take part in the ritual observances of the extended family and usually visit the village home
of their family several times a year, in connection with managing
the joint property and performing the family rituals or to spend
school and office holidays. Children may be sent there during vacation to be fattened up on the wholesome milk and butter, carefully rationed in many urban homes. Occasionally the urban household may be expected to make a financial contribution to the
village household for repair of the family home, purchase of live-
stock, installation of a tube well, or meeting the expenses of a
niece's or nephew's wedding. Regular amounts may be sent for
an elderly parent's support or a young kinsman's education. The
urban household is also frequently expected to board junior kinsmen in the city for education, jobs, or medical treatment.

The extended family usually acts as a ceremonial unit, recognizing its senior member as head, but the primary responsibility for
performing birth, marriage, and death rituals lies with the individual households. Each makes everyday decisions about major
expenditures, children's schooling, trips by household members,
without feeling obligated to obtain the permission of the family
head, although he may be informed of the plans out of courtesy.
Women of the constituent households are under the authority of

their respective husbands, although they defer to the wishes of the head of the extended family when he is present and when they visit the family home.

The usual urban response to inquiries about economic relations with rural members of such extended families is, "How can we give anything to them when we can hardly manage ourselves?" The urban household feels obligated to assist close agnates financially only when obvious need or an explicit request is involved: "When they need it, we send something" or "In emergencies, of course, we try to help." It is aware that one ought to share what one has with others in the extended family, according to traditional Indian norms; nonetheless it believes those who do share openhandedly are the exceptions rather than the rule. The falling away from the traditional ideal of the joint family — what is earned by one belongs to all — is usually justified in terms of changing times ("nowadays no one cares about family obligations any more") and the high cost of living. A stereotyped comment, repeatedly heard, is: "In the old days one person earned and ten could eat. Nowadays all ten have to earn for themselves and still everyone is hungry."

Aid in a coparcenary family does not flow in only one direction. There is a flow of goods, services, and even cash from the village to the city, particularly when the urban household is in a financially more precarious situation. But since the urban household has a legal share in ownership of the family land or business, much of what it receives from the village is regarded as its due, rather than as a gift or assistance. The share of agricultural produce from family land sent to the urban household is usually measured carefully, with an allowance made for the labor invested by family members still engaged in cultivation. The main goods are wheat and clarified butter, staples of this region, but occasionally supplies of other grains, raw sugar, and fresh fruits and vegetables in season may also be sent. With rising prices and grain and sugar rationing in cities, having produce available from his own land is advantageous for the urbanite. But few households can depend upon securing their entire yearly requirements, even of the staple foods, from jointly held land.

Sixty-four of the surveyed households in Ganeshnagar report ownership of land: seven own land only in Meerut (mostly house lots); the rest in rural areas. Fifty-one households own their land jointly with the husband's agnates: twenty-eight with his father or father and brothers, sixteen with brothers and brothers' sons, and five with father's brothers, sons of father's brothers, or relations of more distant lineage.

In addition, one hundred and six households report owning one or more houses (other than their present residence). Three-quarters of these houses are jointly owned, mostly with father and brothers. Others report owning a shop or business, either in Meerut or elsewhere.

TABLE XIII

OWNERSHIP OF REAL PROPERTY BY GANESHNAGAR RESIDENTS

Property	Ownership	Number	Total
Land	Joint	51	
	Single	13	64
House	Joint	77	
	Single	29	106
Shop or Business	Joint	12	
	Single	5	17

The ownership of real property was probably underreported, but these figures are a significant indication of the extent to which joint ownership in family property is retained by neolocal urban householders. These data, combined with evidence from interviews, informal discussion, and observation, suggest that the urban resident who has a claim to family property is reluctant to see the property divided, even if his household is commensally, residentially, and financially severed from other households in the extended family. Gould has suggested that most partitions of joint holdings in northern India occur after the death of the patriarch (1968: 416), and that in fact such partition belongs to the typical developmental cycle of the family (1965b: 39–40), but the present data indicate that partition is commonly delayed by those who have settled in an urban area. Taking the village as his perspective, Lewis has suggested that urban migration typically precipitates the division of joint holdings (1965: 107). Gore's study of Agravāl Baniās in the same region (Delhi State), however, describes a pattern more in accord with the figures given here. Most of the urban residents studied by Gore "have ceased to be seriously interested in the limited property that is left in the village. They are content to leave the house to be occupied by their brothers or cousins and to leave the land to be cultivated by them. They look upon their city incomes as their main support" (1961: 175).

These remarks point to one possible explanation for the prevalence of joint property holders among Ganeshnagar residents. If rural property has little material value, if it is not a significant source of present or potential income but only provides small yearly amounts of foodstuffs, urban residents may prefer to avoid the psychological and social break implied in its partition. This explanation would be primarily applicable to those who own property with brothers and more distant agnates, for those who share in the estate with a living father are in any case restrained by customary norms from requesting partition.

A number of respondents speak of legal rights to village property which they have "left" to brothers or cousins who reside in the village. They maintain that they expect no further return from the land and propose to make no further claim on it. Although not all such statements may be literally true, and many urbanites may simply be in no position to enforce a claim on land effectively passed from their control, these assertions do reflect an attitude widespread even among those who still take a yearly share of the land's produce. Apparently, many see little advantage in formal division of the small rural holdings which can perhaps support the family's villagers and provide some foodstuffs for urban shareholders, but not earn much excess profit. Furthermore, household heads in these mohallās, except possibly a few old men who came to Meerut as adults, have no intention of ever returning to live in the village, nor will their children migrate there. Therefore there is little reason to press a claim on a few acres of land and a mudbrick house with none of the amenities that Ganeshnagar can provide. Yet a further reason for not dividing the land is the practical difficulty of managing a rural estate from the city. Although sharecropping is a common solution, sharing one's land with agnates is deemed preferable; theoretically they can be relied upon to cultivate one's portion adequately and surrender a more-or-less fair share of the produce. An unrelated sharecropper on a singly owned holding requires close supervision that the urban resident is in no position to exercise.

Finally, the Uttar Pradesh Zamindari Abolition Act and the Imposition of Ceilings on Land Holdings Act limit the size and subdivision of holdings, rental of land, and hiring of farm labor by noncultivating owners (Neale 1962; Singh, B. and Misra 1964). The multitudinous effects of this land reform legislation require detailed study, but undoubtedly the provisions also influence decisions about land division or retention by urban residents.

If the relatively low value of rural land to the noncultivating white-collar urbanite probably discourages land division, so too does the high value placed upon the ideal of family "jointness." Previous studies[3] and my own data show clearly that this ideal is widely upheld in urban India, even by persons who neither live in extended households nor own joint property. The ideal cannot prevent division from occurring for compelling reasons, and indeed fission of the coparcenary unit is integral to its normal development over time. However, when segments of the family have established urban residences distant from the family seat, the type of compelling reason likely to precipitate division seldom arises. The kinds of disputes and competition between brothers or cousins or between their wives which are commonly the immediate causes of partition in the rural milieu depend on close proximity and largely disappear when brothers have their own income and control over its expenditure and when each wife is mistress in her own home. The low value of rural land to the urbanite may always threaten its rapid division and sale (as in fact has happened in many cases), but the positive value placed on maintaining a joint estate, coupled with sentimental attachments to the ancestral place, ensures that some urbanites at least will keep their family estate intact.[4]

The ideal of family "jointness" affects more than property holding. Scheffler has cogently pointed out that ideals are not only guides for action; they act as "rhetorical elements in behavior" (1965: 295). Members of a society use them in social transactions

---

[3] See Kapadia 1966: 273–308 for a review of studies focusing on this point. Also see Ames 1970 for a survey of attitudes toward joint family living among an urban industrial population in Bihar.

[4] A similar notion has been expressed by Ames 1970: 29, supported by data on the retention of coparcenary rights in joint rural property by urban industrial workers.

to better their position vis-à-vis others. The concept of jointness is manipulated by its users to gain the advantage over others in the family, both in direct interaction with them and with outsiders. Members of nuclear households, for example, will describe themselves as being "separate" or "together" as a family, depending upon the image they wish to project. Usually for an outsider, they are the traditionally organized family, joint in all important respects and therefore admirable. Also operative, presumably, is the ideal of behavior which prescribes maintaining a solid front, an appearance of family unity before outsiders, regardless of the personal dissension within the group. Within the extended family, the ideology of jointness is used in attempts to control or justify behavior. A woman may criticize the independent decision made by the head of another household of the extended family by saying, "After all, we aren't separate; they should have consulted us on such an important matter." But when she and her husband wish to make a major purchase on their own, her justification is, "Why should we ask anyone? It's no one's business but our own!" Help, financial and otherwise, may be expected of extended kin "because we are 'together'," but denied to them "because we have our own expenses to worry about."

The joint family implies less a problem of definition than of context. The ambiguous status of the residentially distant segments of a legally joint corporation creates undercurrents of unfulfilled expectations. Partly, of course, these are inherent in the fissive process an extended family undergoes even when members group at one place. Physical separation enables the various segments to avert formal breakup for a long time, but meanwhile hard feelings fester and create affective distance among family members.

THE URBAN HOUSEHOLD AND THE KIN NETWORK

The boundaries of the extended family do not mark the limits of effective contact with kin, for the typical mohallā resident interacts frequently and closely with other more distant agnates of the household head and with other consanguines and affines of the head and his wife. Those kin with whom each household member commonly interacts may be called his effective "kin network." *Network* is particularly appropriate here, because interaction with

kin for the urban dweller does not mean only having membership
in bounded kin groups (such as the patrilineal extended family or
lineage), but also using both consanguineal and affinal links, allowing for geographical propinquity and personal compatibility, to
build up a satisfactory circle of associates.[5] Such networks are best
viewed as ego-centered rather than household-centered, because
traditional social segregation of the sexes and prescribed respect
and avoidance relationships encourage husband and wife to have
distinct, though overlapping, effective kin networks.

The Mohallā Kin Cluster

Mohallā residents who have kin living nearby do not necessarily interact with them more than with other neighbors or with
kin farther away, but most women and many men do spend a
greater part of their time with such kin than with anyone else.
In fact a rare person in these mohallās has no kin living in either
the same mohallā or an adjoining one, within walking distance.
Almost all interviewees claimed kinship to at least one other
mohallā resident not of their own household, the exceptions being
mostly recent arrivals from distant districts of Uttar Pradesh. Many
residents are related to two or more different neighborhood households through quite distinct kinship links. Actually my data under-
estimate the extent of interlocking kin ties because few respondents
tried to give an exhaustive listing of their kin. Others deliberately
omitted or neglected to mention kin whom I later discovered residing nearby, because their relationships with these households were
strained or severed or they were unenthusiastic about the survey.

The data, from the perspective of the neighborhood as a
whole, show a large number of what I call kinship clusters; that is,
groups of bilaterally and affinally related households within the
same or closely adjacent mohallās. Within these clusters individual
kin networks begin to be built up, although such networks also go
beyond the immediate neighborhood to include kin in other parts
of Meerut and beyond. The highest frequency of interaction occurs
when kinship, propinquity, and mutual liking, or at least mutual
tolerance, coincide.

---

[5] This term has been used by Bott 1955, 1957 in reference to urban
kin interaction. See also the studies collected in Mitchell, J. C., 1969.

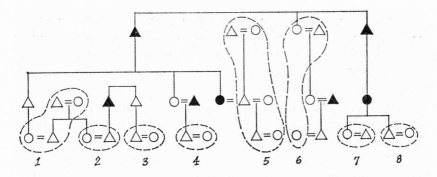

▲ Deceased ◯ Household (minor children have been excluded)

FIGURE 4 Kinship Cluster in Ganeshnagar (Brahman)

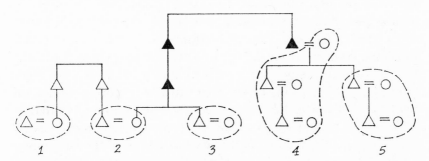

▲ Deceased ◯ Household (minor children have been excluded)

FIGURE 5 Kinship Cluster in Kalyānpurī (Baniā)

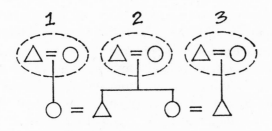

◯ Household
(minor children have been excluded)

FIGURE 6 Kinship Cluster in Ganeshnagar (Kāyastha)

Kinship clusters in the neighborhood are sometimes extensive, consisting of five or more related households, but they are more commonly limited to two or three. The kinship links are both consanguineal and affinal and are traced through both males and females. Such clusters usually center in one mohallā but may also spill over into adjoining neighborhoods. Developmentally they can usually be traced to a household's settlement in the neighborhood and the later addition of kindred households as migrants from the village or the old city arrived. The kin clusters are continually subject to expansion by in-migration and the settlement of newlyweds in or near parents' or another relative's mohallā; perhaps neighbors related to one of the parties have been intermediaries in arranging the marriage. The existence of these residential clusters of kin illustrates an important function of the kinship network for urban migrants: providing a housing and employment service for new arrivals. It also illustrates one of the functions of the neighborhood: providing contacts through which marital alliances may be made.

Within the large kinship clusters, individuals interact with only some of their kin, forming effective kin networks based on personal preference. Personality, age, sex, and common interests are important criteria, and a marked structural determinant is the preference for interaction with one's own rather than the spouse's kindred — a response which belongs particularly to the networks of women. It is related to cultural norms which prescribe restraint in the behavior of a woman toward her conjugal family, especially the custom of pardā and the deference owed to female affines.

Nearby kin not only provide companionship for leisure time; they are also consulted for advice on family matters, including interpersonal difficulties arising within the household. Here certainly one's own kindred are more appropriate than a spouse's. Borrowing household objects, food, and sometimes money is done more casually and easily from kin than from unrelated neighbors. Help is sought from nearby kin in emergencies, and children are left with them when the mother must be away for a short while or even for an out-of-town visit lasting several days. The aid of kin is also sought for domestic projects which require extra labor. Kin who are neighbors are invited as a matter of course to one another's household ceremonies and often act in a quasi-host role on such occasions along with household members. Neighboring kin visit frequently and informally and are likely to know most of the details of one another's daily lives. Among nearby kin are typically found the mohallā resident's closest friends and confidants.

Kin outside the Mohallā

Kin who live in the city but not within walking distance may not be seen daily, but women make casual visits to kinswomen on weekday afternoons, and men often visit with kin in the evening after work. The attendance of all kin who live in Meerut is obligatory at ceremonial affairs. On Sundays and holidays many mohallā families go visiting, particularly to see kin of their own generation. Siblings of husband or wife seem to be favored, after parents (if they also live in Meerut). Young couples often arrange movie outings or trips to city parks or nearby pilgrimage sites with kin. Gatherings of sisters and their husbands or cross-sex siblings and their spouses are particularly relaxing and comfortable for everyone because none of the women are expected to observe pardā.

Kin who live at a greater distance from one another cannot interact on a regular basis, but there is little evidence that the geographic mobility of the people of these mohallās has led to a significant weakening or supplanting of kinship ties. The widespread literacy of this population is advantageous for maintaining close ties between distant households — the mails keep kin informed of the minutest details of everyday life. The important festivals of the Hindu, Muslim, and Christian calendars are marked by schools, offices, and other places of business, and give opportunities for kin from different locales to visit one another or return to the village to visit with relatives there. School holidays provide a chance for children to spend extended periods with paternal and maternal uncles and aunts or grandparents, for wives and their children to visit their natal homes, and for neolocally resident couples to return for a visit to the husband's place of origin. Abundant bus and train facilities reinforce kin ties. Though slow and often uncomfortable, such transportation is immeasurably better and faster than the traditional ox-cart and is relatively inexpensive for the white-collar employee. Rural as well as urban dwellers make frequent and abundant use of the excellent network serving all of northern India. Distant or close kin, friends of kin, and kin of friends are always expected, and usually prepared, to provide a visitor accommodation and meals for a reasonable time on little or no advance notice.

THE BILATERAL TENDENCY IN URBAN KINSHIP

Because, as I have shown, the north Indian kinship system distinguishes sharply in prescribed behavior and in terminology between one's own kindred and the kindred of one's spouse, the members of an individual's kin network are not an undifferentiated group within which interaction may be freely structured. Although in the countryside the spatial or residential correlates of kinship generally coincide with the ideal and behavioral structure, they do not do so for neolocally resident urban households. Consequently one can observe certain changing trends in the behavior of kin toward one another which suggest gradual but fundamental changes in the kinship system. Changes in the norms for kin behavior are slower to come, and the strength of the traditional norms is still quite evident in the neighborhoods studied here.[6]

Patrilateral emphasis is a very obvious feature of the north Indian kinship system. Men are expected to form their most intimate and lasting ties with agnates, and their most important rights and duties are linked with membership in their agnatic extended family and local patrilineage. A wife, however, is expected to interact most frequently and intensively with her affines, agnates of her husband and their wives. Although the system recognizes the strength of a woman's ties to her own kin, it makes these secondary, and limits their expression to limited and specified contexts. A woman's primary obligations are to her conjugal family — even when she is a child, her future husband's family is referred to as "your own people," its home as "your own home." In conflicts of interest a woman is ideally expected to favor her conjugal over her natal family. In practice, of course, it is recognized that a woman will always be drawn by sentiment to help preserve the interests of her natal kin. An important reason for marrying a girl at a distance from her home is to prevent constant communication with natal kin from impeding her adjustment and gradual attachment to her conjugal family. A pronounced change observable in these

[6] For a more detailed discussion of changing trends in Indian urban kinship see my 1971 paper.

urban mohallās is increasing emphasis on the ties between a woman and her natal home and a relaxation of the traditional separation of natal and conjugal spheres of activity. It is shown in the significant number of married women who live near natal kin, in the frequency with which women are able to interact with natal rather than affinal kin, and in the persisting closeness between mother and daughter and between sisters, who in the traditional system and in the rural setting have little opportunity for continued intimacy after marriage.

Very few adult men regard the mohallā as their "real home"; most consider the real one to be some village in the region and say of their present home, "We are living 'in service' "; that is, at their place of employment. Or they say, "We are living 'outside.' " For women living 'outside' with their husbands, neolocally in the city, a third standard of behavior has been added to the traditional standards of natal and conjugal home. As long as a man has not been reared in the mohallā and his parents or other agnates do not live there, it is not regarded as his wife's conjugal home. Therefore, the standards of behavior of the conjugal home do not apply. The wife does not observe pardā in the mohallā as she would if it were the home of her parents-in-law. She is still expected to observe pardā when she visits her husband's home village or town, but such visits are likely to be brief and limited to two or three occasions during the year.

Some men in these mohallās are second-generation residents; during their childhood or earlier their parents settled here. For these men also the mohallā is not the "real home" (because frequent contact with and a sense of belonging to a village home carries over several generations), but it is their wives' conjugal home because the men's parents still live in the mohallā or have lived there until recently. And almost invariably, if their parents still live in the mohallā, the younger couple live in the same house with them, even if commensally separated. Women married to such men must observe pardā for other men in the neighborhood, as I have described earlier. When they make a visit to the home village of the husband, that too counts as the conjugal home, and the same behavioral constraints apply.

For other women the mohallā in which they live is their own natal home. Such women's husbands are not looked down upon like men living matrilocally in the village nor called the somewhat derogatory "son-in-law of the house" (*ghar jamāī*). In some cases the woman's parents have arranged for the younger couple to live nearby, but in no case to live in the parental house. None of the sons-in-law are economically dependent on their wives' parents. Furthermore, harboring people of diverse origins related to one another in a variety of ways, the mohallā does not present a solid agnatic front to an intrusive "sister's husband" like the typical village in the region.

However, residence near the wife's parents in the city does cause certain strains in the traditional affinal relationship. The woman who lives in her natal mohallā — or whose parents have moved nearby after her marriage, as many have done — cannot sharply separate her statuses as daughter and bride as she could in the traditional setting. The strong emotional ties between parents and daughter, which would have been compartmentalized by traditional residence rules and clear role definitions, are allowed active expression when a daughter lives within easy walking distance of her parents. Instead of periodic, extended visits to the natal home, gradually diminishing in frequency, the married woman in this situation can make almost daily ones. Furthermore, if she lives in a nuclear household, her parents and siblings may even visit frequently in her home. Such visiting would be unthinkable for the family of a married woman in a village — or even one living patrilocally in the city — because, unless perhaps she is seriously ill, only her brothers and male cousins should come to the home of her parents-in-law.

For examples of some urban visiting between married women and their parents, a young, childless Brahman woman lives with her husband in a rented room only two alleys away from her parents' home. She spends most of every day with her mother and invalid father while her husband is at work. Her mother occasionally comes to her room, if the son-in-law is absent. In contrast, in another young family the wife's mother spends most of each day at her daughter's home. This elderly woman, whose poor health prevents her from doing any household work, lives in an extended household with her husband, youngest son, and daughter-in-law, not more than five minutes' walk away. Because she does not get along well with her daughter-in-law, she prefers to be in the more compatible surroundings of her daughter's house, although she never accepts food or a bed there. Her son-in-law is often at home because he is self-employed, but he usually keeps out of his mother-in-law's way, and she treats him deferentially. This same family illustrates the greatly restraining effect which a daughter's in-laws have on visiting by and with her family. The old woman's daughter-in-law has parents who live in a neighboring mohallā, but they have never been inside their daughter's conjugal home and they see her rarely because she is not free to visit them without her mother-in-law's permission. When she does visit them it is often for a period of several weeks, according to the traditional pattern. She is not free to drop in on them casually as does her husband's sister in her home. Her husband often visits them alone, however, since hers was a love marriage, and her parents were well acquainted with him before the wedding.

In such situations, in which both sets of parents live in the same or nearby mohallās, residence is almost always with the husband's parents. The wife's parents never visit her, unless she or a member of her conjugal family is very ill, and they do not accept food or drink as guests. The wife typically makes more frequent trips to her parents' home than she would if they lived at a distance, but these trips are made only with the express consent of her husband and parents-in-law and permission may often be denied (as in the previous example), particularly for casual visits.

For young educated couples, the social distance between a man and his parents-in-law — just as between a man and his wife in her natal home — declines in the city. A young man does not normally spend much time in the home of his wife's parents, even if they live nearby, but he does occasionally visit informally with his wife. City-reared young women are increasingly abandoning avoidance of the husband in the natal home: couples may address each other before others or even converse privately. Such behavior is deemed reprehensible in the village. Even in the city, older women particularly find this new trend ominous and shocking and openly criticize parents who condone it.

Most couples in these mohallās, like the married children of most older householders, live distant from both sets of parents. When they have a vacation (usually during the children's school holidays) they return to visit their respective families. They typi-

cally divide their holiday so that the wife spends some time with
her children in her parents' home, and the rest of the time with
her husband in her in-laws' home. Women usually try to extend
the period in the natal home as long as possible but cannot neglect
a visit to the conjugal home altogether. The husband customarily
spends the entire holiday in his parents' home, making a polite
visit to his wife's family when he brings her and another when
he takes her away, to visit his parents or to depart for their "in
service" place of residence. A man rarely spends the night in the
home of his wife's parents if his own parents' home is in the same
city, but in any case he does not remain for more than a few days.

Neighboring parents whose offspring have married do not
casually visit back and forth, although the men and women respectively greet each other warmly should they meet by accident
or at the home of mutual friends. On ceremonial occasions the
wife's parents invite the husband's; his parents do not invite hers.
The women observe pardā for each other's husband, just as they
would do in the village. An elderly Kāyastha woman, an old resident
of Ganeshnagar, explained her relationship with the parents of a
son-in-law:

> The parents of our daughter's husband have moved to Meerut
> recently with her children, because in the mines [where the son-in-
> law is employed as an engineer] there is no good provision for their
> schooling. We found this place for them to live, over in the next
> alley. But we don't visit one another. We never go to their house.
> When we have a ceremony at our house, we invite them and they
> come. Of course, I do pardā in front of him, but I talk to her if we
> meet on the street. When our daughter's son has a birthday he
> comes here and we give him our blessing, but we don't go to his
> party.

The old relationships are changing in the increasing frequency
of overnight visits by women to their daughter's neolocal homes.
The conviction that it is wrong for a mother to visit her married
daughter remains strong among urban residents, but this attitude
may be modified when the daughter lives close by in a nuclear
household, as I have shown. It is also increasingly being modified
to permit visits to a married daughter farther away. The principal
motivation behind such visits is of course the women's desire to
see each other. But because personal sentiment is not generally

considered sufficient justification for breaching custom, a visit is made to coincide with some problem in the daughter's household, some difficulty for which she "needs" her mother. Such needs must always be balanced against the rights of the married woman's affines to attend her and her children in adversity.

During the research year I observed visits by mothers to their daughters because a grandchild had been injured, the daughter was studying for an examination and needed extra help in the house, the son-in-law was confined to bed with an acute illness, or even, in one case, because the daughter was about to have a baby. It would always have been proper to ask some woman of the husband's kindred (his mother, sister, brother's wife, cousin, or aunt) to come to take over the household responsibilities. The right of the husband's kinswomen to be called upon for help is particularly compelling for childbirth, because the new child belongs to his father's descent group and the privilege of caring for his mother is jealously guarded even when patently inconvenient. Inasmuch as in the village a woman ordinarily gives birth in her conjugal home, who is to care for her is never in question there. Most urban families do call upon the husband's kin in situations like those enumerated. But the mothers who came to visit married daughters during my research justified their trips by saying, "No one in his family would come," or "He doesn't have anyone who can help at this time." Young women (sometimes abetted by their husbands) are often willing to cooperate in being unable to find help in their conjugal home, because they feel more at ease with their mothers than with their in-laws, particularly if they have lived neolocally since marriage.

Whatever the circumstances of a woman's visit to her married daughter's home, she is always expected to pay for the food she consumes there. The alternatives — to order ready-made meals from a nearby restaurant or to buy raw ingredients and cook separately — are sometimes resorted to instead. When payment is offered, the exact amount is never reckoned, but the couple is given a sum on departure which is well in excess of what could have been spent on the mother's behalf. For example, a Ganesh-nagar woman visited her daughter in a city two hundred miles away when she heard that her grandson had burned his arm badly in a kitchen accident. She stayed with her daughter for a week and gave her Rs. 50 on her departure. Although conversely a kinswoman of the husband who comes to help must be given presents of clothing and sometimes of cash as well when she departs, no one suggested to me or even implied that such costs encouraged the increasing tendency to call on the wife's mother instead in an emergency.

The segregation of conjugal roles typical of married couples in India is related to the fact that married men and women have distinct social networks among their kindred. It eases the urban adaptation to a shift away from a strong patrilateral emphasis in kinship interaction.[7] A wife may associate daily with kin whom her husband rarely sees, and he may spend copious time with persons to whom she has never spoken because of avoidance constraints. This segregation of social networks is facilitated by men's working outside the mohallā all day, but women's socializing near or at home. Most men do not object to their wives' spending time with natal kin, as long as their socializing does not interfere with the household tasks or cause the men's relatives to be slighted or have their rights disregarded. However, they may object to a wife's attempts to draw them into closer association with her network of natal kin during time which they would prefer to spend with kin and friends of their own choosing.

The wife's siblings and cousins are important members of her kin network, and often close friendships develop between brothers-in-law because of the bond between sisters or between siblings of opposite sex. A woman's brothers are free to accept her husband's hospitality, but her older sisters are subject to the same constraints as are her parents. Because so many kinsmen having this or a similar relationship live in the city in close proximity, attitudes toward their visits are also changing, although women are still reluctant to accept food and drink at a younger sister's or female cousin's home. For example, a middle-aged couple while I was visiting them also received the wife's elder sister, a widow living elsewhere in Meerut with a married brother. She arrived soon after the midday meal, and at four o'clock the ten-year-old daughter of the household was asked by her mother to prepare tea, the usual late afternoon refreshment. When it was ready, the visiting sister refused to take

---

[7] See Bott's similar conclusions for British urban couples (1957).

any. Her brother-in-law insisted, saying "Don't bother about that, it doesn't matter," but she was adamant. Finally he said, "If you feel that way, pay us for it, but at least drink it!" "I can't pay for it — I haven't brought any money with me. You go ahead and have it. I won't drink." Finally the husband became exasperated. Probably if I had not been present he would have dropped the subject at that point or even earlier. But he continued, "Isn't it silly? It's just a cup of tea. Have it and give us the money the next time you come." Relenting, she drank one cup, but carefully avoided the plate of cookies which was also offered.

Younger siblings nowadays commonly make extended visits to the urban neolocal residences of their elder married sisters, particularly during school vacations. In the rural setting such visits would be unusual, although junior members of a woman's kindred are not explicitly barred from accepting the hospitality of her conjugal home as are natal kin older than she. Face-to-face contact between adult sisters appears generally to be more frequent in the city than in the village. Rural sisters remain fond of one another after marriage and keep up indirect contact — through parents, brothers, and their respective children — but opportunities for them to meet are limited. They do not visit one another's conjugal homes and are not expected to invite one another to weddings of their respective children, although a sister's husband is usually invited. (A brother, however, as mentioned earlier, has a prominent role in the wedding of a sister's child.) Married sisters may meet at their natal home, but only coincidentally. I found illiterate middle-aged and elderly women who had effectively lost contact with their married sisters many years ago. And I observed an instance in which two sisters living in villages less than thirty miles apart had planned their respective sons' weddings for the same week; they learned of each other's plans only when both came to Meerut to ask their brother to make preparations for giving bhāt, the wedding gift of the mother's brother. Girls reared in the city keep up much closer contact. They visit freely as long as they reside neolocally, except for the restraint already described on the elder's accepting the younger's hospitality. When they live far apart, they exchange frequent letters and visits by themselves or their respective children on holidays.

In all these respects we see in urban India a trend toward lesser incorporation of a married woman into her husband's kin network, and greater assertion of her ties to her natal kin. It has been suggested (cf. Sweetser 1966) that a trend toward bilateralism is characteristic of urbanizing societies which have traditionally been strongly patrilateral in emphasis, and these data seem to support such a generalization for India. Clearly this trend is still in its early phase, and the strength of the concept of an asymmetrical affinal relationship suggests that it will probably proceed slowly. However, the direction of change seems clear, and probably the trend will become more firmly established as neolocal residence becomes increasingly normal (in both the statistical and ideological sense) for the educated urban middle class.

CHAPTER VI

The Neighborhood

I HAVE translated *mohallā* as "neighborhood," and used the word more or less consistently to refer to a bounded and named area of the city. But for those who live within its boundaries, the mohallā is more than a defined geographical space; it is also a social space. The ways in which residents of Ganeshnagar and Kalyānpurī use *mohallā* give clues to how they view their immediate physical and social surroundings.

These residents do use *mohallā* to refer to the geographically bounded, named area which gives them their address within the larger city. But people speaking of "our mohallā" are frequently referring to a much smaller area which constitutes their immediate neighborhood within the mohallā as a whole: the alley in which they live, or a section of the alley set off by some distinguishing feature. For example, in Ganeshnagar an interviewee of the first alley (galī) who says, "I know everyone in the mohallā," may have meant only that he knows everyone in his alley; further interviewing makes clear that he knows little about the residents of the rest of the mohallā. If he lives in the forward end of the first alley, before the jog in the street at the corner bread shop, he may be referring only to the residents of this end of his alley. He probably has little or no contact with most residents of the other two main alleys. The average mohallā resident can easily identify all the residents of his own alley, but cannot say who lives in each house in the other alleys, although he may know many inhabitants by sight and a few very well. For practical purposes, then, "our mohallā" or even just "the mohallā" means the immediately surrounding neighborhood. Thus a resident of the far corner of Ganeshnagar, where public utilities have yet to be installed or streets paved, responds when I ask whether she has electricity in her home, "Electricity hasn't come to our mohallā yet," or a neighbor complains, "In the rainy season this mohallā is unbearably muddy, because the streets are all unpaved."

Definition of the vaguely bounded, smaller area of the speaker's immediate surroundings as the mohallā depends upon context and on the breadth of the speaker's social contacts. Delineation of the mohallā in this sense is related to geographical features of the neighborhood and to the settlement plan, but is not subject to the drawing of firm boundaries. The area each person refers to as "our mohallā" may be more or less fixed within a given context, but one man's mohallā is large, another's very small, and each man has his own mohallā, which overlaps rather than exactly coinciding with his neighbors'. The mohallā in certain contexts is an egocentrically defined space.

The mohallā is also egocentrically defined in that a speaker's social perspective determines his choice of language to refer to neighbors. Reference to fellow-residents of the mohallā in their role as neighbors is rarely intended to include every resident of the bounded space within the named neighborhood. Rather, people speaking of "the people of the mohallā" or of "my neighbors" refer to the socially significant neighbors, those whose presence in the neighborhood has social meaning for the speaker. For example, the secretary of the Ganeshnagar Association reported to me, "All residents of the mohallā are members of the association," but later cited only forty men as members. It later became clear that "all residents of the mohallā" for him meant "all men of importance in the mohallā who own their own homes here."

The mohallā is commonly referred to as a moral community, a group agreed as to right and wrong and having a body of custom and a character. But what the agreed values or the mores of the mohallā really are, is uncertain. Much contradiction attends the subject. Nonetheless one frequently hears "In our mohallā we do things this way" concerning the customs of gift exchange, the manner of celebrating festivals, and the enforcement of moral standards. Other indications of this sense of the "character" of the mohallā are statements such as "The people in this neighborhood are all country hicks," or "I like Ganeshnagar because people leave you alone here — there isn't all the fighting and squabbling like there is in some neighborhoods," or "I am very careful not to go out with my husband anywhere in the daytime, because the people of this neighborhood don't approve." Other mohallās are also felt to have distinctive characters. A Ganeshnagar woman says of Kalyānpurī that it is a rough neighborhood, "with people always fighting and yelling loudly in the street." Another says that she wouldn't want to live in the adjoining mohallā of Durga Mandir "because they are all low-caste people and illiterates over there," and a man explains a recent move from a predominantly Muslim mohallā nearby "because over there there was no one of the kind my wife could mix with." Awareness of the individual quality of his own mohallā and surrounding ones adds to the resident's sense of belonging, to his sense of community with his neighbors, even though he may happen to scorn the dominant tone of his neighborhood.

Even if residents of other mohallās share a common boundary with oneself and are situated nearer than some residents of one's own mohallā, they are separated by a psychological and social barrier. One knows individuals in other mohallās who are connected by kinship, place of origin (village kinship), friendship, office association, or a combination of these. But one is oneself essentially an outsider in another mohallā, without the sense of being in one's own place, on familiar terrain. Thus women living with or near their parents-in-law, as I have indicated, observe pardā only in the conjugal mohallā and uncover their face once mohallā boundaries are crossed. Obviously a great deal of movement across mohallā boundaries does occur. I have described how kinship networks stretch across these boundaries, and going somewhere usually means passing through adjoining mohallās. One freely patronizes particular businesses elsewhere which one's own mohallā lacks. But formal social activities and home ceremonials in the mohallā rarely draw anyone but kinsmen from other mohallās, and men and women do little informal visiting in other mohallās, except of kinsmen or village kinsmen.

FORMAL MOHALLĀ ORGANIZATION

Because a mohallā is not an administrative division of the city, no representative of a mohallā as such sits on the Meerut Municipal Board, although one Ganeshnagar man is a member as an elected representative of the ward which contains Ganeshnagar. The mohallā has no official governing body or *panchāyat*, such as reputedly exists in some neighborhoods of other north Indian cities (cf. Lynch 1967). However (as I noted in another context) Ganeshnagar does have a mohallā association, a voluntary organization established by the older residents during the early 1940's, ostensibly to arrange for the protection of the mohallā during the Hindu-Muslim conflicts. The mohallā was of course much less populated then, and numerous open spaces between the homes made the residents feel exposed and insecure. The Ganeshnagar Association originally levied a tax of Re. 1 per month on all homeowners and hired a guard to watch the entrances of the mohallā at night and to warn inhabitants of any danger. Since then, the tax has been reduced because the guard is no longer needed. However, all members pay dues of 25 N.P. per month. The Ganeshnagar Association is theoretically open to all, but in fact only homeowners are particularly urged to join. Forty official members exist, about half the homeowners, and only some actively participate in meetings. The association pays a Nāī from Ganeshnagar a monthly wage of Rs. 2 for doing odd jobs for the executive committee, collecting dues, and circulating notices.

The Ganeshnagar Association owns a collection of large cooking pots which it makes available to any Ganeshnagar resident for a wedding or other large feast: members use these without charge; nonmembers pay Rs. 4 rental fee. It also rents out two gas pressure lamps for nighttime marriage processions. Once a year the association organizes a large bonfire on the festival of Holī in which residents of both mohallās participate, worshipping together. The fire is built on the Ganeshnagar side of the main road separating Ganeshnagar from Kalyānpurī. Members of the association solicit donations from householders in both mohallās to buy wood for the fire and sweets to be distributed among those who attend the festivities.

The officers of the Ganeshnagar Association are all high-caste, relatively well-to-do men, very early settlers in the mohallā except for a Baniā contractor who has lived in Ganeshnagar fewer than two years. These men have high status in the neighborhood because of their age, wealth, and long residence, and would doubtless be community leaders if the mohallā had any group activity in which leadership was called for. The association itself, however, has so little practical function for the mohallā as a whole that many tenants and recent arrivals are unaware of its existence. Even its meetings are irregularly held, except just before Holī and during the annual elections for the executive committee. The association has no authority to settle disputes within the mohallā, or to enforce its decisions if it should become involved. Two of its officers, on separate occasions, mentioned to me that they had been instrumental in settling a rent dispute between a member and a tenant several years before, but none could think of another similar instance. Occasionally members have been able to intercede with the municipal board on behalf of the neighborhood about such matters as the paving of streets and upkeep of drainage ditches.

Other formal mohallā organization pertains to temples. Both mohallās studied have temples within their boundaries, owned by private persons who live elsewhere in Meerut. Each temple has a managing committee, partly drawn from the mohallā of its location, which assumes the responsibility of securing a priest's services, keeping up the temple buildings and yard, and organizing periodic religious functions to raise money for the temple's support.

SOCIAL DIFFERENTIATION WITHIN THE MOHALLĀ

The mohallā, a unit within the larger society, has a social structure of its own, and mohallā residents are differentiated along a number of cross-cutting axes.

Caste and Class

An important means of social differentiation within the mohallā, as in Indian society as a whole, is by caste. The caste hierarchy

of the mohallās studied is similar to that of rural areas in this region, modified by the fact that representation of the various castes
is skewed. The high proportion of Brahmans, and particularly of
Baniās in these neighborhoods, the virtual absence of Harijans and
Muslims, and the presence of representatives of a number of non-
local castes is atypical for villages in this region.

Mohallā residents are little concerned in their everyday interaction with minor status differences between castes, although these
are important during the arrangement of marriages. The occasions
which in the village commonly allow explicit ritual recognition of
these differences according to the rules governing commensality
and seating arrangements for feasts (cf. Marriott 1968; Mayer
1960: 33–52) do not serve this function within the mohallā, since
residents do not generally eat at the feasts of their neighbors unless
they are also close family friends. Brahman caterers are usually
hired to cook at feasts by members of all castes, and their food is
acceptable to most, regardless of the caste of the host family.

The primary caste distinction with practical implications in
everyday life is the broad distinction between "high" and "low"
castes (ūc kom and nīc kom). High castes are generally agreed to
include Brahman, Baniā,, Rājpūt, Kāyastha, Tyāgī, and Jāt. Nāī
Dhīvar, Mālī, and Chipī are usually regarded as low. There are a
number of Gūjar and Sunār households in these mohallās whose
position is ambiguous with respect to this binary distinction. The
Sunār particularly regard themselves as high caste, and many have
taken on a Rājpūt caste name to replace the traditional one. Other
persons are less likely to include them in a listing of high castes,
although they might do so for a particular Sunār or Gūjar family
if the family's education, occupation, and economic level gave it
high secular status.

All castes resident in these neighborhoods are officially vegetarian, with the exception of Kāyasthas, some of whom traditionally eat meat. There are individuals who deviate from these caste
norms, however. Meat-eating is normally attempted only in restaurants, and mainly by young men, rather than at home where
neighbors might detect the odor or passers-by see the bones and
scraps in the small piles of refuse which line the drainage ditches
in front of each house. Furthermore, few neighborhood women
eat meat or would agree to cook it in their kitchen, even to please

their menfolk's palate. A number of households which consider themselves modern eat the traditionally forbidden eggs, convinced of their healthful properties. One cannot demonstrate a direct correlation between position in the caste hierarchy and the prevalence of egg- and meat-eating by individual caste members. Economic constraints prevent most low-caste persons and many of high caste in these mohallās from eating these foods, however willing they may be to forgo a strictly vegetarian diet. Furthermore, meat-eating is generally regarded with such abhorrence that few will admit to indulging in it, although they may admit to eating eggs. Between the two largest castes, eggs seem to be eaten more commonly by individual Brahmans than by Baniās. Although traditionally both castes in this region avoid eggs and meat very strictly, Baniās in these neighborhoods are generally even stricter in their food habits than Brahmans. Many more Baniās than Brahmans avoid such foods as onions and garlic, and some avoid all foods with a red or "meaty" color, such as tomatoes and beets.

Although there is no residential segregation within the mohallās on the basis of caste (except for the presence of the low-caste squatter settlement in Kalyānpurī), and landlords and tenants are frequently of different castes, close informal relationships develop primarily among those of approximately equivalent caste status. People of high castes are more likely to congregate with one another than with members of low castes. People of low castes do not normally participate in the social gatherings held in the homes of Brahmans, Baniās, Kāyasthas, and others of similar rank, except in their capacity as ritual servants. The Nāī, or his wife, for example, normally attends every neighborhood ceremony to perform traditional services similar to those performed at village ceremonies. Likewise, high-caste people do not normally attend ceremonies or visit informally in the homes of their low-caste neighbors. Because so few households are low caste, their ceremonies are attended by their own caste-fellows and persons of similar caste rank from surrounding mohallās. Ceremonies in high-caste homes are attended almost exclusively by relatives and people of the same mohallā.

The tendency for social circles to segregate according to broad caste rank is not rigid, however. Because of the high correlation in these neighborhoods between low caste status, low income, menial occupations, and lack of education, it is misleading to assume that caste is the only, or even the primary, operative criterion. Persons of middle castes who are equal or superior to their high-caste neighbors in income, occupation, and education, normally participate in informal social activities on an equal footing with them. Conversely, poor Brahmans or Baniās, particularly if they live in a house owned or tenanted by low-caste persons or work at menial occupations, are usually excluded from the social activities of their well-to-do caste fellows. Class criteria, which include not only income, occupation, and education, but adherence to a middle-class life style, appear on close observation to be of more direct significance than caste in determining patterns of association between neighbors.

An illustrative example is a comparison of the associates of two Sunār women in Ganeshnagar. One of these young women lives with her husband, a clerk in a government office, in a rented room in the home of a Brahman family of moderate means with many kin in the immediate neighborhood. She is always included in the women's social activities of her landlady's family, and is an intimate friend of the strictly secluded daughter-in-law of the family, with whom she spends most of her leisure time. But several houses down the street another young Sunār woman lives with her husband in the ramshackle house of a Mālī gardener which contains a number of Mālī, Nāī, and Baniā tenants. She associates with the women of this house and their kin most of the time and is never included in the Brahman gatherings which the first Sunār woman attends as a matter of course. Nor does she visit her fellow caste woman. Similarly, a Brahman widow who works as a domestic servant for several Ganeshnagar and Kalyānpurī families associates informally with women of low caste who are in a similar economic position. She does not attend ceremonies or gatherings for singing in the homes of her middle-class Brahman neighbors, nor does she ever drop in to chat with these neighbors during the day, except in the course of her work.

Client-Servant

Another socially significant neighborhood distinction exists between "clients" and "servants" (*jajmān* and *kamīn*). These terms properly refer to the hereditary client-servant relationships between families characteristic of Indian village economy (Wiser 1936;

Opler and Singh 1948; Lewis and Barnouw 1956; Beidleman 1959; Kolenda 1963). Actually, Ganeshnagar and Kalyānpurī have not existed long enough for truly hereditary relationships to have been established between client and servant families, and few if any mohallā families have continued to call on the services of those who attended them in their home village. Nevertheless, the relationship between established mohallā residents and members of certain low castes is modeled upon the traditional *jajmānī* system as it is found in the villages of this area and in the old city. The castes primarily functioning as servants in this relationship are the Nāī (traditionally the barber), Bhangī (sweeper), and in some cases the Kumhār (potter). Members of these three castes may be called either "servants" or "serving people" (*kamīn-log*) in certain contexts. The terms may also be used loosely to refer to members of other low castes which are not actually involved in "servant" relationships in the city. In usage, therefore, these terms are often coterminous with "low caste," and may have derogatory connotation when used by upper-caste persons, although persons themselves actually engaged in service as kamīns frequently take pride in using them.

When a mohallā resident speaks of "our kamīns" rather than kamīn-log in general, he refers to members of specific families who serve his own family regularly in an occupational or a ritual capacity or both. An urban family does not have the full range of services provided by kamīns in the village. There such services as carpentry, laundering, haircutting, and shaving, and such goods as pottery and baskets are commonly provided by hereditary servants in return for a fixed annual payment, often in grain rather than in cash, and periodic small ritual gifts from the client. In the city all these and other commodities and services can be obtained only in exchange for cash, in a largely impersonal market setting. However, the traditional system provides a conceptual framework and a prescribed pattern of behavior between employer and servant and between producer and consumer which carries over into the commercial relationship.

Every mohallā household requires a sweeper woman to clean the latrine daily. Although the family's relationship with the sweeper (always a Bhangī by caste) is semi-permanent, in the city she considers herself attached to the house rather than to the occupants. Should the family move, it will be served henceforth by the Bhangin who has rights to the house into which it moves. When a new house is being built, a Bhangin comes to its owner to stake her claim to service its latrine when completed. The family may not replace her or the members of her household with any other member of her caste without her agreement. She may sell or rent or give away in dowry her rights to service a particular house to another Bhangin or use them as security for a loan. She may repay a debt to another Bhangī family by allowing its women to service the latrines of "her" house until the borrowed amount has been repaid. Despite the fact that the Bhangin is attached to the house rather than the householder's family, members of her family are considered kamīns of any family she serves. Each client pays her monthly in cash, negotiating the amount individually. She is also entitled to cooked food from her clients. For cleaning a latrine twice a day, seven days a week, in these neighborhoods she usually earns two to four rupees per month, plus one or two pieces of bread per day, which she comes to collect at noon, and occasional leftovers. On festival days she receives a portion of whatever special foods have been prepared, and her family is entitled to take all the leftovers from feasts in her clients' homes. On certain festivals she also receives small amounts of cash and often requests and occasionally receives presents of old clothing for herself and family members. When her children marry, her jajmāns are expected to give gifts, which she solicits shortly before the wedding.

Men of Bhangī caste are employed by the municipal board to sweep the city streets daily and keep the public drains open. Men of the Muslim Sakar caste work with the Bhangīs, squirting water from goatskin bags onto the edges of the road to keep down the dust and into the drains to keep them flowing smoothly. These men are also loosely referred to as kamīns by mohallā residents, although the relationship with them is much less personal than with the Bhangin who comes to the house thrice daily. Nonetheless, these men do have regular routes, neighborhood people know them at least by sight, and they receive traditional small gifts of cash from all the homes along their route on certain festival occasions. No Bhangīs or Sakars live in either Ganeshnagar or Kalyānpurī; they live in mohallās of their own caste within walking distance.

Persons of the Nāī caste, however, do live within the mohallā and serve residents primarily in a ritual capacity. Many Nāī men do engage in the traditional barbering, mostly in their own shops or stalls at which a haircut costs a set price, although some barbers come to clients' homes to give a haircut and shave for a fee. Nāī women are usually household servants; they scour the brass cooking and eating utensils after meals in a number of houses, and each household pays a monthly wage and sometimes also provides a daily meal. The ritual services provided by the Nāin and her husband make this caste indispensable. For marriages they perform both practical and ritual services and are expected to be at the disposal of the family concerned for several days. As I mentioned earlier, they are paid traditional amounts as their ritual dues at various points in the ceremonial proceedings, plus a lump sum for their labor if they have also helped with the food preparation and cleaning and decorating of the home. A large wedding may earn a Nāī family Rs. 100 or more if both husband and wife have served. A Nāin is called upon even by families who have never employed her for domestic work because parts of every ceremony require her participation. Although she usually serves only certain sections of a mohallā, the Nāin is not firmly attached to a specific house as is the Bhangin. In theory, the householder may call upon any Nāin whose ritual services he needs, but most families always use the same Nāī family.

The Nāin is also the messenger for neighborhood social activities. When a ceremony is to be held, or a gathering for singing or a prayer meeting, the hostess tells the Nāin to announce the event. The Nāin calls out the message from house to house, urging the women to come at a specified time. For larger and more formal events such as weddings, the host may also send a written invitation or personally invite the neighbors to the main phases of the ceremony, but for small gatherings of women the Nāin makes an announcement. Her payment is in small coins; guests first describe a circle around the head of a singer or dancer at the gathering with a coin, then give it to the hostess for later presentation to the Nāin.

Some families regard particular Kumhār (potter) families as their servants and regularly buy the pottery for daily use and for ceremonial occasions from these families. The ceremonial ware consists of disposable unglazed cups and small plates used to serve guests and the large decorated pots traditionally required in the ceremonies surrounding marriage. The potter and his "client" bargain over the cost, although there is a standard price range in the city at any one time. The ostensible reason for setting the essentially commercial relationship of potter and customer in a jajmān-kamīn framework is the customer's need for the Kumhār's ritual services in the "worship of the potter's wheel" (chāk pūjā) which precedes a marriage. Although one may go to any potter for this ritual, more usually one establishes a regular relationship with a particular potter when the first of one's children is married, and deals with him somewhat as one would do with the village potter who is the hereditary servant of one's family. No Kumhār family lives within Ganeshnagar or Kalyānpurī, but there is a small settlement of potters in a nearby mohallā, where most families buy their pottery and have the ritual of the potter's wheel performed.

Hereditary service relationships with priestly families are also customary in the rural area. Although the priest is not referred to as a servant, he refers to his clients as his jajmāns. Some urban families continue to use the services of their village priest or of a member of his family for ceremonial observances, but usually families establish a permanent relationship with a local priest after the move to the city. Only a few Brahmans in Ganeshnagar and Kalyānpurī serve as priests, and almost all have some other occupation as well. Therefore most families engage Brahman priests who live in other parts of the city to perform rituals as needed.

Owners and Tenants

Residents of these neighborhoods make frequent distinction between "real mohallā people" (khās mohallevāle) and "tenants" (kirāyadār), between those who as home owners may be presumed to have a real stake in the neighborhood, and those who just rent rooms temporarily in a neighborhood home. Although tenants as a category are viewed as impermanent residents, whose place in the neighborhood is shifting and whose influence is ephemeral, a number of tenants have actually lived in the mohallā for many years and may be reasonably expected to spend the rest of their lives there. Such people, thought of individually, would normally also be referred to as real mohallā people, even though technically they are tenants.

The prototype of the tenant is the young man in government service, transferred to Meerut for a year or two and soon to be transferred elsewhere. He and his wife and children rent crowded quarters in a permanent resident's home, learning to know intimately only the other residents of the house and perhaps a few close neighbors. Lack of money, responsibility for the care of young children, and fear of the customary disapproval of young married women who spend time outside their homes "without good reason" limit the wife's circle of contacts. The husband, who has little free time, is likely to be on closer terms with his colleagues at work and kin elsewhere in the city than with male neighbors, except those whose house he shares. A remark made by a woman who has lived in Ganeshnagar all her married life, in a home formerly owned by her husband's parents, is indicative of the attitude of real mohallā people toward the transient families: "We come and go in the homes of most of the people in this alley. But I can't tell you anything about the tenants. We don't have anything to do with them." The gulf perceived between a close community of long-time neighbors and the temporary tenants in their midst is expressed in a saying often used in reference to the latter: "here today, where tomorrow?" (āj yahā̃, kal kahā̃?).

I must stress that being a tenant does not mean being totally excluded from neighborhood activities, for most tenants do develop meaningful relationships with some of their fellow residents, who include them in social gatherings. But generally short-term residents have a narrower circle of friendships, participate less often in the ceremonies and gift exchanges of neighbors outside their immediate vicinity, and have less sense of belonging to the neighborhood in which they live.

As an example of social isolation, a young couple, recently married and childless, rents a large room with kitchen in the home of a formerly well-to-do family in Ganeshnagar. The husband, who is employed in a government office, does the shopping daily on his way home and expects his wife to ask his permission if she wishes to go out during the day to visit neighbors or attend a woman's gathering for singing in another house. She is working at home for her B.A. examinations because she was not allowed to complete college before marriage, and she says that studying gives her something to occupy her time. Her constant companions are her landlady and the woman's three unmarried daughters, all in their late teens. She looks to her landlady for guidance and calls her "Mother," regarding her as a fictive mother-in-law. Her landlady's daughters are her fictive sisters-in-law because her husband lived in this mohallā for several years as a bachelor student and calls them "sister." Her landlady has a wide circle of acquaintances in Ganeshnagar and in Kalyānpurī, her natal mohallā, and considers herself a daughter of the neighborhood. She sometimes brings the young tenant along to the gatherings which she attends at nearby neighbors' homes. The young woman has one other real friend in the mohallā, the wife of one of her husband's colleagues, who lives at her mother-in-law's home in another alley of Ganeshnagar; she visits this woman occasionally, but her friend never visits her because of her seclusion at home. Contacts with other mohallā residents are minimal for this young woman, as they are for her husband, even though he has lived in Ganeshnagar for five years.

A tenant family which is even more isolated from mohallā residents than this young couple consists of a young contractor in his late twenties, his wife, and two young children, who have come from another medium-sized city in northern India. Their rented house is small, but it is self-sufficient and they share no facilities with other households. It is situated next door to the larger and more elaborate house of their well-to-do landlord, who is an engineer, an old friend and colleague of the husband's father. The family has lived in Meerut for only one year, and does not expect to remain much longer because the husband's present construction project is almost completed and he is seeking a contract elsewhere. The wife says that she knows very few of the neighbors even to speak to and has no desire to visit with the neighborhood women, with whom she feels she has little in common. She considers most of the neighbors unsophisticated compared with herself and her husband. "To pass the time," as she explains, she is learning machine embroidery from a teacher who comes to her home weekly. She and her husband know their landlord's family well from previous association and were once invited to a ceremony in the home of a retired postmaster, across the alley, but they have never been inside any other homes in the mohallā. I was introduced to this couple by a young man of approximately the husband's age and educational level, who lives almost directly across the alley from their house and whose father is one of Ganeshnagar's original settlers and leading citizens. As the young man introduced me, he also introduced himself to them, saying laughingly, "Isn't it strange — you have lived here for some time, and it is only because I am bringing someone to meet you that we have the opportunity to meet ourselves!" The reason for this couple's isolation from neighbors is partly the husband's devotion to his work and the wife's reserved and solitary nature, partly their house's self-sufficiency; they do not live in unavoidable proximity to any other household. A more gregarious couple would surely have been able to make friends in the neighborhood, had it wished to. This couple's extreme case illustrates how the tenant whose accommodations do not provide ready contacts may remain socially peripheral unless he exerts himself to become acquainted with his neighbors.

Another important consideration in the position of tenants in the neighborhood is the presence of kin living nearby. Kinship is important in providing links to the community of one's neighbors. Neighbors who are related to a newcomer immediately include him in their social network, and he is unlikely to experience the initial isolation which faces those who enter the mohallā as strangers. Even village kinship, a link with persons from one's own village of origin or the village of origin of one's mother or wife, may play such a role for the newcomer. The tenant families described above had neither kin nor village kin in the neighborhood, although they had contacts with friends which had brought them to the mohallā in the first place; without kin they remained essentially apart from mohallā life.

Understandably, the tenant in these mohallās is himself aware of being an outsider, without a secure place in the social milieu. But rather than expressing his resentment at being excluded by the established residents, the tenant often rationalizes his minimal contacts with neighbors by claiming no wish to interact closely with them. The usual reason given is that the neighbors are inferior in social graces, education, or general life style. One woman made the following reply to an enquiry about the extent of her social relationships in the neighborhood:

> I don't like to have a close visiting relationship with anyone in this mohallā. I never go to anyone's house for a wedding, singing, or hymn meeting. To stay in one's own house, to take care of the

children, that in itself is a very big job. The way the people in this neighborhood are, as soon as two women sit down together, they start gossiping about someone or other. I don't like that. . . . Here people aren't very well educated. The way of life is just like in a village. It's only because of my husband's job that we are living here.

A similar attitude toward neighborhood society and preference for solitude and family life are also expressed by some older residents and homeowners, particularly women, who could take a more active role in social life, if they so chose. The traditional and still vital notion that it is not proper for a respectable woman to spend time outside her own home, talking with women outside the family, underlies their attitude. Outside contacts are not in fact shunned or disliked by Indian women, but rather, a positive value attaches to the woman who never leaves her home except "on necessary business." The woman who is admired utilizes all available time in constructive labor and demonstrates a tenacious and single-minded devotion to husband, children, parents-in-law, and home. Idle conversation among women is regarded as a waste of time and a probable source of conflict within and without the family. There is always the assumption, when two women are seen talking to each other, that they are gossiping about the faults of a third. Some women live up to the ideal closely — particularly those who live with a mother-in-law or are newcomers to the neighborhood, like the young woman quoted above. But others are extremely sociable and spend a large part of each day agreeably conversing in neighbor's homes or even in the street. Even these women, however, accept the values which discourage excess informal visiting; they are likely to pretend having little taste for it, should one inquire, and to discourage their own daughter-in-law from overindulging in sociability.

Men take pride in their ability to keep their wives, daughters, and daughters-in-law at home. When I asked about social relations between their household and neighboring ones, many men proudly denied that members of their families had much to do with neighbors. A well-to-do engineer, living with his parents in one of Ganeshnagar's largest and oldest homes, explained that his wife leaves the house only to visit her parents or sisters, who live elsewhere in Meerut, or when the two of them, very rarely, attend an evening movie. He asserted proudly: "Neither she nor my mother ever go to any of the neighbors' homes."

Despite their generally middle-class, white-collar character, these mohallās are, as I have shown earlier, quite heterogeneous in educational level, income, and social background, so that many residents can honestly feel, within their close perspective, that they have little in common with their neighbors' life styles and values. Much of the mohallā population, certainly most of its older women, is composed of first-generation urbanites whose youth and perhaps early adulthood were spent in a village. Their parents were uneducated, and many are themselves uneducated. Their values and manner of life seem alien in many ways to people who grew up in Meerut or in some other city in a family of educated professionals or civil servants. To an outsider the differences may seem small, but not to an upwardly mobile group of people. An aspiring elite, consciously attempting to distinguish itself from the great mass of the rural Indian population, to be regarded as "modern" and "progressive," finds great significance in even small differences of dress, eating habits, and household decoration. Even many persons of rural background, particularly college-educated men, have ceased to identify with village values and pride themselves on being more "educated" and "forward" than their "illiterate" and "backward" cousins.

A Brahman woman in her forties, reared in a small town of the district, married a man who teaches English in a local college. The two have settled permanently in the mohallā in a home they recently built. Although some of her statements about herself were misleading, she revealed a typical perspective as she described her adjustment to the social life of Ganeshnagar:

> I never go anywhere in the mohallā. My ideas and those of the mohallā people don't match at all. Whatever I do, I think that the mohallā people will be against it. Everyone gossips against one another. I go where I like, have tea with my husband's friends [in her own home], but the women in the neighborhood don't like that. . . . When there is a wedding in the mohallā I just go for a few minutes. I give a gift [of money] and return home. In this neighborhood all the women have come from villages. Even those

who have lived here for twenty or twenty-five years haven't got used to the city way of life. They live here just the way they lived in the village.

Actually she has an extensive network of gift exchanges with her neighbors, some exchanges dating from the couple's housewarming ceremony two years ago and others from previous residence for many years in rented rooms elsewhere in the mohallā. Despite her protestations to the contrary, she in fact has many more informal visiting relationships within the mohallā, even with neighbors who live at some distance from her home, than most women have. Doubtless her social network is so extensive partly because of the deviant freedom of movement which she insists upon maintaining. She is probably correct in feeling that most of the women of the mohallā are (or would be) disapproving of some of her "forward" habits, which are symbolized by her way of walking in the street with her head uncovered. (The only other married woman who does this within the mohallā is the socially isolated young contractor's wife referred to earlier.) Whatever the disapproval, apparently it does not make her unwelcome in mohallā homes.

In these neighborhoods at least two major contrasting value orientations obviously exist; difficult to define precisely, but widely recognized and, as I have shown, definitely bearing on the organization of social relationships. The commonest references to the polar orientations are the distinctions made between "rural" and "urban," "illiterate" and "educated," "old-fashioned" and "modern." The characterization of each pole varies with the orientation of the speaker himself, as might be expected; he attaches negative connotations to whatever he wishes to disassociate himself from. These contrasting orientations are particularly relevant to interaction among women. Because almost all men are educated to some extent, they show a higher degree of value consensus, although the values of young and old, country- and city-born men, understandably will differ.

For the educated, cosmopolitan, "modern" man or woman, those of a "rural" orientation are "rustic" in their behavior and have "old-fashioned ideas." These ideas manifest themselves in such diverse spheres of life as dress, hairdo, food preferences, house furnishings, and in a vaguely conceived "traditional life style," which requires much attention to religious observances and ritual prescriptions and avoidances, and a strict code of family and caste morality, particularly for women. To some extent the "old-fashioned" are also the old, but the association is imperfect, for many of the older generation are considerably more "modern" than some of their juniors.

The "modern," "progressive," and "forward" orientation (for which, significantly, the English words are often used in Hindi discourse) is understood to involve such diverse practices as a family's eating together at a table with chairs, one's eating eggs to supplement an otherwise vegetarian diet, and a married couple's going out together to the movies or for social visits. Other of the diverse characteristics are Western clothes for men and a tight blouse and distinctive manner of wrapping the sari for women. The really "modern" woman wears her hair in a bun rather than in a single braid, appears in public with her head not covered by the end of her sari, walks next to her husband rather than behind him when they are together in public, and neglects to observe pardā with friends and colleagues of her husband.

"Modernity" has also less superficial characteristics, such as belief in the fundamental equality of all men, regardless of caste, and consequently disdain (or at least professed disdain) for the traditional structuring of intercaste relationships. It includes belief in the necessity for "raising the position of women," "banishing the evil of dowry," and making other reforms in Indian society. Some of these ideas, like some of the above-mentioned features of the "modern" life style, have Western origin or are associated with Western society, but others are the firm beliefs of people exposed to the Hindu reform movement, the Ārya Samāj, in their youth. Some of those persons most "modern" in their ideology are also among the least Western in their life styles, and the most fearful of the consequences of Westernization on the development of Indian society. Particularly true of many older men, this circumstance shows that the contrast in orientations is not a sharp and simple one.

To the "man of old-fashioned ideas," his "forward" oriented neighbor appears unacceptably deviant from tradition and a portent of impending social disintegration. The symbols of "progressiveness" flaunted by the "modern" man are viewed as precursors of widespread immorality and loss of self-control, and manifestations of diminishing respect for the values of Indian civilization. Conversation in "old-fashioned" circles centers on the follies of "the young people nowadays." Single or married, girls are too "free," too much concerned with fashions and movies. They "wander around needlessly" here and there, and "don't listen to anyone," even their husbands. Young men waste time hanging around in groups on the streets, teasing the girls who go by, and squander money viewing "immoral movies" and eating meat in restaurants. They care nothing for their parents' welfare, have no regard for the tested and proven Indian customs, and are only interested in having love affairs and flouting the authority of their elders. Such an assessment of changing trends characterizes an orientation clearly dominant in these mohallās, although plentiful deviation exists for people of this orientation to condemn. These mohallā people see a flood of change already upon them. Although they sometimes exaggerate the level which the flood has reached, they perceive very clearly the direction in which the waters rush.

INFORMAL INTERPERSONAL RELATIONS AMONG NEIGHBORS

Fictive Kinship

In this region the use of given names is generally avoided, except for young persons and social inferiors. The lower middle class has no title equivalent to the English "Mr." or "Mrs." although the upper-class urban elite uses these English titles or the Hindi *shrī* and *shrīmati*. In these middle-class neighborhoods, caste surnames, caste titles, and terms denoting a person's occupation are frequently used in reference and sometimes in address, as are terms indicating a person's place of origin, such as "Dillivālī," meaning "woman of Delhi." In both reference and address, particularly for women, circumlocutions such as "Rām's mother" or "Prakāsh's wife" are common. But the frequent use of kin terms within the mohallā and with people in adjoining mohallās is striking. An obvious manifestation of the frequently close personal relationships among neighbors is the customary use of kin terms in reference and address.[1]

---

[1] For a fuller discussion of fictive kinship in the urban neighborhood, see Vatuk 1969a.

Freed (1963) and others have shown the prevalent use of kin terms among fellow villagers in rural areas of this region; the choice of terms is determined by an internally more or less consistent and inclusive fictive genealogy linking families of all castes in a given village. I have referred to this above as village kinship. Others have discussed how the use of kin terms by unrelated persons in a village may reflect the presence of a formal ritual kin tie between them (Mayer 1960; Berreman 1963; Okada 1957). Neither village kinship nor ritual ties, however, satisfactorily account for the entire use of kin terms among unrelated neighbors in these urban neighborhoods.

The choice of terms used to refer to or address mohallā neighbors is neither capricious nor determined solely by relative age and sex. Two main factors determine it: childhood residence by the speaker or his spouse in the mohallā, and the existence of real or village kinship ties between him or his spouse and other mohallā residents. If the mohallā is the man's childhood home, his wife regards it as her conjugal home, as I have explained earlier. She will therefore use affinal kin terms for its residents, based on the agnatic terms which her husband uses for them, appropriate to their relative age, generation level, and sex. If the mohallā is the wife's childhood home, she regards herself as a daughter in the neighborhood and addresses neighbors as fictive consanguineal kin. Her husband will therefore consider himself to be living among affines and will use the appropriate terminology for his neighbors. But in either case, if the in-married spouse already has prior kinship ties (either actual or fictive, through common village origin) with anyone in the local community, he will use the terminology appropriate to this prior relationship.

Because most couples are neolocally resident in the neighborhood, newcomers not natives, they establish themselves accordingly, structuring their fictive kin relationships in any way that seems satisfactory to them or to the neighbors who welcome them into the community. Even for them, however, a prior relationship has first consideration — most residents have come to the mohallā through kin or village kin or friends formerly incorporated into the fictive kin network who must be referred to and addressed by the correct term. Often some prior relationship is not obvious immediately. Only belatedly do neighbors discover a tie which links them through some third party: an affine of an affine, a fictive brother of a distant consanguine, a fellow villager of the wife of a kinsman. When one fictive relationship proves to supersede another, sometimes two neighbors will change their usage to conform.

Even if such prior relationships may exist, most relationships for a newcomer to the neighborhood have no precedent. Therefore, men usually begin by using agnatic terms ("brother," "paternal uncle") for new male acquaintances, and either a "sister" term or the appropriate term for the wife of an agnate for their wives. This choice for a man is almost inevitable, since the terms for uterine males ("mother's brother") and affinal males ("wife's father" and "wife's brother") are considered abusive when used in address; even in reference they are uncomplimentary if they have no basis in real or village kinship. A man would certainly not refer to a newly met neighbor as "wife's brother," for example,[2] without having prior justification, such as his wife's having already established a fictive brother relationship with the man, or his proving to be from her cousin's village.

Women who come into a new neighborhood often use affinal terms for neighbors, consistent with their husbands' use of agnatic terms. However, many women prefer to use what they call "natal kinship" (*pīhar kā rishtā*) in structuring fictive relationship in the mohallā. They will thus call a female neighbor "sister" and the latter's husband "sister's husband" or even "brother." Children generally use terminology consistent with their mothers', and therefore children most commonly address a neighbor of the older generation as "mother's sister" or "mother's sister's husband." This practice differs from that of children growing up in a village, where adult neighbors are all "father's brother," "father's brother's wife," "paternal grandfather," and so on. To have a situation in which the core of the community is a group of "sisters" with their hus-

---

[2] The terms for wife's brother (*sālā*) and wife's father (*sasur*), and for mother's brother (*māmā*) used for a person not actually so related are felt to have an obscene connotation. To call someone "mother's brother" suggests that his sister has had illicit relations with one's father. To call him "wife's brother" suggests that one has had illicit relations with his sister, and so on. These implications are insulting because the mother and sister are the epitome of "purity," about whom (or to whom) no sexual suggestions can be tolerated.

bands is anomalous in terms of traditional residence patterns, but such a situation is implied by this fictive terminology.

Married women in these neighborhoods seem to prefer "natal kinship" terms because of the sharp differences in behavior expected of a woman toward those in her natal and in her conjugal homes. Even for fictive relationships, the behavior prescribed toward affines should be adhered to. If male neighbors are fictive "husband's elder brothers," "husband's paternal uncles," and the like, a mohallā woman should properly avoid them, and she should defer to her fictive "husband's sisters" and "husband's paternal uncle's wives." However, if she regards male neighbors as husbands of her fictive "sisters" or as her own fictive "brothers," she is free to move in the neighborhood with uncovered face and to speak to these men when necessary. The use of this terminology therefore promotes easier, more egalitarian, more loosely structured relationships among neighbors than is characteristic of the patrilocal village. It is particularly useful in the typical urban home, where two or more unrelated families live in close juxtaposition, often sharing common household facilities.

Visiting

Informal relations between neighbors provide a day-to-day framework of sociability which is enlivened periodically by formal social gatherings, ceremonial events, and neighborhood gift exchanges. One aspect of these informal relations, as I have already observed, is casual visiting in homes. Men visit largely in the evening after returning from work (for government employees, between six and seven P.M.) or on a Sunday, the usual free day, or a holiday. Visits to sit and chat with a neighbor are seldom prearranged; two or three men who are kin or village kin or simply close neighbors are particularly friendly and expect to meet. They use a sitting room, if available, or, weather permitting, meet in the front of the house or in the courtyard.

Women are most free to meet informally with neighbors in the afternoon, after washing the dishes from the noon meal and before beginning preparations for supper. In the cool season, women who live in the same or neighboring houses gather in the sun of a courtyard or on a roof, bringing knitting, embroidery, mending, spices to pound, or a lump of dough to make hand-rolled noodles, so that the time will not pass in idleness. As they sit, other neighbors wander in and out, their young children on the hip or at their heels. They talk about events in their household or among their kin, weddings, and other ceremonies they have attended or are planning to attend, scandals or near-scandals in the neighborhood, problems with in-laws and husbands, marriage proposals made, received, or contemplated, and their children's school successes and difficulties. The hot season offers less opportunity for such sociability, since the need to rise early makes an afternoon nap imperative and a walk to a neighbor's in the sun a foolish journey. For most women scarcely a day passes without someone's dropping in for a chat, perhaps on an errand, perhaps just passing by. Anyone who feels bored need only stand at his door for a few moments and a passer-by will stop to talk. Walking down an alley in these neighborhoods one commonly meets little groups of women engrossed in conversation.

Women neighbors do not normally entertain one another in the sitting room, or extend invitations to neighbors to visit at specified times, except for formal ceremonial occasions. Neighbors are not invited to come for tea or to share meals, and when a neighbor drops in she is not offered refreshment like a friend or acquaintance come to visit from afar. Men who entertain male neighbors may call to their own wives to have tea prepared or ask a child to bring water to a visitor on a warm day, but as a matter of course neighbors are received casually.

Borrowing of Goods and Exchange of Services

Neighbors in these mohallās borrow and lend various items frequently. For example, few urban households possess the sort of heavy stone hand mill in which village women daily grind their wheat; nearby motorized mills perform this service for a small charge. However, a hand mill is sometimes needed to grind lentils into flour for preparing special dishes and snacks or small quantities of other special grains used for making bread on fast days when wheat is forbidden. Women who own such a hand mill generally share it with neighbors, who use it in the owner's home because it is of course heavy and stationary. Most households own sewing machines, but a woman who does not have a machine can usually find a neighbor who will lend hers. Likewise, a neighbor will lend a thermometer when someone is sick. China tea-sets and chairs can be borrowed when a family has special guests who cannot be expected to sit on string cots or to drink from inexpensive, chipped cups without saucers. Neighbors are usually happy to lend such things, taking vicarious pleasure in the entertainment of someone who needs to be impressed and enjoying the recognition of their own prestige as owners. Whoever subscribes to a daily newspaper counts on sharing it with others. The drums women use to accompany their singing are often sought for gatherings from the few households which own them, but with these affairs so frequent and the drums so subject to breakage, most women are reluctant to lend a drum, particularly if they are not attending. They make various excuses to avoid lending it, though they rarely refuse outright.

Food in small quantities is freely lent to neighbors: uncooked items such as flour, lentils, tea, and spices, and sometimes even cooked food. During my stay, an inconvenient shortage of white sugar caused women to borrow small amounts of sugar from neighbors who had black-market supplies, repayment due when their own ration allotment arrived. Various forms of crude sugar were easily available, but only white sugar is considered suitable for tea, which for most families is a regular morning and afternoon institution. Cooked food is occasionally borrowed from neighbors and repayment is made through a general willingness to reciprocate whenever necessary. Emergencies requiring the loan of prepared food do arise. A woman usually cooks just the amount of food she thinks necessary to feed her family or perhaps even a little less, to avoid leftovers. Only in the cool season can cooked vegetables be kept overnight or from the noon to the evening meal. Bread can of course be kept always, and in many homes last night's bread serves as a morning snack. It is customary to offer a meal to anyone (except a neighbor) arriving near mealtime, and such an offer (usually made by the husband, without first asking his wife what is available) may catch the housewife unprepared. Because kindling a charcoal or wood fire and preparing a fresh meal of bread and vegetables takes at least an hour, a woman commonly goes or sends a child to neighbors to request vegetables from their meal and serves the borrowed vegetables to the guest with leftover bread. She may also borrow food if a fussy child (or more often a fussy grandchild) dislikes his meal, asking close neighbors if they have a different dish "so that he may be pleased." Cooked food is also shared when a housewife makes some special dish for her family which requires lengthy preparation and can be made in large quantities; she commonly sends portions to neighboring households with which she is on intimate terms.

Small amounts of money are sometimes borrowed by neighbors in an emergency. Ration books are shared so that those who do not need or want their total allotment of some item may enable a neighbor to get a supplementary supply. Households which have acquired extra ration books by some ruse are usually generous about sharing the allotments for which they have no use — commonly barley and millet, but even wheat of the "inferior" imported variety.

Neighbors also perform various services for one another. Guarding one another's property is usual. In these mohallās people are reluctant to leave their homes unattended. Families which occupy a single-family dwelling or a self-contained apartment within a building tenanted by others, try to plan their days so that their home is never left unoccupied; usually no problem inasmuch as few married women work, all women are supposed to remain at home most of the time, and a whole family rarely goes anywhere together. An empty house is almost never a problem in extended or supplemented nuclear households which include the husband's mother, for here the daughter-in-law, as I have shown, rarely leaves the home. However, occasionally all members of a family must be absent simultaneously — for example, if there is hymn singing in the afternoon while a woman's husband is at work and the children are in school, or if there is a wedding of kin or close friends elsewhere in the city. The woman then padlocks the doors and notifies a neighbor to keep watch. For absences lasting all evening or for several days, someone in the neighborhood (usually a young man) may be asked to occupy the house as guard, or a boy of a servant family may be paid a small sum to camp in front of the house or in the courtyard, all its doors padlocked.

Unlike guard duty, I might mention, child care services are almost never exchanged. Children are regarded as either young enough to accompany their mother anywhere or old enough to stay alone. If not, extended households and those with a widowed grandparent or aunt almost always have an adult at home to mind youngsters, and among a usually wide range of children, nuclear households are likely to include young adolescent boys and girls who are able to care for younger siblings in their parents' absence. Occasionally fathers remain home with children when their mothers have an evening gathering for singing or a ceremonial event to attend. The possibility of leaving a child with a neighbor rarely occurs to anyone. When I asked about it, the answer was, "Oh, we never do that!" The general feeling, usually not verbalized, seems to be that children belong with their own kinsmen; leaving them with someone else, even familiar neighbors, seems somehow risky and irresponsible. No one in these middle-class mohallās has hired help for child care, common servants for the Indian upper classes.

Children do frequent close neighbor's homes, walking in without asking permission; they join in children's play and occasionally in adult conversation, or simply sit quietly and listen. Children are taught, however, not to eat anything casually offered in a neighbor's home because to do so is ill-mannered and also implies that one is not fed properly at home. Children do not normally take meals or spend the night in their friends' homes, except those of kinsmen.

Neighbors do occasionally provide one domestic service: preparing meals when a woman is sick or observing menstrual taboos. To help out the husbands who cannot or will not cook, friendly neighbors are often willing to prepare bread (if flour is provided) and vegetables, normally doing so for two or three days. Should a woman be seriously incapacitated, a kinswoman (preferably someone from the husband's kindred) would be asked to stay in the home to perform the household duties.

Neighbors also share nonmaterial possessions such as medicinal and ritual knowledge and medical advice. Every family has a favorite physician or practitioner, and every housewife has her own set of remedies for common ills. Some women in the mohallā are considered experts in curing anything, or at least specialists in some branch of medicine. Some are deemed experts at childbirth. There is no need to inquire about good doctors for a sick person because once neighbors learn about him they will come to comfort the patient and offer their advice, often bringing some special potion or food that they believe will relieve his suffering. If the sickness seems serious, neighbors will suggest their favorite doctors or other medical practitioners and will sometimes offer to give the patient the personal introduction which is felt to ensure better attention. Because people commonly try out numerous remedies for a single illness, simultaneously or in rapid succession, they welcome neighbors' suggestions.

On any ritual occasion, particularly observances of household rites which do not require a priest's services, women neighbors consult at length about the proper procedure, the items to be prepared, the manner of making offerings, the timing, and so on. When festivals and minor rituals occur in a village, each household has a standard to follow: the way that this ritual has always been performed in this household. Ritual knowledge is handed down in the agnatic line through the women who have married into the household. No matter what the procedures in their natal village, married women are supposed to observe the traditions of their conjugal household. Although even each village household has individual peculiarities, a certain amount of uniformity is likely among households, at least within a single caste. Urban women are conscious of their duty to do as their conjugal household does, but also uncertain about the procedures — many women are remote from that household or have never learned the proper performance for that household of all the minor rituals of the annual cycle. Their uncertainty is compounded by the variety of detail from household to household, even among nearby districts. Hardly a festival or rite goes by, either a private family one or one which forms part of a major ceremonial occasion, that does not involve considerable discussion about procedure, with each woman contributing her version of "how it is done in our [conjugal] village." The opinions of women regarded as specialists are normally deferred to. Considered to be particularly devout and knowledgeable about ritual, these usually elderly women play a quasi-mother-in-law role for young wives. In Kalyānpurī one such specialist is the wife of a Brahman priest, a Sanskrit scholar and teacher who frequently performs at ceremonies in mohallā homes. In her fifties and childless, the scholar-teacher's wife has little to occupy her except attending gatherings for devotional singing and readings of the *Rāmāyana* and keeping an eye on mohallā residents' affairs. She is sometimes jokingly referred to as the "mohallā policeman," but she is respected for her ritual knowledge and often even directs the major rituals aloud while her husband performs them. In Ganeshnagar two Brahman sisters are the experts. One is widowed and childless and has become increasingly religious in recent years. A circle of neighborhood women who regard her as their guru gather regularly at her home for inspirational talk, religious recitations, and devotional singing, but also others turn to her and her sister for advice on spiritual and ritual matters.

FORMAL INTERACTION AMONG NEIGHBORS

I have described informal neighborly relations; a number of occasions provide periodic opportunities for more formal association of neighbors amidst planned socio-religious gatherings. Most such occasions are ceremonial observances of various life crises. The others occur in conjunction with the yearly festival cycle or are religiously motivated gatherings for devotional singing or recitations, held at a householder's convenience.

Devotional Singing

The most frequent event of formal interaction in Ganeshnagar and Kalyānpurī is the devotional- or hymn-singing gathering (kirtan). Most such gatherings are segregated by sex and those I attended were for women only. A hymn singing may take place regularly at the temple, as occurred weekly at the Ganeshnagar temple during my research year, in addition to the periodic gatherings held in conjunction with the major festivals. However, most gatherings for hymn singing are held in private homes and arranged to celebrate some special event in the hostess's family, such as the birthday of a male grandchild or the opening of a new shop, or to acknowledge any success which divine assistance is felt to have been instrumental in effecting. Particularly religious women often organize a weekly or monthly hymn singing, to which a regular group of neighbors is expected to come. The Brahman sisters referred to above hold a regular hymn singing late in the evening of their monthly fast day. A middle-aged Baniā woman in Ganeshnagar holds a regular Tuesday afternoon hymn singing which a group of her special friends are in the habit of attending.

A woman arranging a hymn singing invites neighbors personally or asks the Nāin to serve as messenger. She sets up an altar in a room or in the courtyard of her home, a table or cot covered with rugs or fine cloths, religious pictures, and real or artificial flowers in decorative vases. On the floor she spreads rugs or mats for the guests, dressed in their better clothes, who sit in a semi-circle facing the altar. For one or two hours the women sing devotional hymns (*bhajan*) to the rhythm of a drum and hand cymbals, talking between songs about local happenings. Between songs women often make short inspirational comments or offer brief discourses on spiritual matters. The general atmosphere is reverent and pious, but the occasion is nonetheless regarded as a social one, an opportunity to meet with friends and catch up on recent events in their families and in the neighborhood. Sometimes, if the hostess wishes to celebrate an occasion in a more elaborate manner, she invites a professional bhajan singer, a singing and dancing group, or a person well known as an inspirational preacher. The performer is paid by the hostess, and a singer or dancer may also receive contributions from the audience.

Rāmāyana Readings

The reading of the *Rāmāyana* is an occasion even more serious than the hymn singing. A woman vows to read the entire *Rāmāyana* without stopping and invites her neighbors to gather on a certain day for this purpose. One woman begins, and when she tires, signals for another to continue. Often several women read in unison, or one woman reads while the others join in on the refrain. Such gatherings are usually much smaller than those for hymn singing, as they go on for many hours and women will drop in for a short time, then leave. Arrangements, however, are similar: a decorated altar and rugs for participants to sit on, no refreshments served and no gifts presented to the hostess. The guests may offer small coins to the deity, and when they depart receive *prasād*, in the form of small sugar candies or other sweets which have first been offered to the deity by the hostess.

Ceremonial Events and Gift Exchange

The other common event of formal interaction among neighbors takes place because of ceremonial functions connected with the observance of life crises. An important aspect of neighborly interaction is the obligation to attend one another's ceremonies and, on specified occasions and in specified amounts, give one another gifts of money and other items, primarily sweets. These reciprocal obligations, closely linked, are called *ānā-jānā* ("coming-going") and *lenā-denā* ("taking-giving"). The terms are used in this way: "We have coming-going with most of the families in this alley" or "Our coming-going with them has ceased since she fought with me about our little boy dirtying the water pump" or "Most of our taking-giving is with people in our own caste." Coming-going refers to mutual visiting, mainly on formal occasions, and taking-giving to the gift exchange which accompanies it. The existence of coming-going and taking-giving between households rests on the prior existence of a friendly informal relationship between them, and if the obligations of coming-going and taking-giving are neglected, the informal relationship will suffer. Although both these terms have wider application with reference to general sociability and gift-giving within the kinship circle, I will apply them to refer only to their use among neighbors.

The main ceremonial occasions which require the attendance of neighbors (particularly women neighbors) are life-crisis ceremonies: a ritual celebration and a feast presented by the host family, primarily for kinsmen and close friends. Kin, friends, and neighbors participate according to their distinct statuses in the various stages of each occasion. In addition to the various marriage rituals, the most frequent life crises celebrated in Ganeshnagar and Kalyānpurī are *jasūtan* (following the birth of a child), *mundan* (the child's first haircut), *kān bindhvānā* (the child's ear-piercing), *janmdin* (the birthday), first *barāt* (a boy's first trip with the men of his family to the wedding of a male kinsman), and *muhurat* (housewarming for the consecration of a newly-built house). Although the last is not conventionally considered a life-crisis rite, it has this function for mohallā residents, and furthermore it is the occasion at which taking-giving and coming-going within the mohallā most often begin for a newly resident homeowner.

For me to describe these ceremonies in detail is unnecessary and inappropriate because ample writings already exist. However, I should point out that Hindu tradition provides for a large number of life-crisis rituals, but only a sample few are observed in these mohallās. In comparison with local rural practice, the variety of rituals performed by most families in the city is limited. However, certain ceremonies which have minor if any significance in the hinterland of Meerut have come to be celebrated here with elaborate pomp. The most obvious example is the treatment of the ear-piercing. Despite the fact that boys of this class no longer wear earrings, and that in the rural area itinerant peddlers pierce ears without ceremony, this ritual has importance in these mohallās "second only to a marriage," according to some informants.

No household attempts to celebrate all these ceremonies on a large scale, and most households can be counted on only to provide marriage rites for their children. The ceremonies for young children are entirely optional and are ignored by most families: rarely held to honor a girl child, and normally for only a first-born son. The birthday has no traditional precedent, but influenced by Western practices some families now annually celebrate the birthday of one or more of their children, usually a son. Although in more Westernized circles the practice of a children's birthday party with an elaborately frosted cake is beginning to gain popularity, in these mohallās the occasion is celebrated, as are other traditional ceremonies, by feasting kinsmen and adult friends of the child's parents.

Cost is a major consideration, and only the well-to-do aspire to celebrate minor events on a large scale. Ceremonial observance is a form of conspicuous consumption in that it requires feasting large numbers of persons and gift-giving within the kinship circle. The compensation is enhanced prestige and social influence, more extensive taking-giving ties within the neighborhood, and a widened social network. Because an observance obliges others to invite one to their ceremonies, it is a form of social investment — a possible explanation for the celebration of events like the ear-piercing, which keep the social exchange active during the many years between one's own and one's children's nuptials.

Although each of these ceremonies differs in detail, the recurrence of certain generalized procedures enables one to speak of the life-crisis ceremony as a uniform class of events. First come a number of days during which neighborhood women gather at the invitation of the hostess to sing appropriate folk songs. These are the ones sung in rural areas for the various rites of passage, although film songs have greatly influenced their style and content. The number of days for such singing (gavānā) is planned in advance and indicates the scale on which the ceremony will be celebrated. Five to eight days would be typical, but sometimes twelve days are allotted. The singing usually takes place late in the evening, after women have cleared away the evening meal. Earlier in the day the Nāin goes from house to house to invite the guests, following general instructions about what parts of the mohallā to include rather than a specific list. From long attendance at such functions and her intimate knowledge of local social life, she usually knows whom to invite to a given house. Normally no one who lives in the same alley as the hostess is excluded; a woman with a wide circle of acquaintances or the desire for a large crowd may ask the Nāin to extend invitations also to other alleys or even to certain houses in an adjoining mohallā. Invitations are not private, nor do they require an answer. The Nāin normally comes to the courtyard door and shouts her message as a general announcement to anyone within hearing, who then decides whether she wishes to continue (or to begin) a relationship of coming-going by attending the singing. If the hostess is a newcomer, this liberal manner of invitation enables her to invite neighbors with whom she is not yet personally acquainted, and they can express an interest in her friendship or reject it by coming or not. To attend one night out of the series suffices for all except close friends. Such gatherings usually consist mainly of elderly women who have daughters-in-law or grown daughters to stay at home, and of adolescent girls who have been sent by busy or tired mothers as "family representatives" in their stead. The women sing to the rhythm of a double drum, passed from one woman to another during the evening. Although singing is continuous, most women spend much of the hour or two chatting about family and neighborhood affairs. Refreshments are not served, although occasionally a hostess will offer pan to chew. All guests give a few small coins (five or ten N.P.) to the hostess, and when they leave she gives them ten small sugar candies, or two to four large ones, of the type used for routine ritual offerings. Almost never eaten, except by children, these are hoarded by the guests for use in future exchanges or temple worship.

For a child's birthday or a boy's first trip to a wedding, ceremonial singing may be the extent of the celebration. But for the more important life crises — childbirth, ear-piercing, marriage, and housewarming — a second and major feature is the religious rite, which may have several phases. A particular ceremonial event may include several distinct, sequential rituals, some the province mainly of men and requiring the services of a Brahman priest, others performed by women alone, without a ritual specialist. The multiplicity of women's ritual is particularly evident for marriage and childbirth. Neighborhood men may attend the priestly ceremonies, but more important to the host family is the participation of neighborhood women in the ceremonies which are the prerogative of their sex. The Nāin again invites the neighbors, but for major celebrations in well-to-do households, her summons is merely a reminder of the hand-delivered, advance printed invitation requesting the family's attendance at the appropriate parts of the ceremony. Special friends, or women who consider themselves of higher status than the hostess, may expect the hostess herself or some member of her family to deliver the oral invitation personally, or to come to fetch them just before the ceremony. Although the late-evening singing gatherings in honor of birth or impending marriage require only informal clothes, the major phases of the ceremony, which usually occur during daytime, demand better dress — artificial silk, rayon, or nylon saris for women and bright rayon dresses and suits for young children. Certain rituals — worship at the well by a new mother, worship of the potter's wheel before a marriage, accompanying a couple to their newly-built home — require a parade of neighborhood women, often accompanied by a hired brass band, through the mohallā streets to the ritual site. As the procession passes their houses, women rush out to join it. Most have heads and faces covered, a few are bare-headed; the difference depends on age, education, and kinship position in the mohallā.

At some point during the rituals accompanying each of the major ceremonies, a guest will present a gift of money to the host's family, either because a taking-giving relationship already exists or because he wishes to establish one. The general name for the gift is *tīkā*. For childbirth, ear-piercing, and housewarming, it is usually presented by the women, rather than the men, upon arrival at the host's home to participate in the ceremony. At a wedding for a girl of the mohallā, tīkā is given to her new bridegroom on the morning after the nuptial rites, before the two leave for his home (*bidā*). If a mohallā youth is being married, tīkā is given at the ritual called "mounting the horse" (ghurcharhī), just before he leaves with his male kinsmen for the trip to his betrothed's home. When he brings home his bride and the neighborhood women come to see her for the first time, they give her a gift of money called "seeing the face" (mũh-dikhāī), which is also reckoned as part of the gift exchange between the neighbor families and the groom's family.

The amounts given in tīkā are the major items in the "taking-giving" relationship. They can range from Re. 1 to Rs. 21 and more, but usually range between Rs. 1 and 5 unless the neighborly relationship is of some years' standing and intensified by close friendship, perhaps through some additional external tie. Although much depends on the giver's finances and her calculations about the likely future of the relationship, usually a woman initiates taking-giving with a one- or two-rupee gift. As the relationship continues, one party or both parties to the exchange may increase the amount. Both carefully record the amounts exchanged; the recipient or a member of her household usually enters them immediately in a notebook or the traditional ledger, though some women prefer to keep such records mentally. The tīkā is conceived of in terms of amounts due and owed; to ensure the continuance of a relationship the amounts should never balance. Hence an initial gift of Re. 1 usually elicits a return of Rs. 2 (the Re. 1 owed plus a Re.1 gift). The exchange continues on this Re. 2 basis thereafter unless one party decides on an increase.

Considerable calculation is involved in deciding whether to initiate taking-giving with a particular family, on what scale to participate, and, occasionally, whether to break off a relationship by allowing it to lapse (usually by repaying what is owed without the additional gift that creates a further debt). The speculations of one woman as she prepared to attend an ear-piercing ceremony for the young grandson and granddaughter of a fellow Brahmani in the next alley are indicative:

> I gave her Re. 1 when her only son got married, and she gave Rs. 2 when our second daughter was married. Now I owe her Re. 1. I can return this amount and our account will be even. But our third daughter's marriage is coming soon and our two sons will also marry before these grandchildren of hers. If I only return her Re.

1 she may think I don't want to continue taking-giving with her. Or she may just not give anything when they marry, since nothing will be owing. So I should really give her Rs. 2 this time.

Her next-door neighbor, a young Tyāgin, mother of five daughters all under six years, made plans to attend the singing, but to forego the ear-piercing ritual and not to give any money. She would be unlikely to receive tīkā from the grandmother in the near future, so "What is the use? They are here 'in service.' Here today, where tomorrow? Who gives [in such a situation]?" On a larger scale, another woman made plans to give Rs. 15 at the marriage of a girl from the adjoining mohallā, whose father is also a colleague of her husband. She had received Rs. 11 (an initial gift) from this family when her older daughter was married and reasoned, "If we only give Rs. 11 this time, they will understand that we don't want to add to the amount." Because relations are warm, she could reasonably expect the relationship to continue — had she given only Rs. 11 the girl's family might justifiably feel offended. Keeping the relationship alive is particularly important to this woman because she has other children who will be married in the next few years.

The third and final phase of the major ceremonial is the feast which follows the ritual, usually on the same day. Relatives, friends and colleagues of the host, and any out-of-town guests who come for the ceremony are fed at the host's home. *Pakkā* food (fried bread, several varieties of vegetables cooked in clarified butter, and milk sweets) is served, usually prepared by a professional Brahman caterer at the home. Neighbors do not generally stay for the feast, although an insistent host may prevail upon close male neighbors to do so. Instead, after the feast is over, food packets called *parosā* containing eight pieces of fried bread, some cooked vegetables, and a selection of four sweets are delivered to each home which has taking-giving relations with the family. A fixed number of food packets per household is given, regardless of the number of its members, except by families on particularly close terms, who may send a food packet for each person, or if some members stay to eat at the wedding, may send them home with food packets for the rest. Failure to send food packets after a feast is regarded as a serious lapse in neighborly social obligations, and constitutes a

breach of taking-giving, just as does failure to attend the ceremony
and to bring tīkā.

Another transaction which forms part of the taking-giving relationship is the distribution of *bhājī*, sweets received from kin on
certain occasions. At a marriage, sweets in quantity are received
from affines and distributed among neighbors with whom one has
taking-giving. When a girl goes to visit her natal household from
the home of her husband's family, sweets should be sent with her,
and likewise sweets sent back with her when she returns to her
husband's home. Providing these sweets is the responsibility of a
couple's parents rather than the couple. These sweets are distributed to neighbors according to the amount of sweets available
on a particular occasion, the closeness of the relationship, and the
scale of past distributions made by the recipients. If the amount is
insufficient for distribution among all with whom one has taking-
giving, sweets are given only to the nearest neighbors, those most
clearly aware that a daughter or daughter-in-law has come or that a
supply of sweets has been received. Distribution of sweets is an
obligation taken more seriously in the rural areas; in the urban
mohallā frequently sweets are not received from kin and are less
conscientiously given out. I was told that one should even buy
sweets to distribute on the appropriate occasions if they are not sent
or prove insufficient, but I have never observed such purchases and
doubt that many families make this much effort to maintain the
traditional bhājī exchange.

The various items in taking-giving exchanges form distinct
but related transactional cycles, in which cash is given in exchange
for cash, for example, or food packets for food packets, even though
on any one occasion the transaction may have the superficial appearance of being an exchange of cash for food packets. Eglar
points out in her discussion of a similar type of gift exchange in
rural Punjab that "The gift given and the gift received [on any
one occasion] are parts of two separate transactions, each of which
can be completed only on some other occasion" (1960:127). Actually, to speak of the "completion" of a taking-giving transaction is
misleading, for taking-giving is ideally a protracted and *incomplete*
set of transactional cycles, completed only when the relationship
itself comes to an end. The exact nature and amount of the gift

may be structured, but they are not so rigidly standardized as to leave no room for the play of individual strategies. Whether to give Rs. 2 or Rs. 5, whether to send food packets to each member of a household or the more usual one or two, whether to add a handful of sugar candies and a dried coconut to a cash gift — these decisions are made on the basis of past transactional events and speculations about the future. Each gift in the cycle is simultaneously a return for a previous gift and a solicitation of future ones. At the same time it is inextricably bound to the exchange of formal visits and ceremonial attendances which are required for full participation in neighborhood social life. As one middle-aged Brahman woman complained when a neighbor failed to attend one of the minor rituals preceding her daughter's marriage: "After all, no one's giving is finished. There will be giving in the future and there has been giving in the past. Hers isn't finished, and neither is mine." The woman was not so much expressing displeasure at her neighbor's failure to return the ten N.P. that were her due on this occasion, as voicing the basic principle of the exchange cycle — it should continue, unbalanced and unbroken; the social relationship punctuated by periodic exchange of gifts and visits should not thoughtlessly be allowed to lapse.

Obviously no family can practicably maintain coming-going and the accompanying taking-giving relationship with all other families in the mohallā. These relationships occur most frequently with close neighbors, with members of one's caste living elsewhere in the mohallā, and with families related by village kinship. The number of families with whom any one family maintains exchange varies greatly. Some can count twenty to thirty families in the neighborhood whose ceremonies they habitually attend and with whom they exchange gifts; others limit taking-giving to three or four families. The number depends on a family's length of residence in the mohallā and, in a less direct way, on its current stage in the family developmental cycle, on home ownership (whether a family constitutes real mohallā people or transients), and on the housewife's choice as to whether she wishes to establish and maintain a wide network. Some women are too retiring by nature to make the informal contacts important as a basis for the more formal relationships. Others — few in number — regard the system as time-consuming, expensive, and meaningless. As one such woman expressed it: "Everyone knows I don't give and I don't take."

Home ownership is so important in ensuring a wide taking-giving network because of the institution of the housewarming, which I have chosen to consider here as a life-crisis ceremony. When a new house (or an old house remodeled for new owners) is ready for occupancy, the owners fix a date for its consecration. On the morning of the rites the owner and his wife set out with a procession of women, kin and neighbors from the owner's present mohallā, to advance from their old residence to the new. Upon arrival at the new house, the procession of women, together with some women of the new neighborhood, sit in one room or in a corner of the courtyard to sing while in another room the priest conducts the consecration ceremony in front of the couple and some observers, mainly men. That evening the owner gives a feast to which he invites relatives, friends, and men of the new neighborhood, often by a formal printed invitation sent some days in advance. At the feast or earlier in the day, householders in the new neighborhood bring the cash gifts to their new neighbor which form the basis for future taking-giving. Thus a newcomer, who may never have met some of his new neighbors, has a ready-made network of relationships and a set of obligations to attend future neighborhood ceremonies. Because such a procedure for immediate integration of the new neighbor is not available for tenants, they must build up similar relationships gradually, on the basis of new friendships made and old village kinship ties reactivated.

This differentiation of owner and tenant in the initiation of taking-giving relationships necessarily influences the extent to which tenants participate in taking-giving in these mohallās. Temporary tenants are in effect ignored. Even if more permanent residents do not exclude them from general invitations to ceremonial functions, they are not particularly urged or expected to attend, and permanent residents show open reluctance to participate in their ceremonies. Although one may attend without giving tīkā, doing so is awkward. And giving it is a risky investment because (as both sides know) the recipient may move away before returning it. Tenant women who feel that their husband is likely to be transferred after a year or two will only reluctantly begin taking-giving in the mohallā.

Reciprocity and the "Pure Gift"

Selectivity in the composition of taking-giving networks derives also from the concept of reciprocity which underlies this system of gift exchange. Reciprocity or *adal-badal* characterizes gift exchanges in which a return is expected in the same form and in roughly equivalent amount. Taking-giving is clearly reciprocal, but not all gift-giving is. Gifts given in reciprocal exchanges are sharply distinguished from "pure gifts" or *dān*: gifts for which no equivalent material return may be accepted. For dān, the only return is a gift in another form — either as spiritual merit (*punya*), the granting of a desire through supernatural intervention, or as worldly prestige (*izzat*), or possibly as personal service and devotion from those who accept dān and are in no position to return it materially. The ideal dān is given without thought of even spiritual return — for such gifts the spiritual merit acquired is vastly greater.

The term *dān* is used to characterize the gifts from bride-givers to bride-takers (specifically the dowry). It is present in the term *kanya dān*, "gift of a virgin," by which a certain stage in the wedding ceremony, and in a broad sense the wedding itself, is known. Dān is also used to characterize gifts to Brahmans, and Bania families in these mohallās are particularly aware of the merit to be earned by such gifts and of the sin (*pāp*) incurred by the (even inadvertent) acceptance of return gifts from Brahmans. Although Brahmans and Baniās participate in taking-giving, Baniās do not accept gifts outside this reciprocal context from Brahman neighbors and friends, and some refuse even to eat at the homes of Brahman neighbors on ceremonial occasions because of their reluctance to appear to be taking anything from a Brahman, and the fear that what they have given earlier to the Brahman family may be returned to them now in the form of the meal.

Dān also includes gifts to persons of low economic or caste status. A destitute Brahman widow in Ganeshnagar lives on the gifts of food which neighbors present as dān. Gifts to servants are considered dān, even though they may be offered in the same form and ostensibly in the same contexts as taking-giving gifts are given to others. The obligation to give dān to Bhangī and Nāī families with whom one has a quasi-client relationship is very strong. When the children of servants marry, Brahmans, Baniās, and other high-caste families give presents of clothes, utensils, and cash but expect no direct return. In fact, they will refuse to accept similar gifts offered on their own ceremonial occasions, for "there is no reciprocity with servants." Servant households do participate in taking-giving relationships, however, with other households of roughly equivalent status.

CHAPTER VII

Conclusions

M Y study has focused on two prominent issues in the anthropology of urbanization: the impact of urbanization on the family and kinship system and the significance of the urban neighborhood in a changing society. The data I have presented do not support assumptions that rapid or radical change in the traditional Indian family system has occurred, or that the Indian urbanite is an anonymous inhabitant of his neighborhood, isolated from primary contacts outside his nuclear family.

I have shown that patterns of interaction between kin (at all levels of the system) and, to a lesser extent, the values and norms associated with kinship roles, differ in some respects from what other anthropologists have reported as characteristic of the rural districts of this region. One discerns in these differences incipient changes in the kinship system, which undoubtedly one can relate to the forces of urbanization. I should voice a caution, however, before detailing these differences and the changing trends they suggest. It would be a mistake to assume that the alterations result only from the transplantation of ruralities to an urban milieu. First, these differences are not a necessary concomitant of urban living. What evidence I have shows that kinship organization in the old mohallās of Meerut in the past and among lower socioeconomic groups in the city even today still resembles that of the rural districts in all important respects. Second, the changes in kinship organization in Ganeshnagar and Kalyānpurī and in other middle-class neighborhoods of their type do not result primarily from their being city neighborhoods, but rather from an underlying chain of forces which begins with education and permits occupational mobility, consequent geographical mobility, and neolocal residence patterns. Urban residence is intermediate in the causal chain leading toward changed kinship organization. The changes I have described are intimately connected to the recent rise in India of a substantial white-collar middle class from the peasantry. Whether similar changes in kinship organization are associated with Indian urbanization in general must await research among other categories of urbanites.

I have remarked that kinship organization in the older and poorer parts of Meerut substantially resembles that of the countryside. This fact is consistent with the notion that no sharp cultural discontinuity exists between the masses of the preindustrial or orthogenetic city and the peasants of its hinterland (cf. Redfield and Singer 1954; Sjoberg 1960: 145–181). And for this reason it is misleading to speak of a rural-urban dichotomy in family and kinship organization in India (cf. Lynch 1963, 1967; Pocock 1960). Furthermore, I have perhaps given the misleading impression of a static rural scene by often contrasting urban practices with rural ones. The "traditional rural kinship system" of this region is unlikely ever to have been static. Certainly today one cannot simply equate "traditional" with "modern-day rural." As the village absorbs the growing impact of Western education and industrial civilization from Indian metropolitan centers, neat contrasts between rural and urban kinship systems or any other aspect of social structure become increasingly untenable.

THE IMPACT OF URBANIZATION ON THE FAMILY AND KINSHIP SYSTEM

Goode (1963a, 1963b) has been particularly concerned with universal family change associated with urbanization. He sees a general move toward what he calls a "conjugal pattern" of the family, whose most important feature is the exclusion of "a wide range of affinal kin and blood relatives from its everyday affairs

[and] . . . no great *extension* of the kin network" (1963a:240). In this formulation, though not necessarily in its terminology, he echoes many other sociologists with an interest in the family (Parsons 1949; Nimkoff 1965; Burgess and Locke 1953). Among a number of specific changes which he finds in the "institutional structure" (1963b:26) of the family in Western and non-Western society, he includes some changes relevant to the present study: Increased freedom of marital choice, with a rising age of marriage; disappearance of dowry; decline of polygyny; rise in the divorce rate; increase in the remarriage of the widowed and divorced (1963a: 250ff.; cf. Nimkoff 1965:343–356).

The present study has not found marked change in the direction of these hypothesized trends. Even if increased freedom of marital choice may be indicated by the small, but probably rising number of love marriages and by an increasing tendency to allow the educated young person to veto his parents' choice, the changes in marriage arrangement do not approach those reported for other countries: Japan, for example (Blood 1967; Vogel 1967; Dore 1958). The urban lower middle class in India still depends overwhelmingly on parental arrangement of marriage. Adaptation to changing circumstances does appear in new criteria for mates, however, and in the concomitant rise in marital age, also predicted by Goode. But contrary to another prediction, the dowry is flourishing rather than declining in the Indian urban middle class, largely because of the persistence of arranged marriages and the value placed on the scarce good represented by the educated, salaried employee, who epitomizes class aspirations. Traditional restrictions on a free choice of spouse — caste endogamy, gotra exogamy, the bar to the marriage of known consanguines and to the exchange of women — exacerbate the problem of selection in a field severely limited by secular considerations. The force of these restrictions has hardly weakened, except for gotra exogamy, which is increasingly evaded. Admittedly the difficulty of finding a suitable mate, which encourages high dowries, is partly offset by a willingness to contract alliances at a considerable distance, thus expanding a marriage circle which has traditionally been territorially limited.[1]

[1] For example, Gould gives an average distance between mates' place of origin as 10.5 miles for an eastern Uttar Pradesh village (1960:481) and Rowe gives a figure of 12 miles, with a range of between 3 and 55 miles, for another village of the same region (1969:301).

In the absence of reliable statistics, it is difficult to say whether polygyny is declining. The legal prohibition of the act impedes data-collecting. Polygyny probably is on the decline in the middle class; however it is still acceptable alternative behavior, allowing for the fact that in this society it has never been common or considered particularly desirable.[2] The same statistical difficulty hinders an assessment of the divorce rate. Most estrangements between husband and wife do not result in legal divorce, but in permanent separation (and remarriage for the man), and it is impossible to say whether the "separation rate" in these mohallās is greater now than it was in the past or than it is in rural areas. Certainly divorce remains strongly disapproved of, although residents increasingly recognize its desirability when a marriage produces extreme hardship for one or both partners. As long as a divorcee is as disadvantaged as she still is in this class and her remarriage is practically impossible, there is little reason to expect that women or their parents will take significant initiative in availing themselves of legal provisions. But conversely, increasing awareness among men of the existing legal strictures against polygyny should gradually cause some rise in the divorce rate in coming decades. Contrary to the last of Goode's predictions, there is still little evidence of change in attitudes toward the remarriage of either divorcees or widows, and little remarriage occurs. Changes in Indian family law have indeed been in the direction of Goode's predictions, and legal changes may be reinforcing inherent social processes, but as yet the law appears to be far ahead of accepted norms and behavior.

To turn to relations between kin now, they have been subjected to strain by changing modes of life. Of course a pattern of kinship behavior based on strong, localized patrilineages and patrilocal residence can be expected to show strain when asked to serve in a situation which forces close proximity upon kin who tradi-

[2] Pakrasi and Halder (1970), in a study of the National Sample Survey 1960–61, found that a total of 116 men out of the all-India sample of 16,159 had more than one wife. In Uttar Pradesh the prevalence of polygyny was found to be 4.52% among married men, men of over forty-six years accounting for 42% of the polygynous marriages, though they form only 25% of the total sample population. These figures could be interpreted as evidence of a decline in polygyny, but may instead indicate that polygynous marriages are typically contracted in middle age or later rather than within a short time after the first marriage. Interestingly, 71.85% of the polygynous males surveyed were Hindus.

tionally would rarely have had contact, except in a highly structured context. Strain is also predictable when kin who have traditionally lived in a common household or nearby one another must adjust to the neolocal, nuclear household which urban, white-collar employment usually necessitates.

But the social system can employ a countering mechanism and mitigate the pressures: keeping structural closeness between the spatially separated, and structural distance between the spatially close. The persistence of interdependent relationships, of mutual rights and obligations for urban households and agnates living elsewhere, sustains close ties between kin despite occupational and geographical mobility. Many urban householders, as the mohallās show, retain joint ownership of rural land and homes, and urbanites frequently use their income for maintaining rural estates and making rural investments. The exchange of money, goods, and services between rural and urban segments of the agnatic extended family, as the mohallās also indicate, is not only normatively prescribed but common in practice, particularly if the rural residents are the urban household head's parents. Visits between the family segments are frequent, and a chain of gossip links kin who may seldom see one another in person.

Typically, rural kindred are dispersed over numerous villages, perhaps within a twenty-five-mile radius; the kindred of the mohallā residents, however, are dispersed throughout northern India, and some are even in central or southern India or abroad. Such a wide dispersion of their kindred is particularly characteristic of those who have lived in the city for a generation or more. The people of these mohallās, however, do not lose contact with distant kin, even if they cannot frequently meet. This literate population uses the mails extensively and travels to visit kin. Particularly during school holidays, kin gather to attend weddings, children are sent for visits to grandparents, and women return to their natal homes. News of sickness will bring close kin from hundreds of miles away. No doubt with the wide dispersal of the kindred, relationships with genealogically distant relatives are attenuated. Conversely, however, the urbanite whose range of locally available close kin is narrow often draws those linked by distant ties into his intimate circle if they happen to live nearby.

Migration to urban areas, in India as elsewhere, is associational;

migrants come to the city with kin or, more commonly, seek out kin for practical and emotional assistance upon arriving there. Accordingly, in these mohallās there are kin clusters whose members are linked by both consanguineal and affinal ties. Newcomers exploit distant kin ties, those involving many intermediate affinal and consanguineal links, and even the ties of village kinship in their search for accommodations and congenial social intercourse. Whether they are agnates, uterine kin, or affines, kin who are spatially close usually are included in the effective kin network of the mohallā resident. But traditional considerations, particularly those which prescribe asymmetry between bride-givers and bride-takers, continue to assure social distance between those who in the countryside would also be spatially distant. Social interaction between persons related through the marriage of their children or of other junior kinsmen continues to be limited and rigidly structured.

However, in an increasingly acceptable practice, parents exchange frequent visits with their married daughters who live neolocally in the city. The increasing tendency toward neolocal residence has stimulated other tendencies in turn. The traditional kinship system is yielding under the pressure of the emotional bond which ties a woman to her natal kin. There is evidence that natal bonds are gradually asserting themselves, lessening a bride's incorporation into the affinal kindred; more important, a blurring of the contextual separation of natal and affinal relationships is occurring. The norm prescribing that a woman's loyalties should be with her conjugal family remains substantially unchanged, however, and is preserved in linguistic usages, so that a married woman speaking of "our family" or "family people" is still understood to be referring to her conjugal family or lineage rather than to her natal family. Likewise, the right to attend a woman in childbirth or other difficulties is still felt to reside properly in her husband's kindred. Yet even here some behavioral changes are evident in that the urban middle-class family increasingly acknowledges the woman's preference for interaction with natal rather than conjugal kin because of the traditional double standard of behavior for "daughter" and "bride."

Of course with men's and women's roles, and consequently husband's and wife's social networks, kept segregated, the preference need not necessarily lead to men's increased association with their wives' kin. Association is unlikely to occur between a man and his wife's senior kinsmen because of still vital norms which prescribe deference toward the son-in-law. However, no barrier divides kin of the same generation, who have traditionally had a relationship of joking and familiarity, and a man who is willing finds himself easily incorporated into a social network which includes his wife's younger kin. A neolocally resident husband usually shows considerable tolerance of his wife's natal relationships, as long as these do not interfere with her obligations to his kin. However, the patrilocally resident woman is restrained by the same obligations to her husband's family in the city as in the countryside. I conclude, cautiously, that the Indian kinship system in urban areas is undergoing an increasing bilateral emphasis, which is likely to be magnified in the future in conjunction with increasing neolocal residence.

There is limited evidence of an increasingly companionable relationship between husband and wife in nuclear households and those which include a junior kinsman of either spouse. Such a development is particularly marked for couples in love marriages, of course, but also for couples who have resided neolocally since their marriage and have thus depended only on each other for primary emotional sustenance in the early years of marriage, rather than on extended household members of the same sex.

The extent of role parity and companionship between husband and wife may be affected somewhat by the "conjugal family ideal" cited by Goode (1963a:19–20) as a powerful cause of changing familial patterns in societies with a traditional ideal of extended family living. Indian young people learn about this ideal through movies and popular literature and as they gain increasing familiarity in other ways with the Western way of life. Working against wholehearted acceptance of such an ideal are strong forces rooted in values which place the interests of the group (i.e., the extended family and particularly the parents) above those of the individual. Nevertheless it has some appeal for those who deem the ties of the extended family a hindrance to ambition or personal emotional fulfillment.

However, as I have already implied, even more effective than this ideal in promoting change in the structure and functioning of the family is neolocal residence, a usual consequence of acquiring the education which leads to urban employment. In some American cities the exigencies of occupational mobility do not necessarily include geographical mobility, simply because the cities offer occupational opportunities of all kinds within their boundaries (Mitchell and Leichter 1961:10). But employment opportunities for educated young men in India are less numerous and occupational choice almost always depends on a willingness to accept geographical mobility. Minimally, a man must be willing to leave the village for a nearby city because employment for the educated in rural areas is limited and what jobs there are in the village almost always subject an employee to frequent transfers. The problem of unemployment and underemployment of the educated and the transfer system have made neolocal residence commonplace for the white-collar middle class.

Yet, as I have shown, neolocal residence does not mean the isolation of the nuclear family from other kin. I have remarked on the extent to which kin predominate in social networks, on the strength of ties within the extended family, and on the frequency and ease with which neolocally resident couples add junior kin to their urban household. Another important sign of the vitality of family unity is the way in which urban households provide for the comfort of elderly parents. The "stem families" modify the norm which says "Married sons should live with their parents" to read, "At least one son should remain with the parents — they should not be left to live alone." In the absence of a "stem" structure, elderly parents may visit from one son to another or an elderly couple may split up, each living with a different son. The practice of sending young grandchildren to be brought up by paternal grandparents serves a similar function. However, a substantial number of old couples do in fact live alone because their sons have moved elsewhere and have not made alternative provisions for them.

In patterns of household residence as well as in those of kin network, choice and selectivity have increasing significance and a tendency somewhat to supersede traditional structural determinants. Other societies which are becoming urbanized show the same phenomena (Firth 1964; Baric 1967; Schwab 1965) and they will doubtless be increasingly important for the future urban Indian family.

SOCIAL FUNCTIONS OF THE URBAN
NEIGHBORHOOD

I should restate a caution before reviewing the social functions of the neighborhood. New mohallās in an old city, both Ganeshnagar and Kalyānpurī are neighborhoods of private homes, largely owner-occupied even when tenanted, whose inhabitants are primarily first- and second-generation urbanites of the white-collar middle class. They are not necessarily typical of Indian urban neighborhoods as a whole. Although some of what I have said about them is also true of mohallās described by other researchers (cf. Woodruff 1959; Bopegamage 1957; Lynch 1967; Doshi 1968), these other neighborhoods differ significantly from Ganeshnagar and Kalyānpurī in historical development, in caste and class composition, in internal organization, and in degree and kind of social integration. One would expect to find marked differences between these mohallās and neighborhoods of new towns, particularly towns which draw migrants from many linguistic regions (cf. Bopegamage 1957). Probable differences from old neighborhoods in old cities have already been alluded to. These qualifications cast further doubt on the utility of a simple rural-urban contrast for understanding the social characteristics of Indian urbanization.

The mohallās studied here, however atypical, have been shown to function in many respects as a social community for their residents. Migrants to Ganeshnagar and Kalyānpurī from rural areas or other cities do not normally find themselves isolated from social intercourse with their neighbors, but, if they are receptive to what the mohallā offers, soon become caught up in a web of social obligations for visiting and gift exchange. The pattern is familiar from their place of origin although it differs in details. Social integration in these neighborhoods does not typically mean incorporating complete strangers. Most newcomers have previous social ties through kinship, village kinship, or friendship with some resident of the mohallā into which they move. Prior relationships determine the choice of kinship terms for reference and address among neighbors, although new patterns are emerging in the way in which fictive kinship terms are selected for neighbors with whom no prior relationship can be traced.

Various axes of social differentiation within the mohallā affect the extent of an individual's web of obligations and the composition of the social network which it reinforces. The social organization of the neighborhood is segregated by sex. Although men and women may participate in the same neighborhood events and relationships, they do so separately, and they have distinct roles to play as neighbors. The neighborhood generally has greater significance for women than for men. Women know their neighbors and interact frequently with them, whereas men are likely to have closer relationships with work colleagues and friends outside the mohallā. For women the neighborhood is a source of primary relationships second in importance only to their kinship network.

Status differences within the generally middle-class group in these neighborhoods are also important in determining social networks. An important criterion for establishing status is caste, with a broad distinction made between high and low castes. But education, occupation, and economic status are probably more important than caste alone to a family's position in the mohallā. Ordinarily high caste status coincides with high rank in these other criteria and, if not, caste yields to them. Because people of high castes and white-collar occupations predominate in these mohallās, their social networks are usually localized within the mohallā or within a section of it. Those of low caste and low socioeconomic status usually exchange gifts and ceremonial attendance over a geographically wider area, including low-status residents of neighboring mohallās in their activities rather than high-status residents of their own. This segregation by caste and socioeconomic status is related to traditional concepts of the client-servant relationship, which proscribe equivalent exchanges and balanced reciprocity for those of greatly unequal status.

A social distinction is also made between homeowners or "real mohallā people" and transient residents or tenants; broadly a distinction between residents permanently committed to the mohallā as a social community and temporary residents with no real stake in its preservation. This distinction is buttressed by the custom of the housewarming gift that initiates homeowners' participation in gift exchanges, or taking-giving. Tenants are initiated in a more random way. Because their inclusion depends on their personal inclinations and their initiative in establishing social relationships if they have no prior ties within the mohallā, a minority of tenants find themselves almost completely outside the network of reciprocal ceremonial visits and gifts.

Family and other kindred have primary functions of social control; the role of the neighborhood is limited essentially to gossip and face-to-face disapproval. Residents' tendency to form semi-exclusive social networks means that effective control of behavior is commonly insulated within these networks, rather than responsive to any overall mohallā standard. Formal mechanisms of control hardly exist. Ganeshnagar's mohallā association has no authority over deviants within the neighborhood at large. Kalyānpurī has no association.

I have tried to show that although the middle-class urban neighborhood in India has become the setting for considerable social change, urbanization has not had a radical impact on the family or the kinship system. The degree of social stability is as noteworthy as that of change. The urbanite still operates within a familiar social framework and voices familiar values, although he is becoming gradually aware that his behavior, or at least his neighbor's, is beginning to deviate from those values. The residents of these urban neighborhoods certainly differ in many of their assumptions and way of life, despite similarities in background and livelihood. No complete consensus exists. But neither is the mohallā an undefined or an impersonal place where community social control is absent and primary relationships are lost. In the social organization of the neighborhood, as in the kinship system, we observe an adaptation of traditional means to the requirements of a new life.

APPENDIX I

The Field Research

The research for this study was carried out from September 1966
to August 1967 while I was living in Meerut. My husband, an
Indian national, is a former resident of the city. Although he was
unable to spend the entire research period with me, he did accompany me and our children to India and established us in a rented
apartment on the street in Kalyānpurī where his brother and sister-
in-law reside. As he knew the area well, he was able to help me
select in the vicinity a mohallā of manageable size and suitable
population for my study. He and his brother introduced me to a
number of persons in this adjoining mohallā, Ganeshnagar, and
there I began my formal research. In the meantime I was becoming
informally acquainted with my own neighbors in Kalyānpurī, with
my husband's kin, and with their friends. My study was thus
inevitably broadened to include both mohallās. Although I drew
all my quantitative data from a house-to-house survey of Ganeshnagar, I derived abundant data from observation and nondirective
interviews in both neighborhoods. Because I was a resident of
Kalyānpurī and a participant in the daily life of two of its families
(my landlord's and my brother-in-law's), in some respects that
mohallā afforded me more intimate and continuous insight into
Indian urban social life.

During the entire year I lived with our children on the second floor of a substantial house in Kalyānpurī. Our landlord was a successful businessman who lived with his wife and seven children on the ground floor. Our children played with his constantly, and his wife was a ready conversationalist and an understanding neighbor, who greatly helped my research with hours of talk and invitations to ceremonies in the homes of her many kinsmen in Kalyānpurī and nearby mohallās. When I was not working or visiting in Ganeshnagar and Kalyānpurī, I spent most of my time at my brother-in-law's home with his wife and adolescent children. Their contribution to my research was of course greater than any other person's, and much of my intimate data, as well as help in its interpretation, has come from discussions with them and from the kind of observation that only participation in a family's life can bring. During the year I was able to make several short visits to my husband's village home and to the homes of relatives and friends in other villages of the district. Thus I was able to observe something of the rural life of this area to supplement what I learned through interviews and reading. However, I made no formal attempt to investigate village social organization for direct comparison with urban data.

I spent the first two months of my stay improving my facility in Hindi, becoming acquainted with residents of the two mohallās, and, with the information I was obtaining by observation, constructing a census schedule appropriate to the population I had chosen to study. Afterwards I arranged through the University of Delhi to hire as research assistant a young woman graduate student in anthropology, who worked with me for six months. She spoke both Hindi and English well and was able to serve as an interpreter when necessary. Her role in the research was varied. She filled out census schedules, either alone or with me, and participated in the loosely structured interviews on subjects of primary interest. Late in my stay a young woman from Ganeshnagar assisted me for one month, completing the census survey in households which my research assistant and I had been unable to contact earlier.

In general, I avoided taking notes during interviews lest I seriously hinder spontaneity of response. However, when I was eliciting precise information, such as in enquiries about ritual procedure, kinship terms, or genealogies, often I could take notes or use a tape recorder. I also used the tape recorder frequently to record folk songs and traditional stories associated with the festival cycle, both at gatherings where they were being performed for ceremonial purposes and at impromptu gatherings of women in the neighborhood. I was able to record some lengthy interviews and conversations among groups of people, which my assistant later transcribed in Hindi. Otherwise, we both committed interviews to memory as accurately as possible and later wrote them down. When both my assistant and I were present, each wrote down her own recollections, trying as far as possible to reproduce the exact words of conversations, and her observations and tentative interpretations. Each evening we compared impressions of the events of the day.

I found the cooperation of the people of Kalyānpurī and Ganeshnagar gratifying. Even those who understandably had reservations about my intentions were warm and hospitable and open in their willingness to talk to me about their lives (although understandably some were reluctant to have detailed personal data, such as information about their finances, recorded on paper). I, in turn, spent many hours telling about life in America, for I found mohallā residents as curious about our society as I was about theirs.

Because I was in a society where considerable segregation of the sexes is customary I obtained most of my data from talking to women and observing their activities. The consequent bias is perhaps useful so far as it captures aspects of urban life that might escape the male anthropologist's data, but it is nevertheless a bias, and to counter it I did try to get the male point of view whenever possible. In certain situations my status as outsider superseded my status as woman, so that I was not expected to conform strictly to the feminine role assigned to mohallā women, even to those equally well educated. This freedom was particularly important because my situation was complicated by my being also a "bride" of the mohallā (that is, a woman married to a local man), whose role normally includes strict avoidance of elder mohallā men. Doubtless my own awareness of my kinship position in the neighborhood modified my approach to my work and the image I tried to project, but conformity to local restraints on a bride's freedom was not explicitly demanded of me. Although I cannot test my impression, I feel that my having a kinship link to the people of the mohallās was actually a distinct advantage, causing aspects of life to be revealed to me that would possibly have been closed to a person whose only status was foreign social researcher. Most important perhaps was that kinship enabled me to establish relationships of equality and mutual trust and to put people at ease in a way that might not have been as easy had I been a complete outsider.

Census Schedule
Used in Ganeshnagar

1. Name of each household member:
   a. Relationship to household head
   b. Age
   c. Sex
   d. Religion
   e. Caste
   f. Subcaste
   g. Gotra (natal gotra for married women)
   h. Marital status
   i. Age at marriage
   j. Age at gaunā
   k. Last school class completed
   l. Place of last school (name of school if in Meerut)
   m. Mother tongue
   n. Language spoken in the home
   o. Occupation
   p. Place of employment
   q. Monthly earnings
2. Homeowners:
   a. Did you build or buy this house?
   b. In what year?
   c. In what year did you begin to live in this house?
   d. In what year did you begin to live in this mohallā?
   e. Do you have tenants in this house?
   f. How many?
   g. How much rent does each pay?
   h. Are any of your tenants re-

lated to you, and if so, how?

i. Do you have kinsmen living in this mohallā?

j. Who are they and how are they related to you?

3. Tenants:

a. In what year did you begin to live in this house?

b. In what year did you begin to live in this mohallā?

c. How much rent do you pay?

d. Are you related to the landlord, and if so, how?

e. If the landlord is not a kinsman, did you know him before you moved to this house, and if so, how?

f. Do you have kinsmen living in this mohallā?

g. Who are they and how are they related to you?

h. How did you find these accommodations?

4. Housing facilities:

a. How many rooms do you have for your own use?

b. Do you have a kitchen?

c. Do you share any facilities with other households?

d. What facilities do you share?

5. Ownership of real property:

a. Do you own any house(s) other than this house?

b. Where is it (are they) located?

c. Do you own it (them) jointly with anyone?

d. If you own it (them) jointly, what is the relationship of the other owners to you?

e. Do you own any land?

f. Where is it located?

g. What is its acreage?

h. Do you own this land jointly with anyone?

i. If you own it jointly, what is the relationship of the other owners to you?

j. Do you own any other real property, such as a shop or factory?

k. Where is it located?

l. Do you own it jointly with anyone?

m. If you own it jointly, what is the relationship of the other owners to you?

6. Household amenities and consumer goods:

a. Electricity

b. Hand pump

c. Piped water

d. Bicycle

e. Scooter

f. Motorcycle

g. Automobile

h. Electric fan

i. Radio

j. Sewing machine

k. Electric iron

l. Tea set

m. Stainless steel utensils

n. Sofa set
o. Steel cabinet
p. Cow or buffalo
q. Full-time servant
r. Part-time servant

7. Support of relatives:
   a. Do you regularly aid financially any person who does not live in this household?
   b. What is his relationship to you?
   c. Where does he live?
   d. With whom does he live?
   e. What is the reason for your financial aid?
   f. What amount do you give him?

8. Financial assistance from relatives:
   a. Does any person who does not live in this household regularly aid you financially?
   b. What is his relationship to you?
   c. Where does he live?
   d. With whom does he live?
   e. What is the reason for his financial aid?
   f. What amount does he give to you?

9. Residential history of household head and housewife, from birth to present:
   a. Place of residence (name of mohallā if in Meerut)
   b. Relationship of other members of household
   c. Year of change of residence
   d. Reason for change of residence

NOTE: This census schedule has been translated from the Hindi original. As explained in the text, questions concerning earnings, rental income and payments, extent of landholdings, and details of financial obligations to kinsmen were omitted from most interviews although they appear on the schedule as reproduced here.

References Cited

I have tried to keep bibliographic references to a minimum for the convenience of the reader. Although my study obviously is indebted to the extensive writings on urbanization and its social consequences in Western and non-Western societies, I list here only those works which I have specifically mentioned in the text.

Ahmed, E.
1958   A note on the size and function of towns in India: Uttar Pradesh — a case study. Journal of Social Research 1: 54–58.

Ames, M.
1970   Structural dimensions of family life in the steel city of Jamshedpur, India. Unpublished paper prepared for the Conference on Occupational Cultures in Changing South Asia, Chicago.

Bailey, F. G.
1960   The joint family in India: a framework for discussion. Economic Weekly 12: 8.

Baric, L.
1967   Levels of change in Yugoslav kinship. In Social organisation. M. Freedman, ed. Chicago, Aldine.

Beidelman, T.
1959   A comparative analysis of the jajmani system. New York, J. J. Augustin.

Berreman, G.
1963   Hindus of the Himalayas. Berkeley and Los Angeles, University of California Press.

Beteille, A.
1964   Family and social change in India and other South Asian countries. Economic Weekly 16: 237–244.

Bhat, J. N.
    1956 The middle class in India. *In* Development of a middle class in tropical and subtropical countries. Brussels, International Institute of Differing Civilizations, 29th session.

Blood, R. O., Jr.
    1967 Love match and arranged marriage: a Tokyo-Detroit comparison. New York, Free Press.

Bopegamage, A.
    1957 Delhi: a study in urban sociology. Bombay, University of Bombay Publications in Sociology 7.

Bott, E.
    1955 Urban families: conjugal roles and social networks. Human Relations 8: 345–384.
    1957 Family and social network. London, Tavistock.

Breese, G.
    1966 Urbanization in newly developing countries. Englewood Cliffs, Prentice-Hall.

Burgess, E. W. and H. J. Locke
    1953 The family. New York, American Book Company.

Census of India 1961
    1965 Volume XV, Uttar Pradesh.
    1965 District Census Handbook. Uttar Pradesh 18: Meerut District. Lucknow, Superintendent of Printing and Stationery.

Cohn, B. S.
    1961 Chamar family in a north Indian village: a structural contingent. Economic Weekly 13: 1051–1055.

Collver, A.
    1963 The family cycle in India and the United States. American Sociological Review 28: 89–96.

Department of Statistics
    1964 Report on the middle-class family living survey 1958–59. New Delhi, Central Statistical Organisation, Government of India.

Derrett, J. D. M.
    1957 Hindu law past and present. Calcutta, A. Mukherjee.
    1963 Introduction to modern Hindu law. Bombay, Oxford University Press.

Desai, I. P.
    1964 Some aspects of family in Mahuva: a sociological study of jointness in a small town. New York, Asia Publishing House.

Dore, R.
    1958 City life in Japan. Berkeley and Los Angeles, University of California Press.

Doshi, H. C.
    1968 Industrialization and neighbourhood communities in a western Indian city — challenge and response. Sociological Bulletin 17: 18–34.

Driver, E. D.
    1963   Differential fertility in Central India. Princeton, Princeton University Press.

Dube, S. C.
    1955   Indian village. London, Routledge & Kegan Paul.
    1963   Men's and women's roles in India: a sociological review. In Women in the new Asia. B. Ward, ed. Paris, UNESCO.

Dumont, L.
    1962   Le vocabulaire de parenté dans l'Inde du Nord. L'Homme 2: 5–48.
    1966   Marriage in India: the present state of the question. Contributions to Indian Sociology 9: 90–114.

Eglar, Z.
    1960   A Punjabi village in Pakistan. New York, Columbia University Press.

Firth, R.
    1964   Family and kinship in industrial society. The Sociological Review (Keele) Monograph 8: 65–87.

Fonseca, M.
    1966   Counselling for marital happiness. Bombay, Manaktalas.

Fortes, M.
    1949a   The web of kinship among the Tallensi. London, Oxford University Press.
    1949b   Time and social structure. In Social structure. M. Fortes, ed. Oxford, Oxford University Press.
    1966   Introduction. In The developmental cycle in domestic groups. J. Goody, ed. Cambridge, Cambridge University Press.

Freed, S. A.
    1963   Fictive kinship in a north Indian village. Ethnology 2: 86–103.

Goode, W. J.
    1963a   World revolution and family patterns. New York, Free Press.
    1963b   Industrialization and family change. In Industrialization and society. B. F. Hoselitz and W. E. Moore, eds. Paris, UNESCO.

Goodenough, W. H.
    1956   Residence rules. Southwestern Journal of Anthropology 12: 22–37.

Goody, J., ed.
    1966   The developmental cycle in domestic groups. Cambridge, Cambridge University Press.

Gore, M. S.
    1961   Impact of industrialization and urbanization on the Aggarwal family in the Delhi area. Unpublished PhD dissertation, Columbia University.
    1965   The traditional Indian family. In Comparative family systems. M. F. Nimkoff, ed. Boston, Houghton Mifflin.
    1969   Urbanization and family change. Bombay, Popular Prakashan.

Gould, H. A.
 1960 The micro-demography of marriages in a North Indian area. Southwestern Journal of Anthropology 16: 476–491.
 1961 A further note on village exogamy in north India. Southwestern Journal of Anthropology 17: 297–300.
 1963 The adaptive functions of caste in contemporary Indian society. Asian Survey 3: 427–438.
 1965a True structural change and the time dimension in the north Indian kinship system. Studies on Asia 6: 179–192.
 1965b Lucknow rickshawallas: the social organization of an occupational category. International Journal of Comparative Sociology 6: 24–47.
 1968 Time dimension and structural change in an Indian kinship system: a problem of conceptual refinement. In Structure and change in Indian society. M. Singer and B. S. Cohn, ed. Chicago, Aldine.
Green, B. F.
 1954 Attitude measurement. In Handbook of social psychology. I. G. Lindzey, ed. Cambridge, Addison Wesley.
Hammel, E. A.
 1961 The family cycle in a coastal Peruvian slum and village. American Anthropologist 63: 989–1005.
Hazlehurst, L. W.
 1966 Entrepreneurship and the merchant castes in a Punjabi city. Duke University Program in Comparative Studies on Southern Asia, Monograph 1.
Hitchcock, J. T.
 1957 The Rajputs of Khaalaapur: a study of kinship, social stratification and politics. Unpublished PhD dissertation, Cornell University.
Imperial Gazetteer of India
 1908 New Edition, Vol. 17. Oxford, Clarendon Press.
Joshi, E. B., ed.
 1965 Uttar Pradesh District Gazetteer: Meerut. Lucknow, Government of Uttar Pradesh.
Kannan, C. T.
 1963 Intercaste and intercommunity marriages in India. Bombay, Allied Publishers.
Kapadia, K. M.
 1956 Rural family patterns: a study in urban-rural relations. Sociological Bulletin 5: 111–126.
 1966 Marriage and family in India. 3rd. ed. Bombay, Oxford University Press.
Kapoor, S.
 1965 Family and kinship groups among the Khatris in Delhi. Sociological Bulletin 14: 54–63.

Kapur, P.
    1970   Marriage and the working woman in India. Delhi, Vikas Publi-
            cations.
Karve, I.
    1965   Kinship organisation in India. 2nd ed. Bombay, Asia Publishing
            House.
Kay, P.
    1964   A Guttman scale model of Tahitian consumer behavior. South-
            western Journal of Anthropology 20: 160–167.
Khare, R. S.
    1970   The changing Brahmans. Chicago, University of Chicago Press.
Klass, M.
    1966   Marriage rules in Bengal. American Anthropologist 68: 951–
            970.
Kolenda, P.
    1963   Toward a model of the Hindu jajmani system. Human Organ-
            ization 22: 11–31.
    1967   Regional differences in Indian family structure. In Regions and
            regionalism in South Asian studies: an exploratory study. R. I.
            Crane, ed. Durham, Duke University Program in Comparative
            Studies on Southern Asia, Monograph 5.
    1968a   Region, caste and family structure: a comparative study of the
            Indian "joint family." In Structure and change in Indian soci-
            ety. M. Singer and B. S. Cohn, eds. Chicago, Aldine.
    1968b   Census indices showing regional differences in Indian family
            structure. Unpublished paper presented to the annual meeting
            of the American Anthropological Association, Seattle.
    1970   Family structure in village Lonikand, India: 1819, 1958, and
            1967. Unpublished paper presented to an Indisciplinary Con-
            ference on Processes of Change in Contemporary Asian So-
            cieties, Urbana.
Lewis, O.
    1965   Village life in northern India. New York, Random House.
Lewis, O. and V. Barnouw
    1956   Caste and the jajmani system in a north Indian village. The
            Scientific Monthly 83: 66–81.
Luschinsky, M. S.
    1962   The life of women in a village of north India. Unpublished
            PhD dissertation, Cornell University.
    1963   The impact of some recent Indian government legislation on
            the women of an Indian village. Asian Survey 3: 573–583.
Lynch, O. M.
    1963   Some aspects of rural-urban continuum in India. In Anthro-
            pology on the march. B. Ratnam, ed. Madras, Book Centre.
    1967   Rural cities in India: continuities and discontinuities. In India

and Ceylon: unity and diversity. P. Mason, ed. London, Oxford University Press.

Madan, T. N.

1962a Is the Brahmanic *gotra* a grouping of kin? Southwestern Journal of Anthropology 18: 59–77.

1962b The Hindu joint family. Man 62: 88–89.

1963 The joint family: a terminological clarification. International Journal of Comparative Sociology 3: 1–16.

1965 Family and kinship: a study of the Pandits of rural Kashmir. Bombay: Asia Publishing House.

Mandelbaum, D. G.

1949 The Hindu family. *In* The family, its functions and destiny. R. Anshen, ed. New York, Harper & Row.

Marriott, M.

1968 Caste ranking and food transactions: a matrix analysis. *In* Structure and change in Indian society. M. Singer and B. S. Cohn, eds. Chicago, Aldine.

Mayer, A. C.

1960 Caste and kinship in central India. Berkeley and Los Angeles, University of California Press.

Mehta, S. K.

1968 Patterns of residence in Poona (India) by income, education and occupation (1937–1965). American Journal of Sociology 73: 496–508.

Metcalf, T. R.

1967 Landlords without land: the U. P. zamindars today. Pacific Affairs 40: 5–18.

Mitchell, J. C., ed.

1969 Social networks in urban situations. Manchester, Manchester University Press.

Mitchell, W. E. and H. J. Leichter

1961 Urban ambilineages and social mobility. Unpublished paper presented to the annual meeting of the Eastern Sociological Society, New York.

Montgomery, E.

1971 A local population approach to questions about the extended family in India. Unpublished paper presented to the annual meeting of the Association of Asian Studies, Washington.

Mukherjee, R.

1964 Urbanization and social transformation in India. *In* Urbanism and urbanization. N. Anderson, ed. Leiden, E. J. Brill.

National Council of Applied Economic Research

1965 Techno-economic survey of Uttar Pradesh. New Delhi.

Neale, W. C.

1962 Economic change in rural India: land tenure and reform in Uttar Pradesh, 1800–1955. New Haven, Yale University Press.

Nevill, H. R., ed.
  1904 Meerut: a gazetteer. District gazetteers of the United Provinces of Agra and Oudh, IV. Allahabad, Superintendent of Printing and Stationery.
Nicholas, R. W.
  1961 Economics of family types in two West Bengal villages. Economic Weekly 13: 1057–1060.
Nimkoff, M. F., ed.
  1965 Comparative family systems. Boston, Houghton Mifflin.
Okada, F. E.
  1957 Ritual brotherhood: a cohesive factor in Nepalese society. Southwestern Journal of Anthropology 13: 212–222.
Opler, M. E. and R. D. Singh
  1948 The division of labor in an Indian village. In A reader in general anthropology. C. S. Coon, ed. New York, Holt.
Orenstein, H.
  1961 The recent history of the extended family in India. Social Problems 8: 341–350.
  1965 Gaon: conflict and cohesion in an Indian village. Princeton, Princeton University Press.
Orenstein, H. and M. Micklin
  1966 The Hindu joint family: the norms and the numbers. Pacific Affairs 39: 314–325.
Owens, R.
  1970 Peasant entrepreneurs in a north Indian industrial city. Unpublished paper presented at the Conference on Occupational Cultures in Changing South Asia, Chicago.
Pakrasi, K. and A. Halder
  1970 Polygynists of Urban India, 1960–61. Indian Journal of Social Work 31: 49–62.
Parsons, T.
  1949 The social structure of the family. In The family, its function and destiny. R. Anshen, ed. New York, Harper & Row.
Pocock, D. F.
  1960 Sociologies, urban and rural. Contributions to Indian Sociology 4: 63–81.
Redfield, R.
  1947 The folk society. American Journal of Sociology 52: 293–308.
Redfield, R. and M. Singer
  1954 The cultural role of cities. Economic Development and Cultural Change 3: 53–73.
Rosen, G.
  1967 Democracy and social change in India. Berkeley and Los Angeles, University of California Press.
Ross, A.
  1961 The Hindu family in its urban setting. Toronto, University of Toronto Press.

Rowe, W.
1960 The marriage network and structural change in a north Indian community. Southwestern Journal of Anthropology 16: 299–311.
1968 Mobility in the 19th century caste system. *In* Structure and change in Indian society. M. Singer and B. S. Cohn, eds. Chicago, Aldine.

Sarma, J.
1964 The nuclearization of joint family households in West Bengal. Man in India 44: 193–206.

Saxena, N. P.
1968 Zonal characteristics of the spread of professions and services at an urban centre: a case study of the Meerut town group. The Geographical Observer 4: 5–18.

Scheffler, H. W.
1965 Choiseul Island social structure. Berkeley and Los Angeles, University of California Press.

Schwab, W. B.
1965 Oshogbo — an urban community? *In* Urbanization and migration in West Africa. H. Kuper, ed. Berkeley and Los Angeles, University of California Press.

Singer, M.
1968 The Indian joint family in modern industry. *In* Structure and change in Indian society. M. Singer and B. S. Cohn, eds. Chicago, Aldine.

Singh, B. and S. Misra
1964 A study of land reforms in Uttar Pradesh. Honolulu, East-West Center Press.

Singh, K. N.
1959 Functions and functional classification of towns in Uttar Pradesh. The National Geographic Journal of India 5: 121–148.

Singh, M.
1964 Urban field of Meerut. Deccan Geographer 2: 85–99.

Singh, R. D.
1962 Family organization in a north Indian village. Unpublished PhD dissertation, Cornell University.

Sjoberg, G.
1960 The preindustrial city: past and present. New York, Free Press.

Srinivas, M. N.
1967 Social change in modern India. Berkeley and Los Angeles, University of California Press.

Straus, M. A. and D. Winkelmann
1969 Social class, fertility and authority in nuclear and joint households in Bombay. Journal of Asian and African Studies 4: 61–74.

Sweetser, D. A.
  1966 The effect of industrialization on intergenerational solidarity. Rural Sociology 31: 156–170.
Thornton, E.
  1854 A gazetteer of the territories under the government of the East Indian Company and of the native states on the continent of India. London, W. H. Allen.
Tiemann, G.
  1970 The four-*got*-rule among the Jat of Haryana in northern India. Anthropos 65: 166–177.
Vatuk, S. J.
  1969a Reference, address, and fictive kinship in urban north India. Ethnology 8: 255–272.
  1969b A structural analysis of the Hindi kinship terminology. Contributions to Indian Sociology N.S. 3: 94–115.
  1971 Trends in north Indian urban kinship: the "matrilateral asymmetry" hypothesis. Southwestern Journal of Anthropology 27: 287–307.
Vogel, E. F.
  1967 Japan's new middle class. Berkeley and Los Angeles, University of California Press.
Wirth, L.
  1938 Urbanism as a way of life. American Journal of Sociology 44: 1–24.
Wiser, W. H.
  1936 The Hindu jajmani system. Lucknow, Lucknow Publishing House.
Woodruff, G. M.
  1959 An Adidravida settlement in Bangalore, India. Unpublished PhD dissertation, Radcliffe College.

Index